WELL SUITED

Dress with Confidence
Live Well Suited

Margo Martinez

Well Suited
Dress With Confidence · Live Well Suited
Margo Martinez
Be the Man LLC

Published by Be the Man LLC, St. Louis, MO

Copyright ©2024 Margo Martinez
All rights reserved.

No part of this publication may be reproduced, stored in a retrieval system, or transmitted in any form or by any means, electronic, mechanical, photocopying, recording, scanning, or otherwise, except as permitted under Section 107 or 108 of the 1976 United States Copyright Act, without the prior written permission of the Publisher. Requests to the Publisher for permission should be addressed to the Permissions Department, Be the Man LLC, Margo Martinez, margo@bethemanllc.com.

Limit of Liability/Disclaimer of Warranty: While the publisher and author have used their best efforts in preparing this book, they make no representations or warranties with respect to the accuracy or completeness of the contents of this book and specifically disclaim any implied warranties of merchantability or fitness for a particular purpose. No warranty may be created or extended by sales representatives or written sales materials. The advice and strategies contained herein may not be suitable for your situation. You should consult with a professional where appropriate. Neither the publisher nor the author shall be liable for any loss of profit or any other commercial damages, including but not limited to special, incidental, consequential, or other damages.

The product information and advice provided (in this book) are intended for general informational purposes only. The author and publisher of this book have made every effort to ensure that the content is accurate and up-to-date at the time of publication. However, they make no representations or warranties of any kind, express or implied, about the completeness, accuracy, reliability, suitability, or availability of the information, products, or services contained in this book for any purpose.

Project Management and Book Design: Davis Creative, LLC, dba: DavisCreativePublishing.com
Photography: Rebecca Charbonneau
Shoes: Armin Oehler LLC

Library of Congress Cataloging-in-Publication Data
(Provided by Cassidy Cataloguing Services, Inc.).

Names: Martinez, Margo, author.
Title: Well suited : dress with confidence, live well suited / Margo Martinez.
Description: St. Louis, MO : Be the Man LLC, [2024]
Identifiers: ISBN: 979-8-9907135-0-5 (hardcover) | 979-8-9907135-2-9 (paperback) |
                979-8-9907135-1-2 (ebook) | LCCN: 2024909784
Subjects: LCSH: Men's clothing--Pictorial works. | Grooming for men--Pictorial works. | Fashion--
                Pictorial works. | Clothing and dress--Social aspects--Pictorial works. | LCGFT: Illustrated
                works. | BISAC: PHOTOGRAPHY / Subjects & Themes / Fashion. | DESIGN / Fashion &
                Accessories. | SELF-HELP / Fashion & Style.
Classification: LCC: TT617 .M37 2024 | DDC: 646.32--dc23

ATTENTION CORPORATIONS, UNIVERSITIES, COLLEGES, AND PROFESSIONAL ORGANIZATIONS: Quantity discounts are available on bulk purchases of this book for educational, gift purposes, or as premiums for increasing magazine subscriptions or renewals. Special books or book excerpts can also be created to fit specific needs. For information, please contact Margo Martinez, Be the Man LLC, margo@bethemanllc.com, www.bethemanllc.com.

To my clients and friends who are now officially fashion models.

Allan Ivie	Oscar Martinez
John Banjak	Bill Schmidt
Keith Williamson	Russell Browning
Preston Davis	Kevin Lathrop
Ryan Barr	Joe Larrew
Willie Evans	John Jennings
Andy Bagnall	Paul Yarns
John Drexler	John Weber
Kent Heintz	

Table of Contents

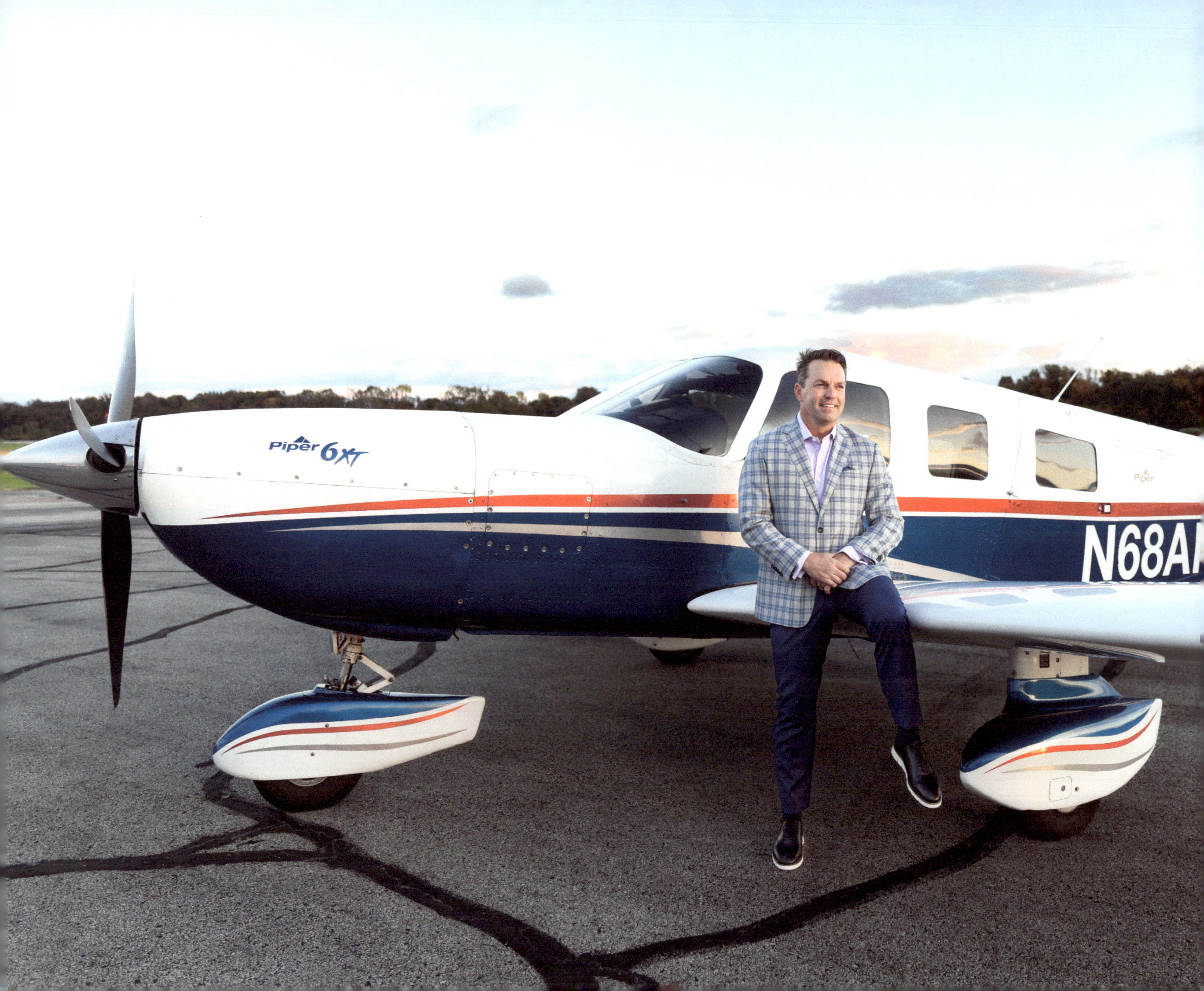

Foreword

To all the men who regularly question, "Do these pants go with this jacket?" Fear not. Help has arrived.

In my years of working in the men's custom clothing industry, I have discovered that my role revolves just as much around how men think and feel as it does about haberdashery. I have to admit, when I first started in men's clothing, I was mainly focused on becoming a salesperson. There are numerous career opportunities in sales to choose from, and I was thrilled to begin my career by offering a product that was as enjoyable, personal, and creative as men's clothing. However, I quickly learned that my role is more about the client and their self-image than their clothes. Clothing is my product, but it does not define my true service. It is about cultivating relationships and fostering the confidence, assurance, and peace clients gain after working with me.

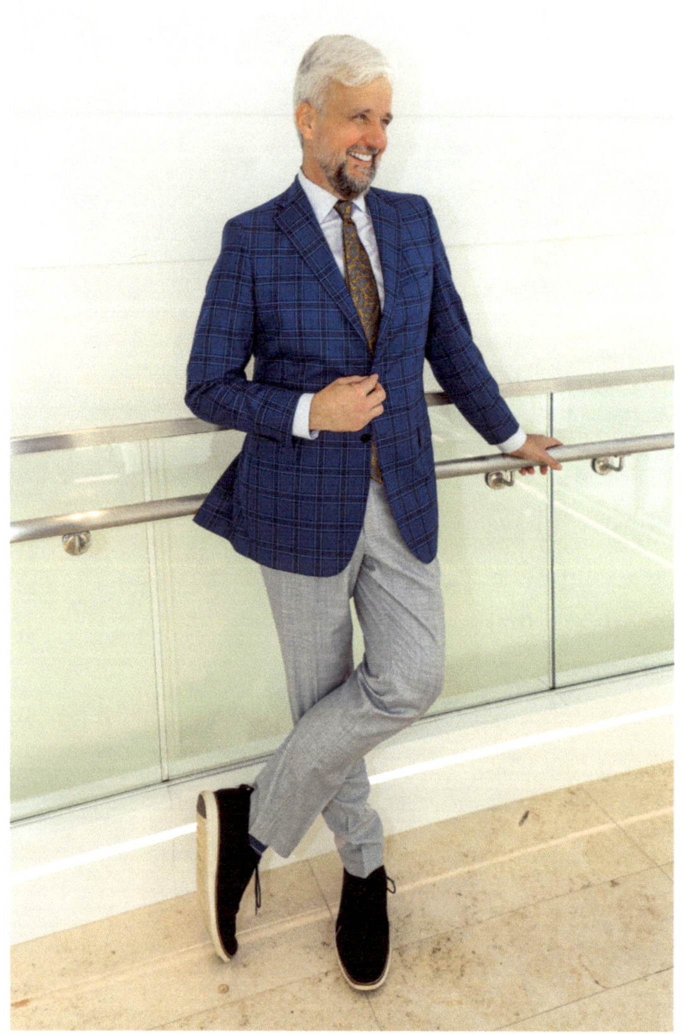

When it comes to fashion and men's dressing, only a small percentage of my clients are blessed with fashion acumen. These select few individuals have more clothes and shoes than many women I know, and they can put impressive outfits together with ease. However, that instinct is foreign to the majority of my custom clothing clientele. I've noticed a few common themes in my work over the years:

1. *Most* men could use a visual guide on how to pair colors and patterns.

2. *Many* men don't feel confident putting together an outfit.

3. *All* men want to look and feel good in what they wear!

These observations inspired me to write this book, 'Well Suited'!

I regularly explain to clients which colors and patterns make an aesthetic outfit. Understandably, it's difficult for them to remember what we discussed. They might try their best and then ask their significant other to approve before walking out the door. I want this book to be a visual guide on how to put together an outfit confidently and quickly. Learn the principles of dressing, so you can combine pattern and color like a pro!

One disclaimer: Many menswear books cover the history of men's clothing, accessories, grooming, and style. For this book, we will save the history and evolution of men's dressings, pleats, cuffs, collars, accessories, and hygiene tips for another time.

What we WILL talk about is:

1. What occasions are appropriate for each look.

2. How color theory plays a role in dressing appropriately.

3. My philosophy on pairing certain patterns and colors together for the most common garments men wear.

The models in *Well Suited* are my clients and friends. None of them are professional fashion models (although perhaps they should be). Instead, they are everyday lawyers, bankers, executives, business owners, and wealth management advisors who live in the Midwest. Their garments are included in their regular rotation (yes, even the purple sport coat outfit and the red suit)! Consider *Well Suited* your golden ticket to dressing with the confidence you seek.

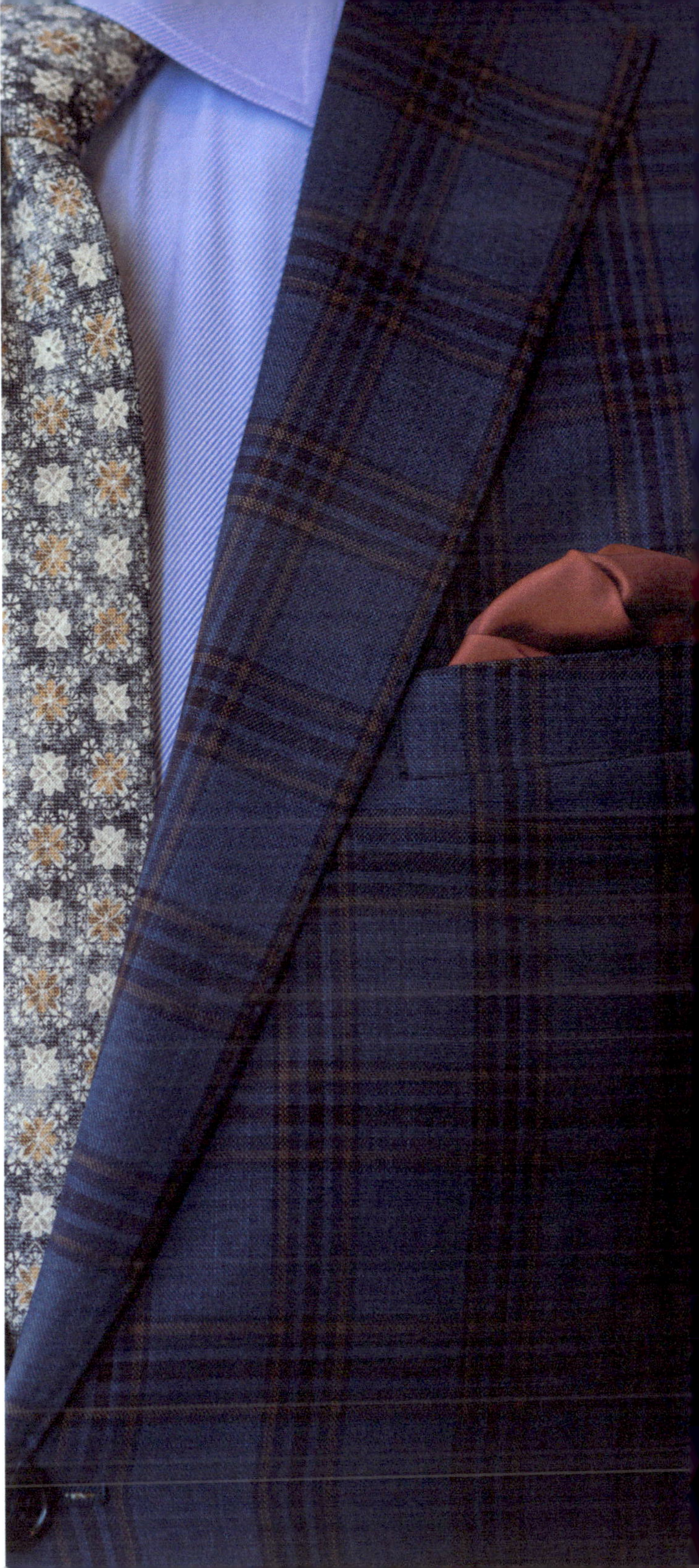

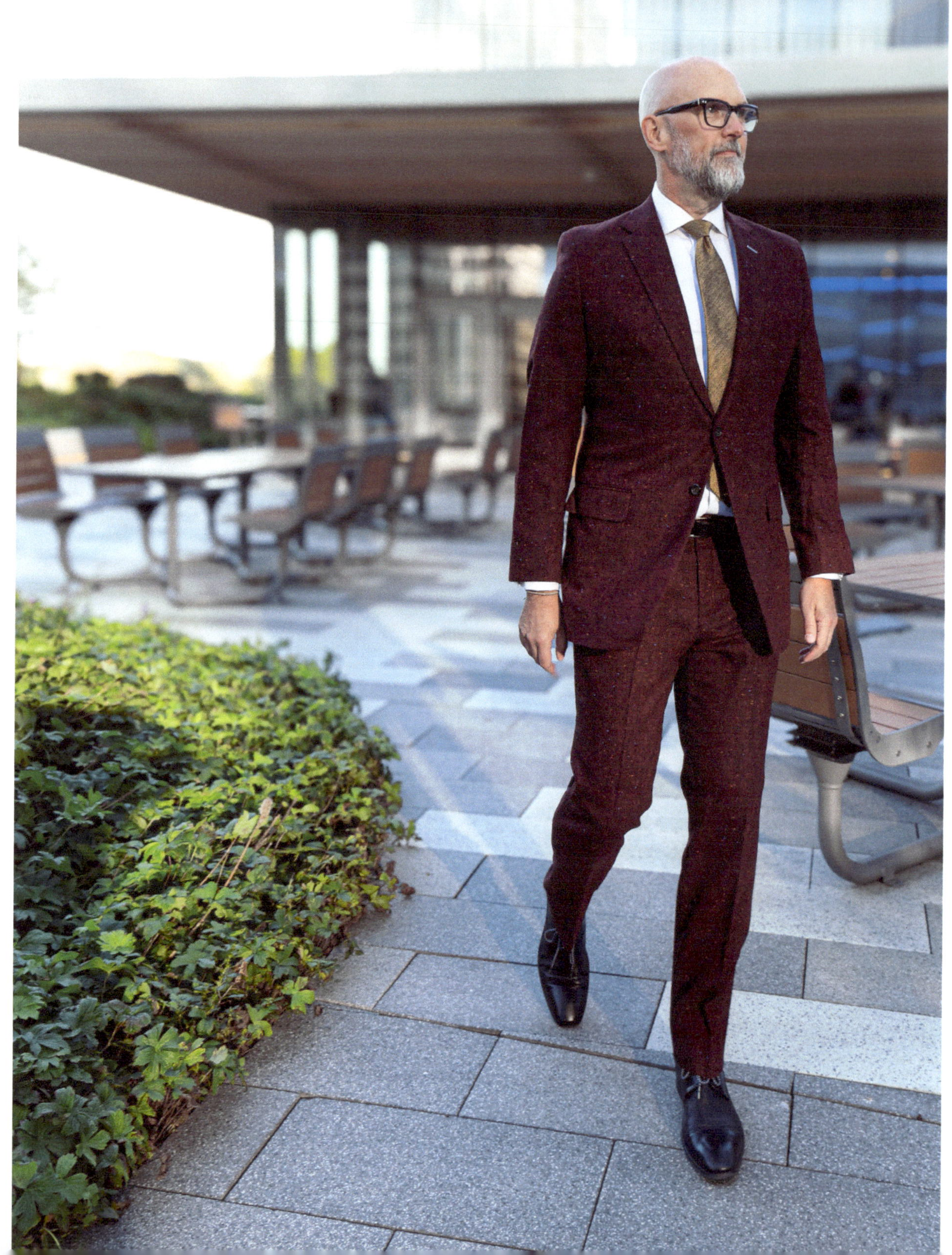

Introduction

Picture it—you have both personal and professional social events on the calendar, and some mysterious dress code terms are being bandied about.

Black tie.
Black tie optional.
Cocktail attire.
Business casual.
Smart Casual. ("That's new…" you comment to yourself).

You attempt a Google search to educate yourself. You click the Image tab, and ads from Shein and Men's Wearhouse pop up with photos of men wearing clothes that are, at best, kind of like things you have in your closet and, at worst, tie-dye vests and sequined blazers. Not exactly a trustworthy source.

If this sounds like you, do not worry. You are not alone! You want to feel good in your clothes regardless of personality, age, weight, height, or career. You might want to avoid standing out but want the confidence to create an outfit that feels like YOU and will fit the occasion.

I, with a few of my dearest clients and friends, am here to visually show how to mix and match patterns and colors with the *most common garments* you will wear on the *most common occasions*.

With each page turn, I hope you gain inspiration and confidence to mix colors and patterns you may not have considered before and leave the solid white shirts behind. And who knows? You may even be inspired to wear a tie. (Or go sockless).

SUITS

*Looking good isn't self-importance;
it's self-respect.*

CHARLES HIX

Suits are defined as a jacket and trouser made of matching fabric. For decades, the suit was considered everyday wear, like a uniform, but has evolved to have a different purpose in modern times. They are often avoided and seen as too formal, stodgy, or uncomfortable. However, modern gentlemen navigate a myriad of occasions that are best attended in a suit, including client meetings, board meetings, trade shows, job interviews, representing a client in court appearances, or weddings and funerals. When pressed to tackle an important occasion, there is nothing better than a tidy and well-fitting suit. The styles and trends vary, but the suit remains a timeless staple.

Start with the fundamentals when curating your suit collection. Invest in a solid navy or grey first, then add pinstripes or chalk stripes. Avoid double-breasted suits or more aggressive windowpane patterns until you have your basic rotation in place. But by all means, once you do, confidently choose a variety of patterns, styles, and colors!

If you are looking for inspiration on what direction to go next with your suits,
 there are three ways to diversify: style, color, and pattern.

To diversify the style, try:

- Two-inch cuffs, single pleat, and buckle side tabs (instead of belt loops)
- Center vent jacket with a ticket pocket and five buttons on the sleeve instead of four
- Double-breasted coat
- Style a vest with lapels to elevate any suit

To incorporate other colors and patterns, choose a different shade of grey or blue with some color and pattern to branch out from a place of comfort. For example:

- Charcoal suit with a lavender plaid
- Light blue suit with magenta windowpane
- Grey with tan and brown glen plaid
- Navy with pink stripe

For something even more adventurous, choose a fabric that is not in the blue or grey family. For example:

- Green glen plaid
- Aubergine stripe
- Red plaid with teal windowpane
- Pink with purple plaid

In this section, we will review some of the most common suits and occasions for wearing them. We will also review the psychological impact of each one and include a visual representation for reference.

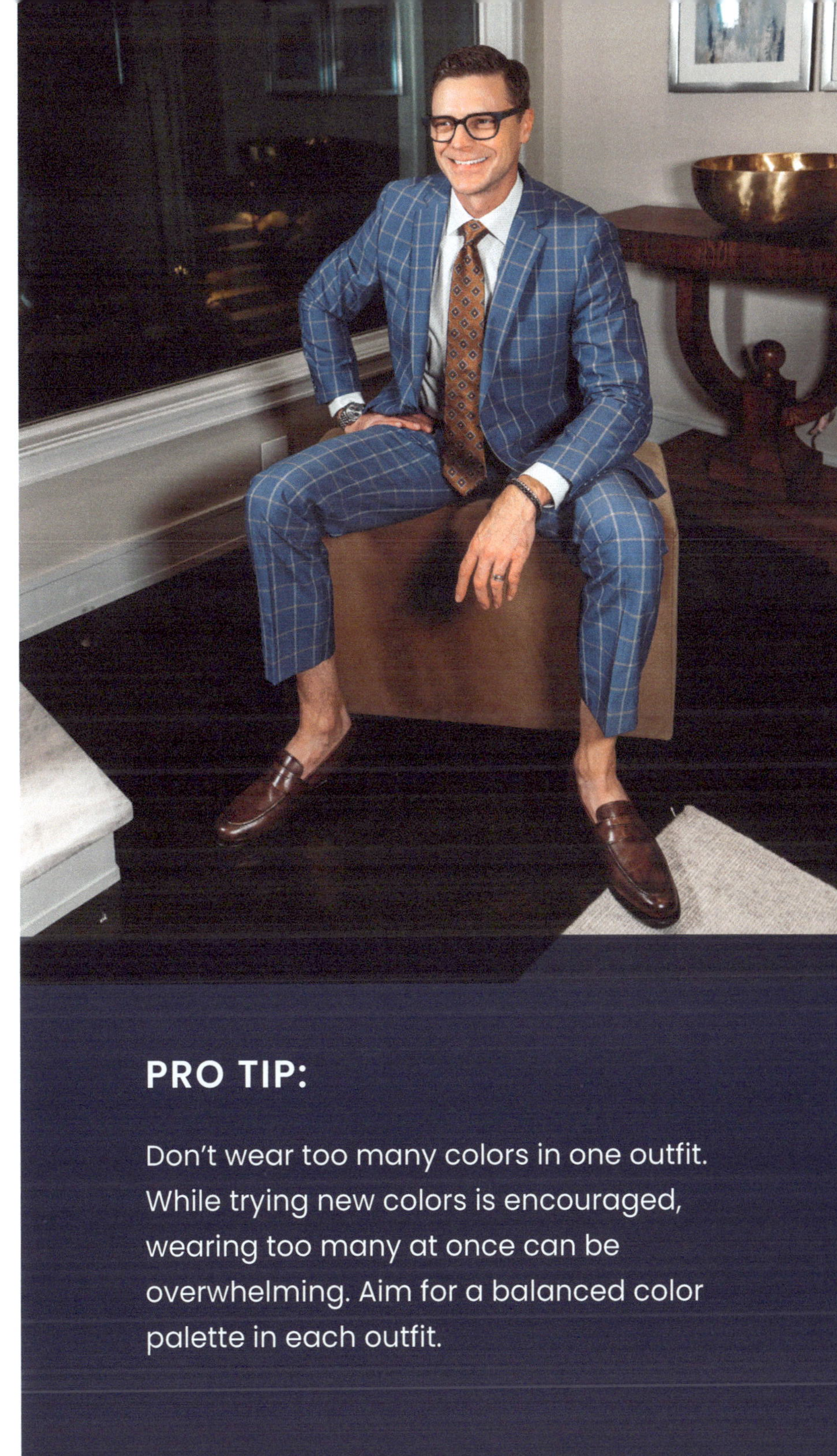

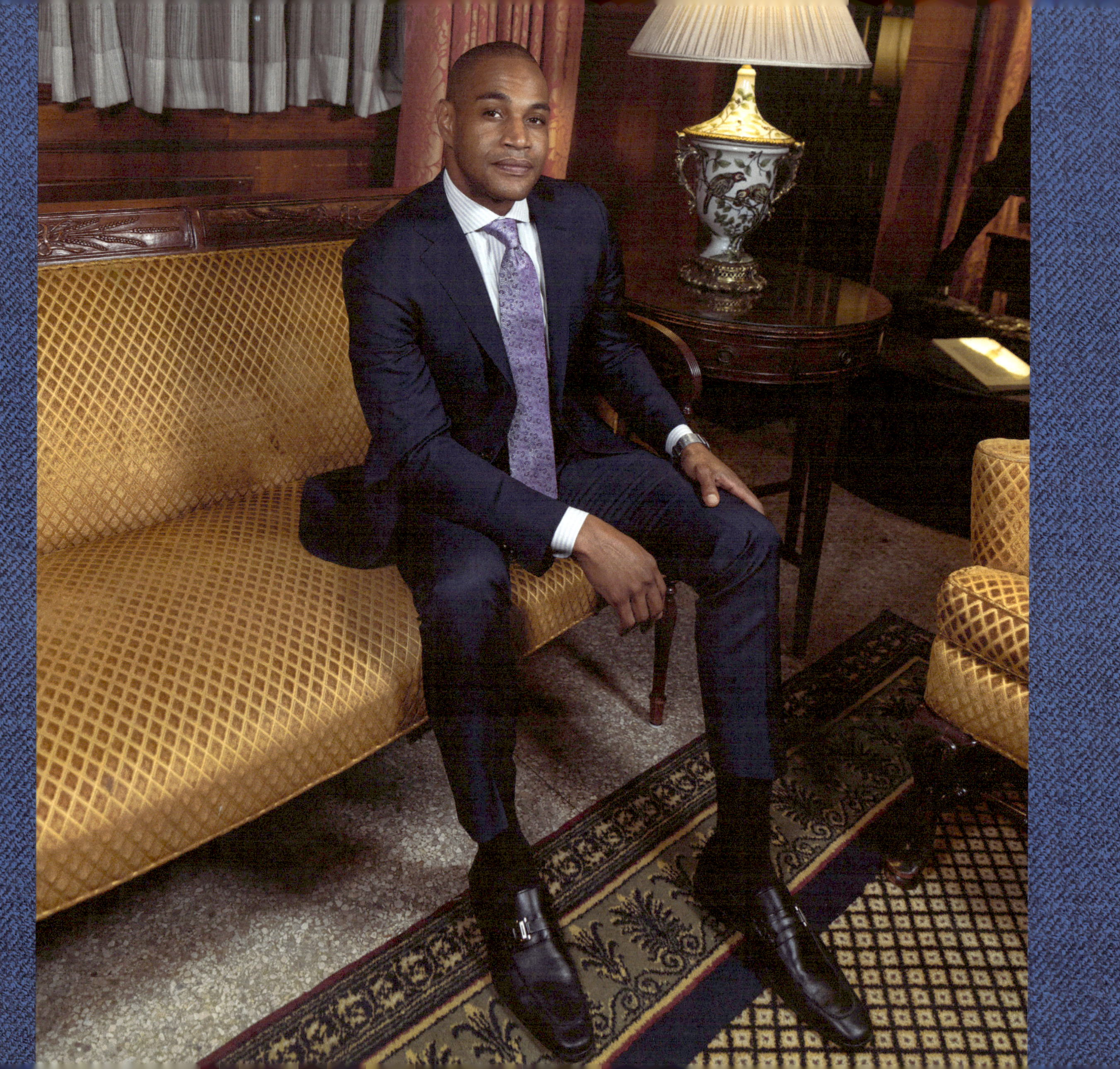

NAVY SOLID

CREDIBILITY • INFLUENCE • HONOR • ELEGANCE • POWER

The perfect business suit, the navy solid is a tried and true staple. It is typically the first suit to add to the wardrobe, and can be worn for many different professional occasions. Navy solid suits project power and influence and should be worn when you do not want to stand out, but want to be taken seriously.

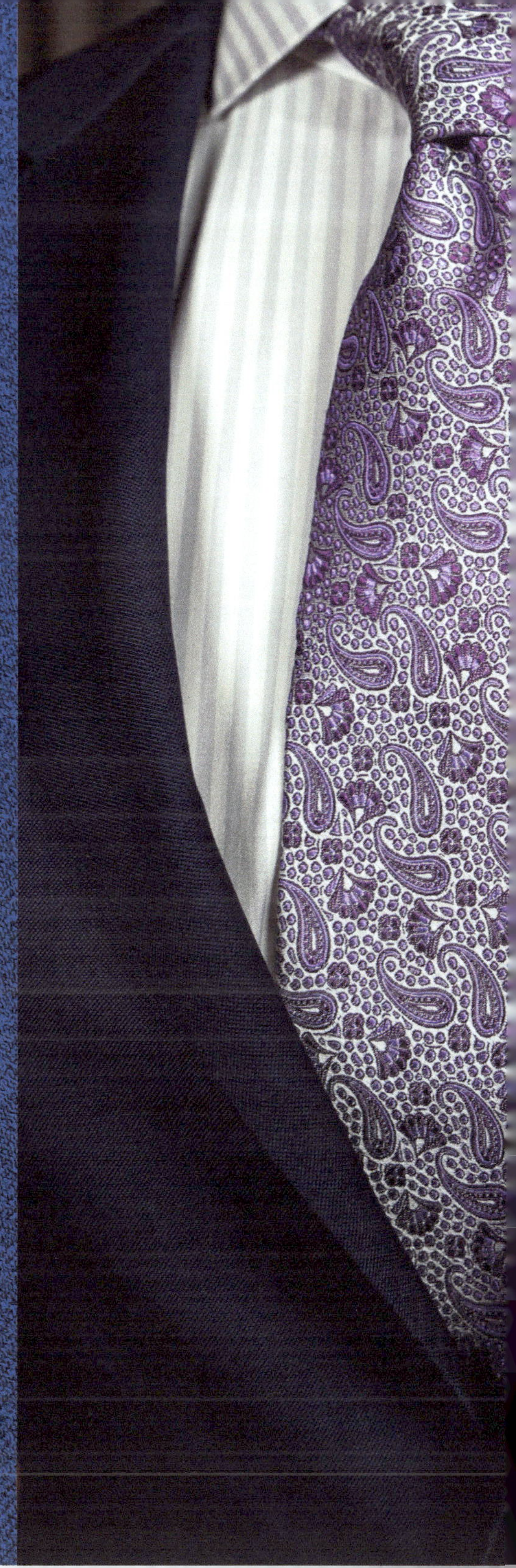

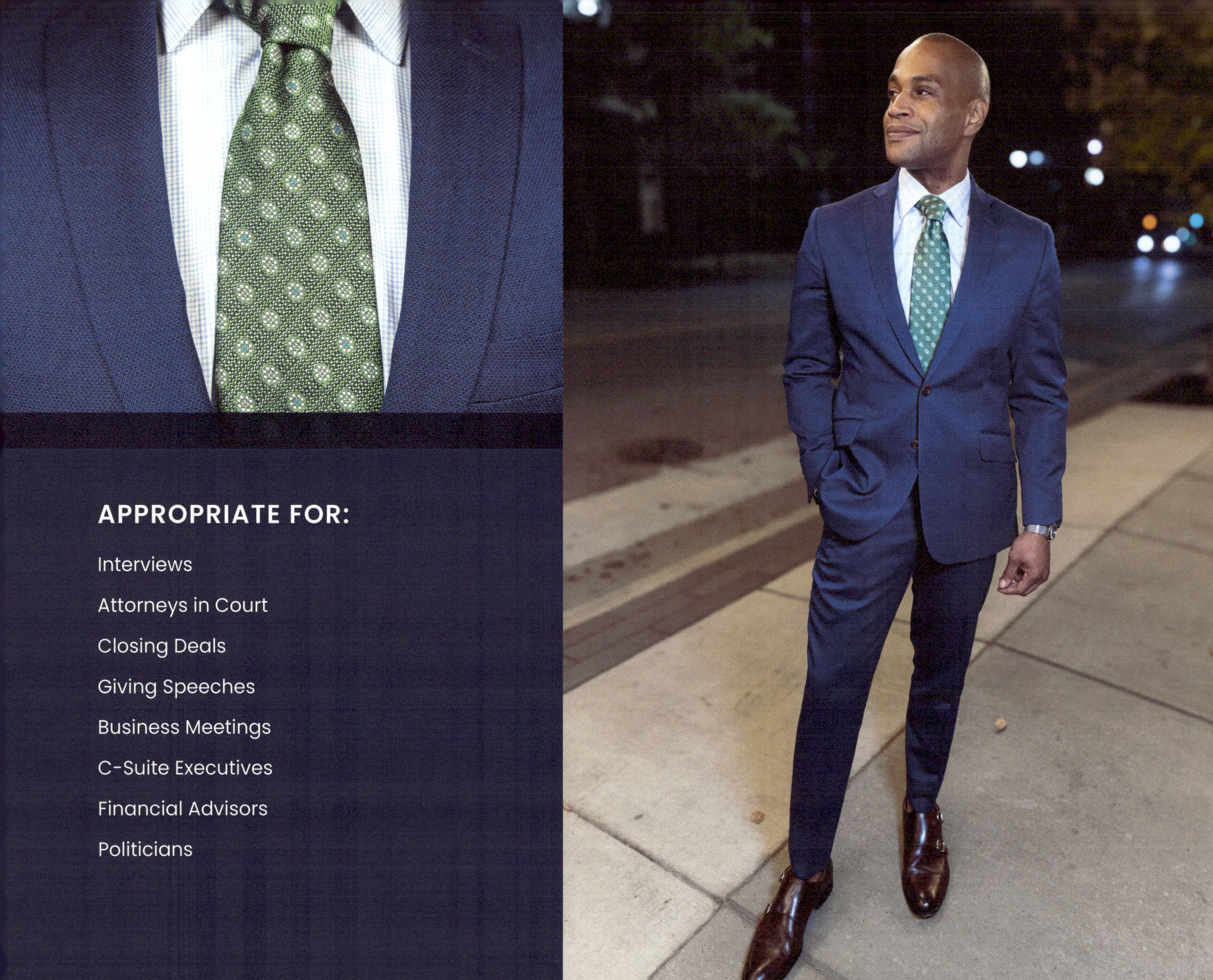
APPROPRIATE FOR:

Interviews

Attorneys in Court

Closing Deals

Giving Speeches

Business Meetings

C-Suite Executives

Financial Advisors

Politicians

NAVY SOLID SUIT

SHIRTS TO MATCH

Solid Colors

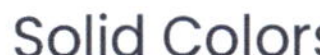

White - Color Stripe or Pattern

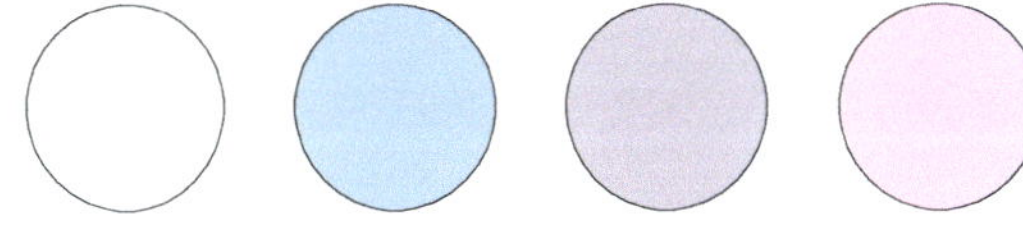

Blue - Color Stripe or Pattern

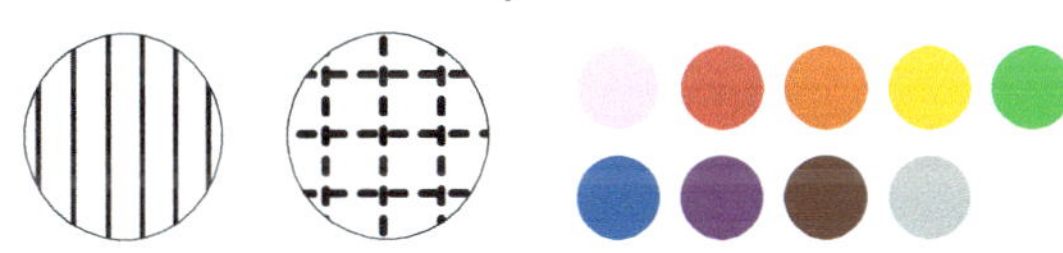
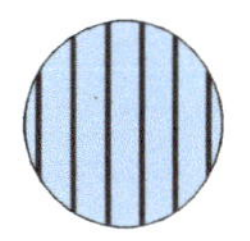
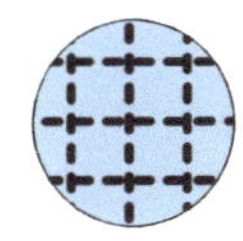
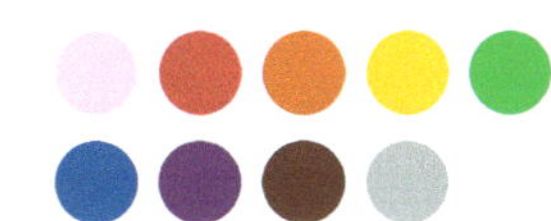

TIE COLORS

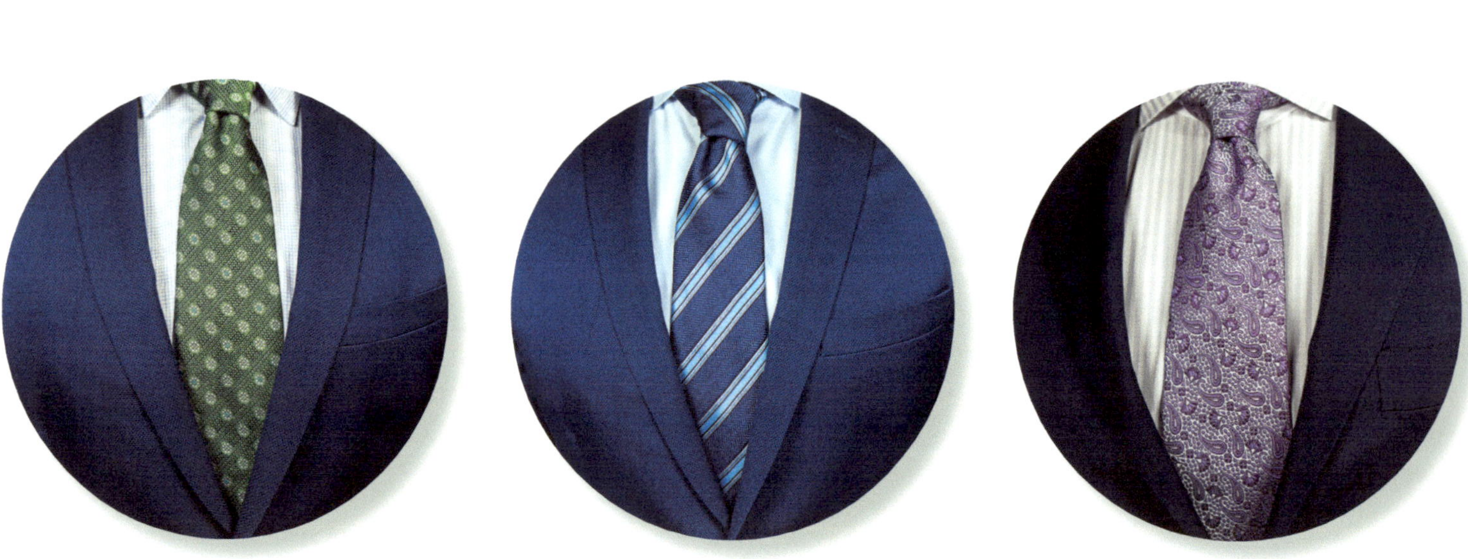

FOOTWEAR

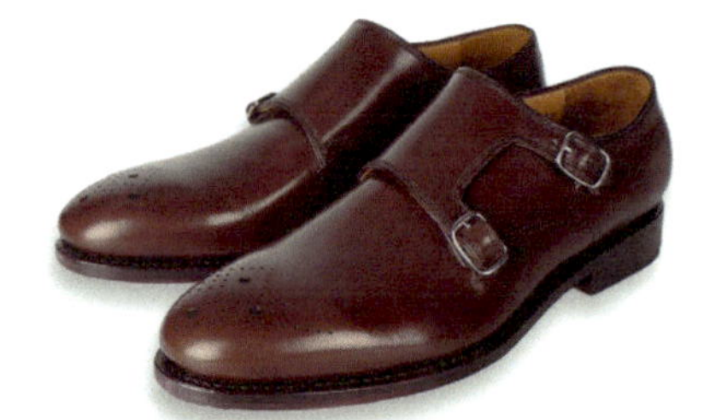 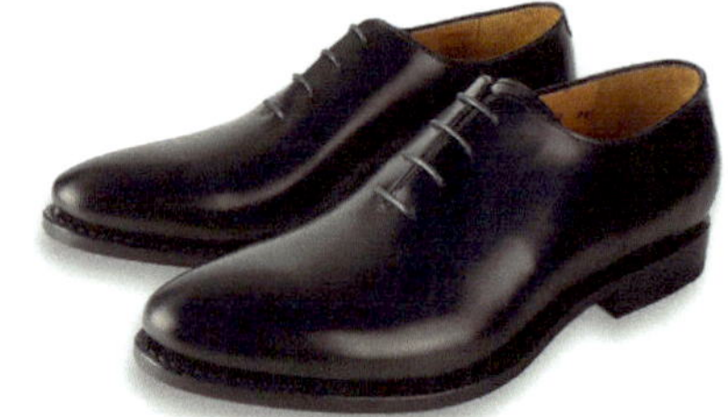 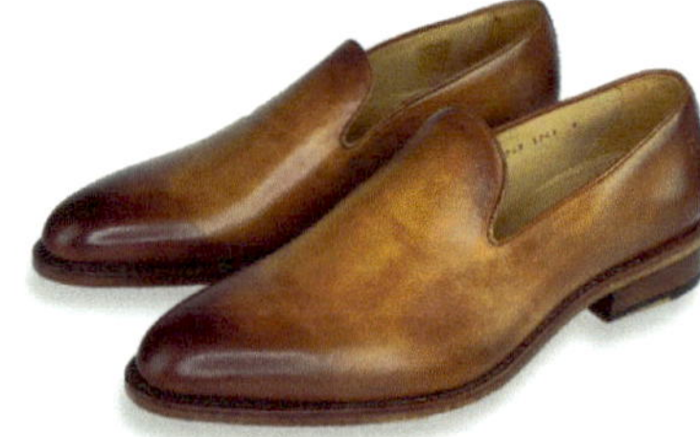

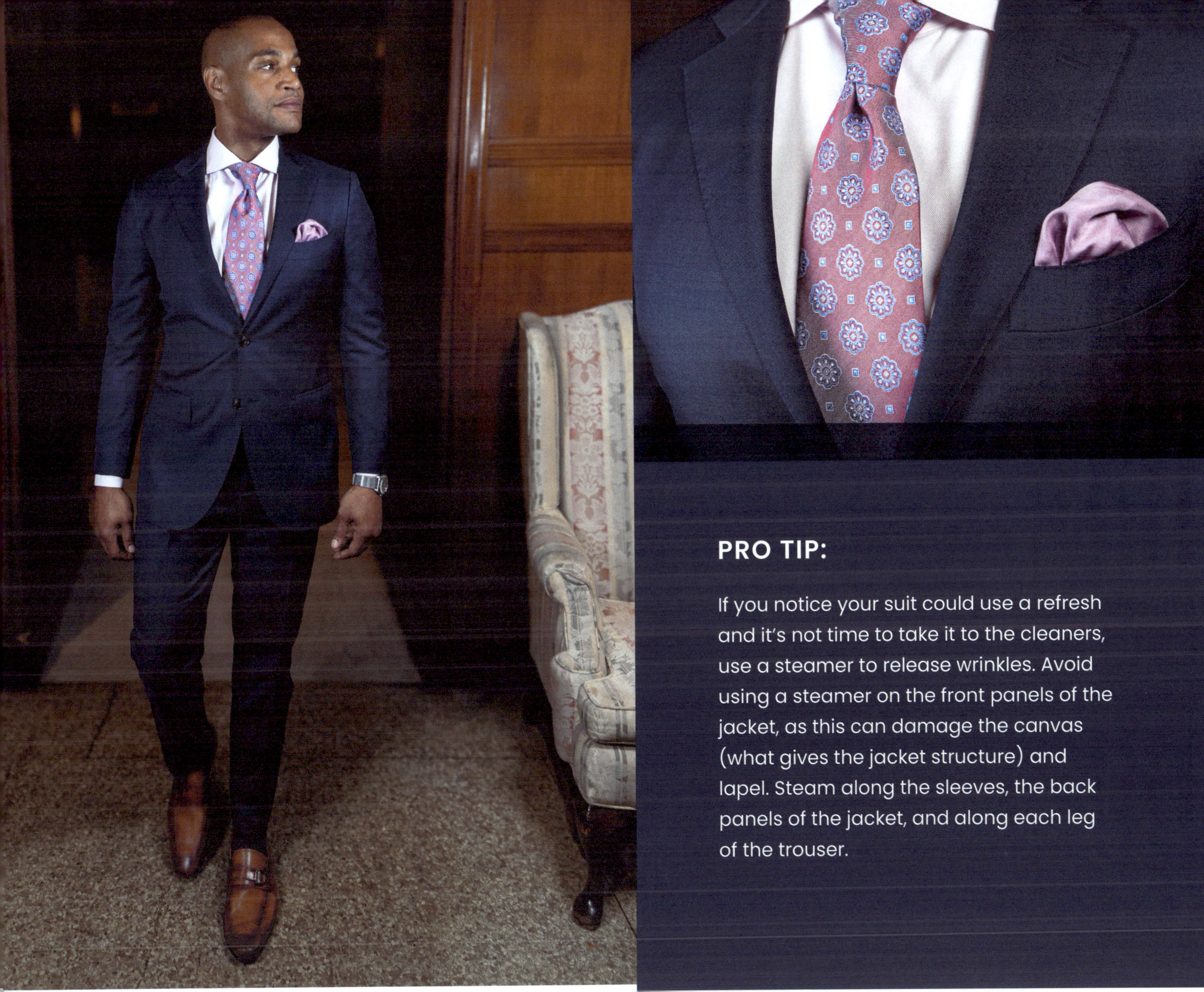

PRO TIP:

If you notice your suit could use a refresh and it's not time to take it to the cleaners, use a steamer to release wrinkles. Avoid using a steamer on the front panels of the jacket, as this can damage the canvas (what gives the jacket structure) and lapel. Steam along the sleeves, the back panels of the jacket, and along each leg of the trouser.

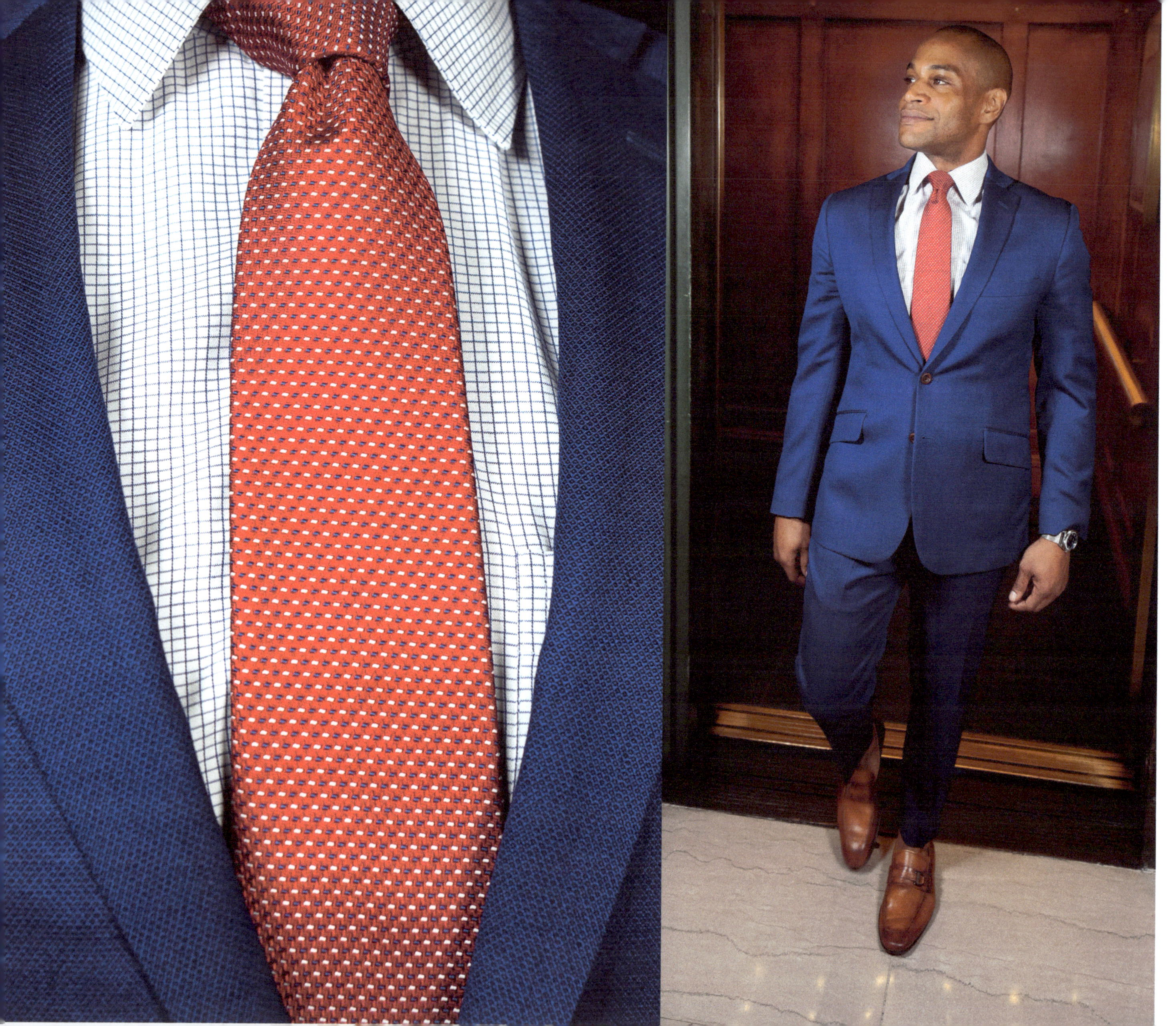

Preston Davis

WHAT IS YOUR OCCUPATION?

Private Banker

WHAT ARE YOUR HOBBIES AND INTERESTS?

I enjoy all sports, playing racquetball, golfing, skiing, traveling, reading, volunteering, and spending time with family.

WHAT IS YOUR FAVORITE TRAVEL EXPERIENCE?

South Africa because of the culture, scenic geography, Nelson Mandela, and the safari!

WHAT'S YOUR FAVORITE PIECE IN YOUR WARDROBE TO WEAR?

My custom green sport coat from Be the Man!

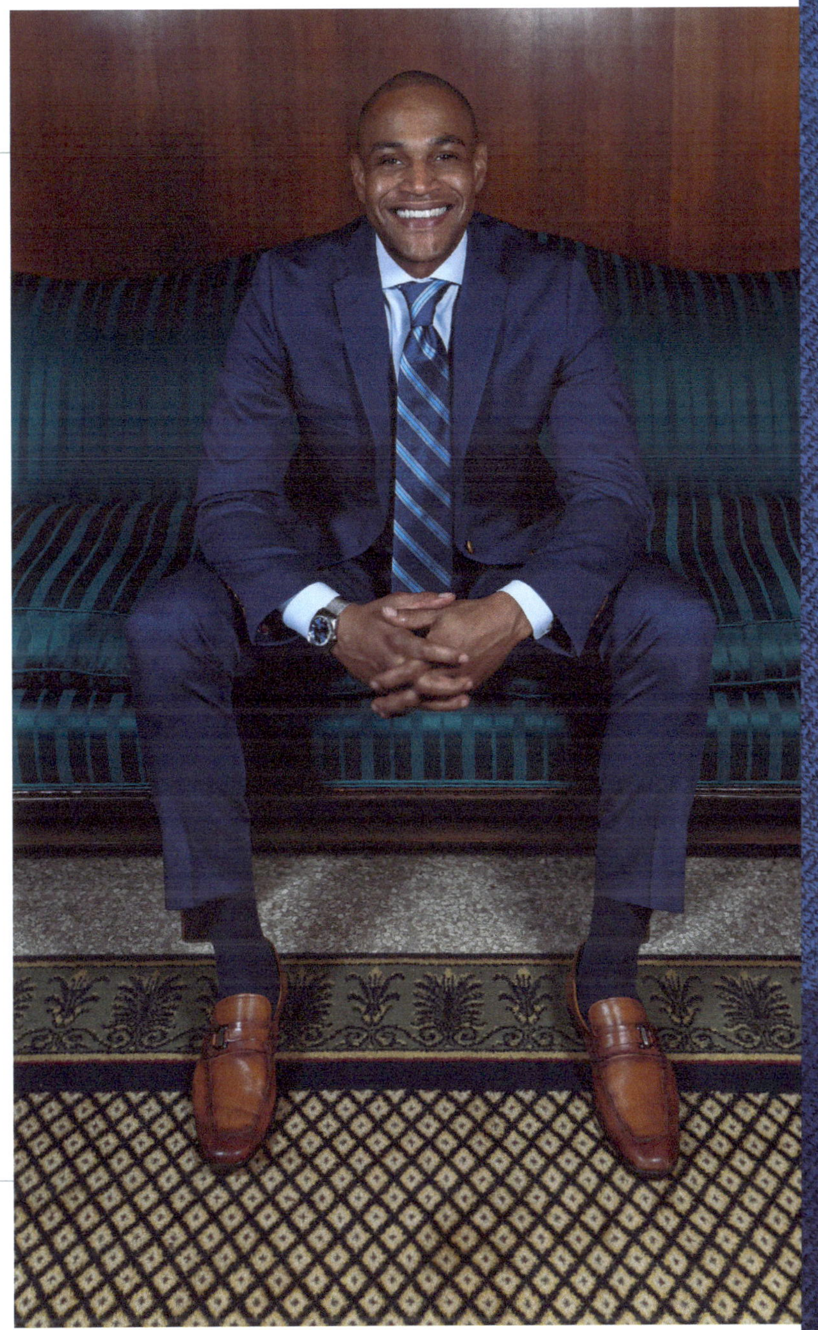

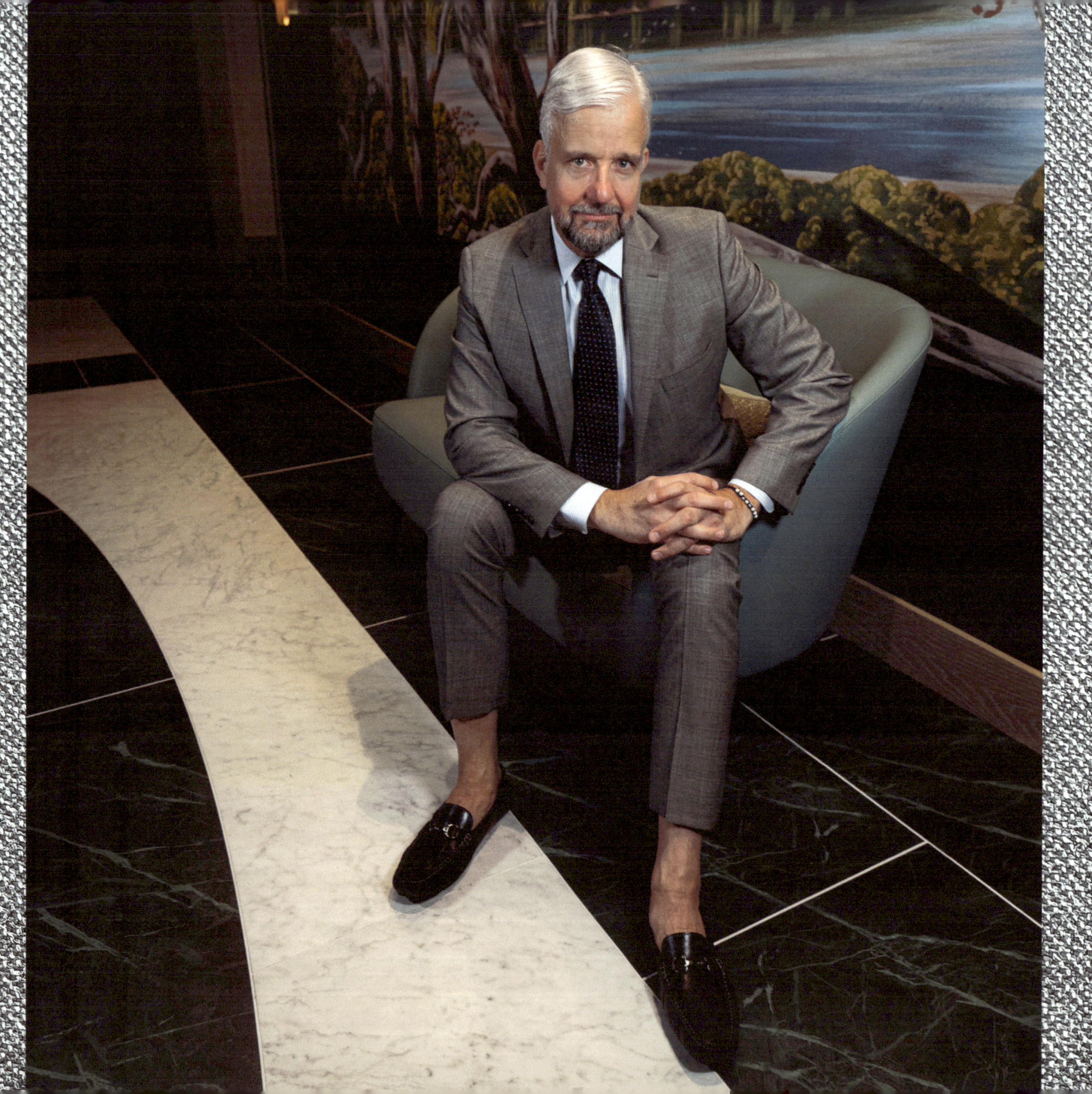

GREY SOLID

LONGEVITY • STRENGTH • WISDOM • EXPERIENCE

Grey solid suits are a traditional and classic staple. Worn mainly for business purposes, they exude strength, stability, and credibility. Grey solid suits are available in a wide spectrum of shades, so it is wise to invest in a light grey, banker's grey (medium grey), and charcoal grey for a variety that allows you to dress for any occasion. Opt for charcoal in more traditional and conservative settings and lighter grey for a more casual audience. Banker's grey is effortless on both ends of the spectrum.

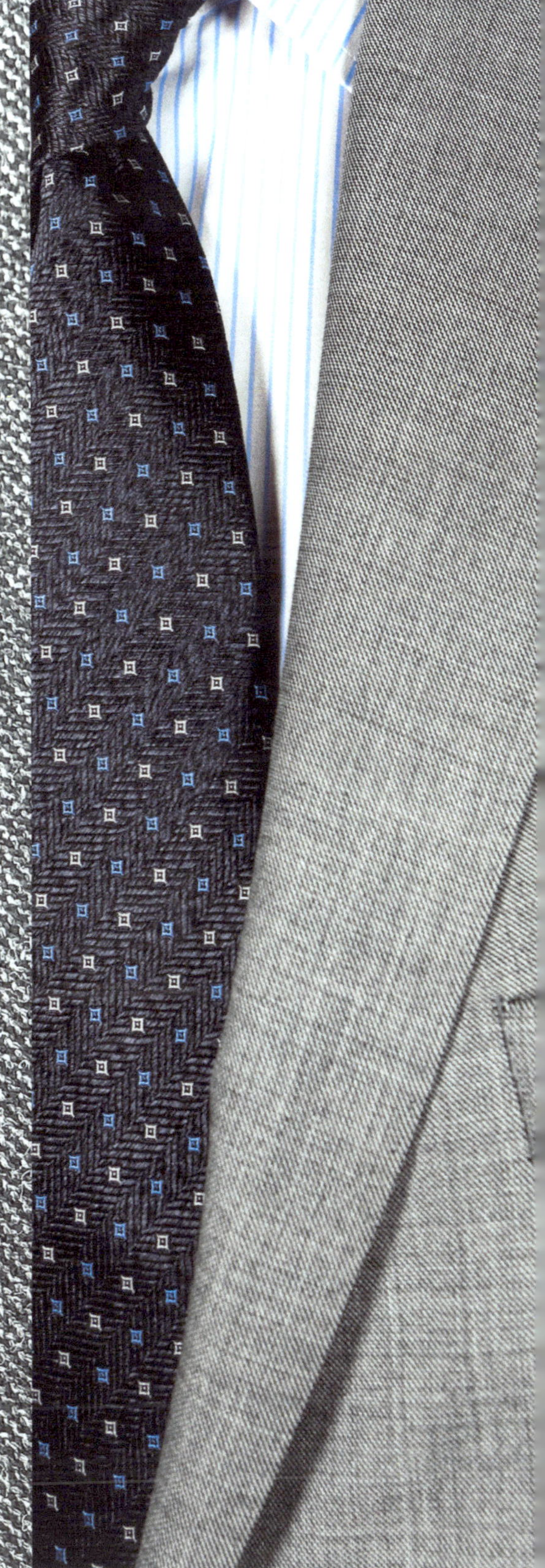

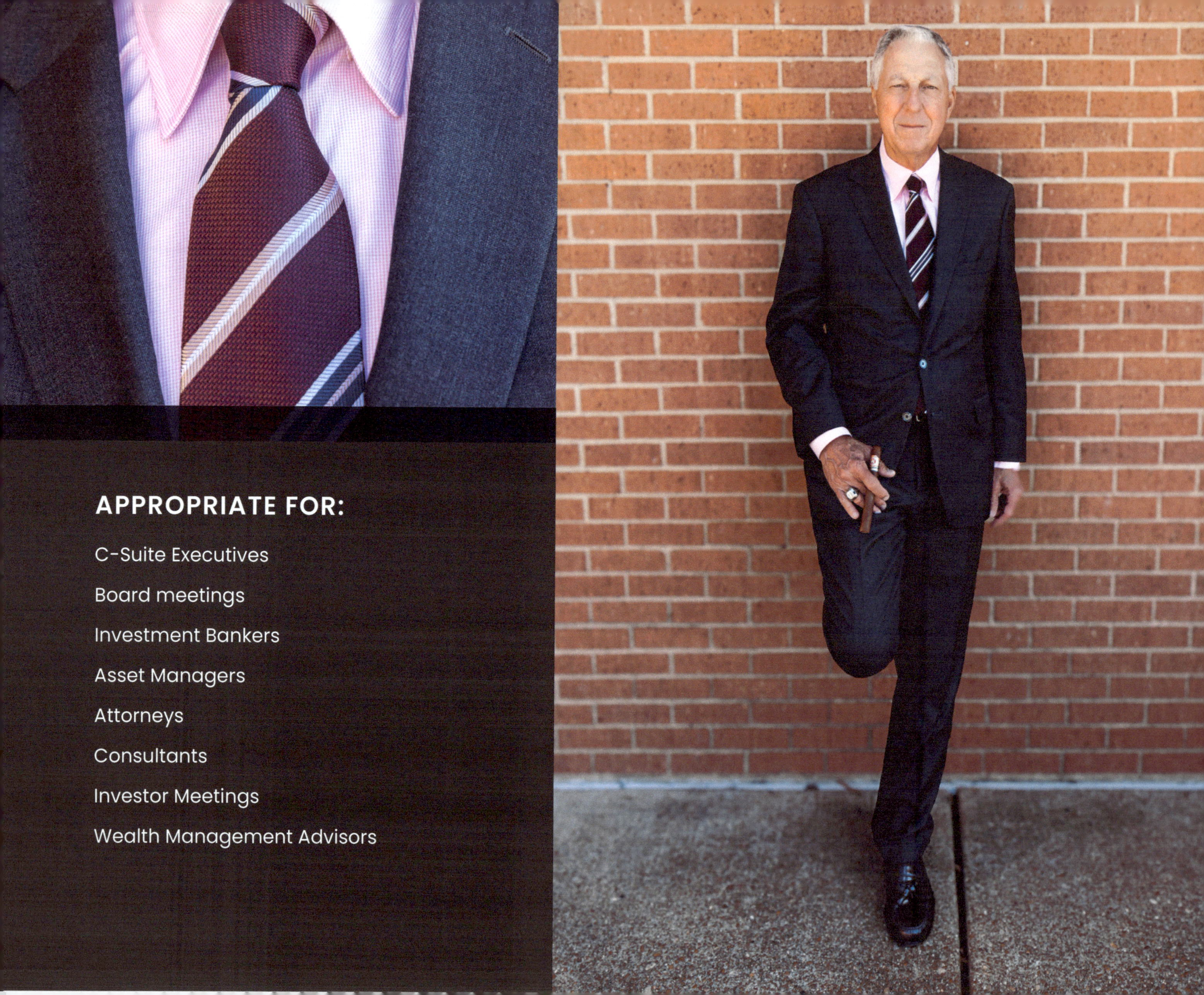
APPROPRIATE FOR:

C-Suite Executives

Board meetings

Investment Bankers

Asset Managers

Attorneys

Consultants

Investor Meetings

Wealth Management Advisors

GREY SOLID SUIT

SHIRTS TO MATCH

Solid Colors

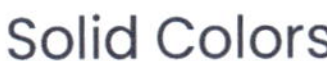

White - Color Stripe or Pattern

Blue - Color Stripe or Pattern

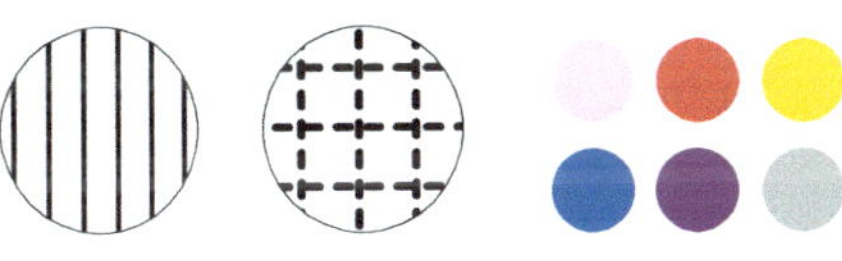

TIE COLORS

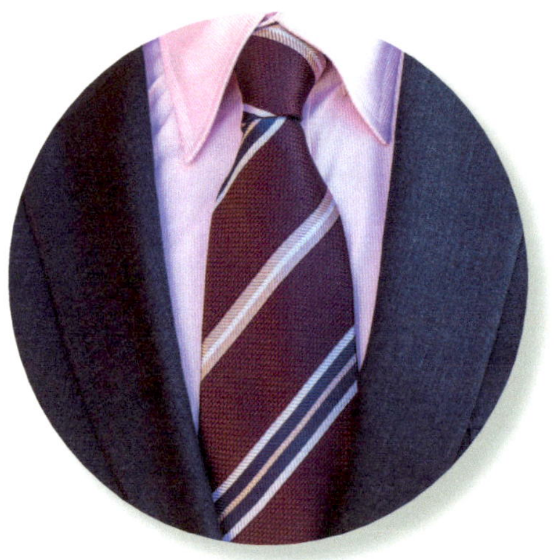

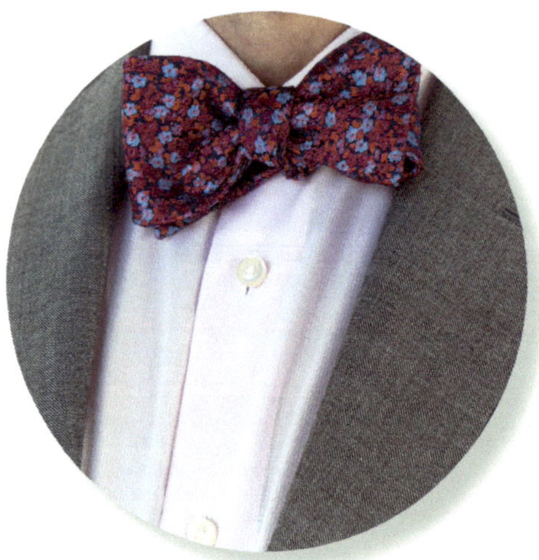

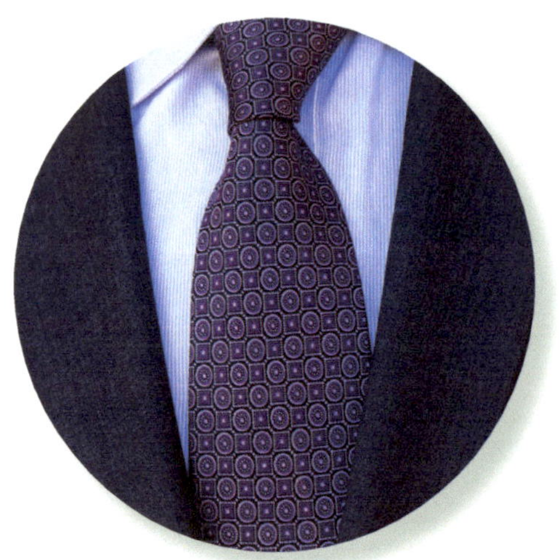

FOOTWEAR

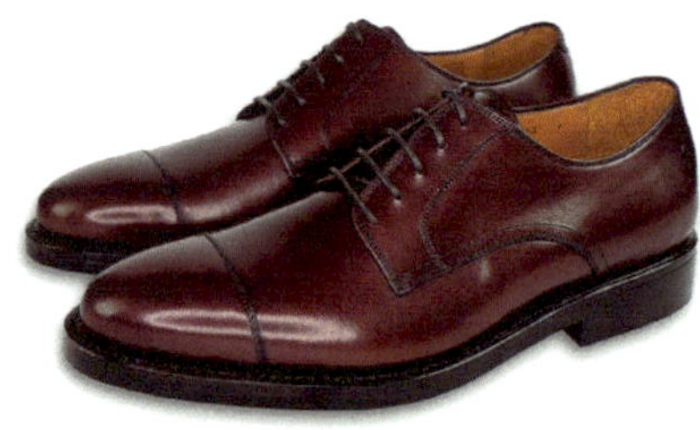

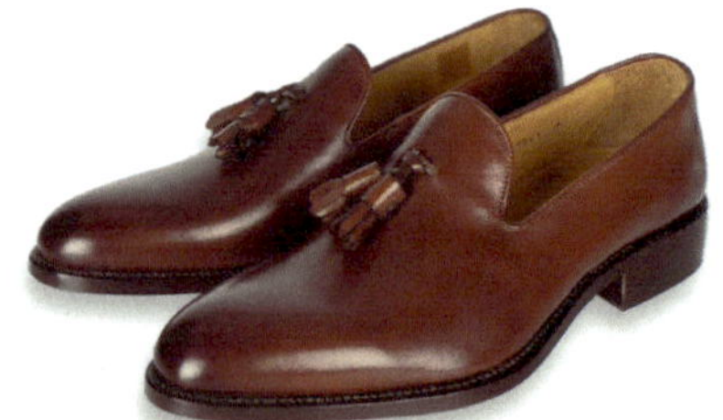

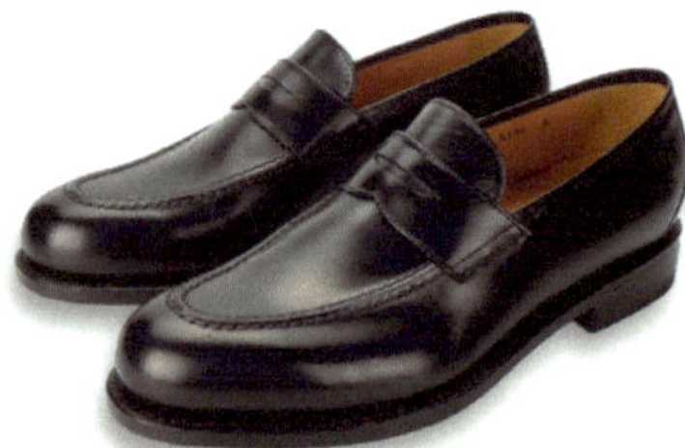

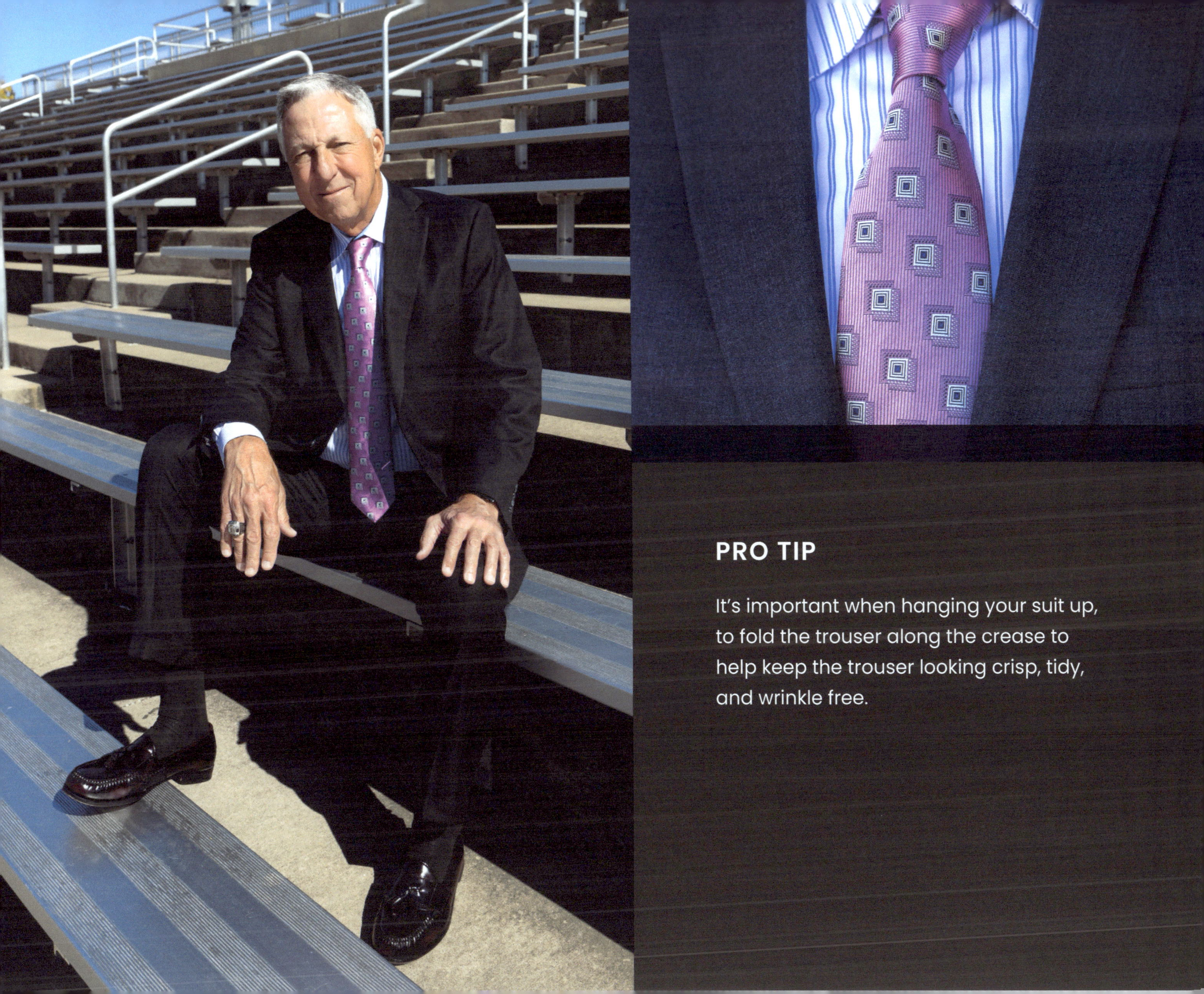

PRO TIP

It's important when hanging your suit up,
to fold the trouser along the crease to
help keep the trouser looking crisp, tidy,
and wrinkle free.

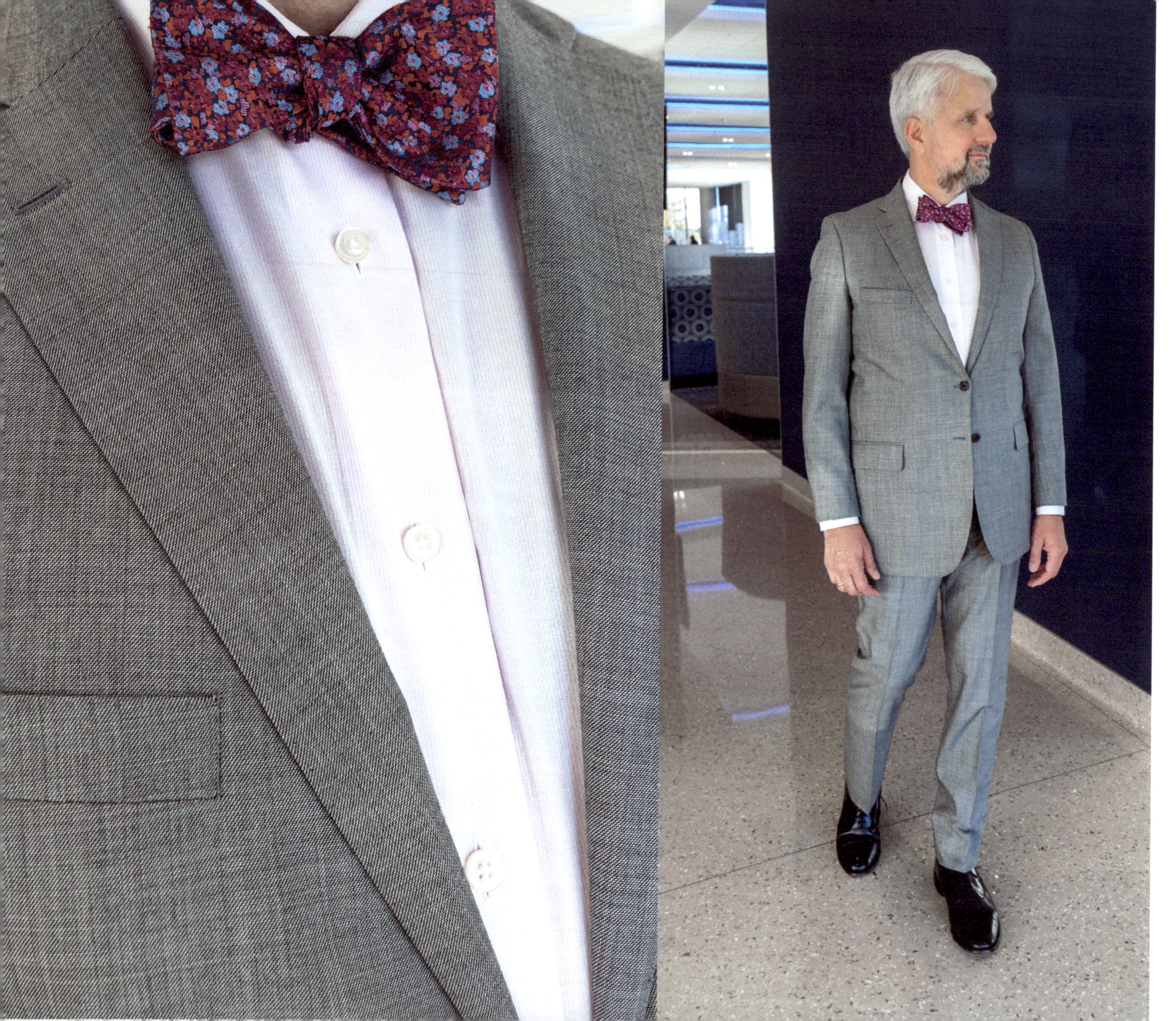

Oscar Martinez

WHAT IS YOUR OCCUPATION?

Corporate Financial Consultant, Chief Financial Partner

WHAT ARE YOUR HOBBIES AND INTERESTS?

Skiing, reading, politics, traveling, wine, bourbon, sports, exercising, cooking, grilling, and most of all, family activities.

WHAT IS A FUN FACT ABOUT YOU?

I've climbed twenty-five 14ers in Colorado. The term 14ers refers to mountains that are over 14,000 feet high. I can also fold fitted sheets!

HOW HAS YOUR WARDROBE CHANGED IN THE LAST 10 YEARS?

I used to focus on conservative suits as I mostly dealt with bankers and investors who were similarly dressed. Over the last 7 years, I've really enjoyed adding more color and pattern to my wardrobe especially when it comes to sport coat outfits.

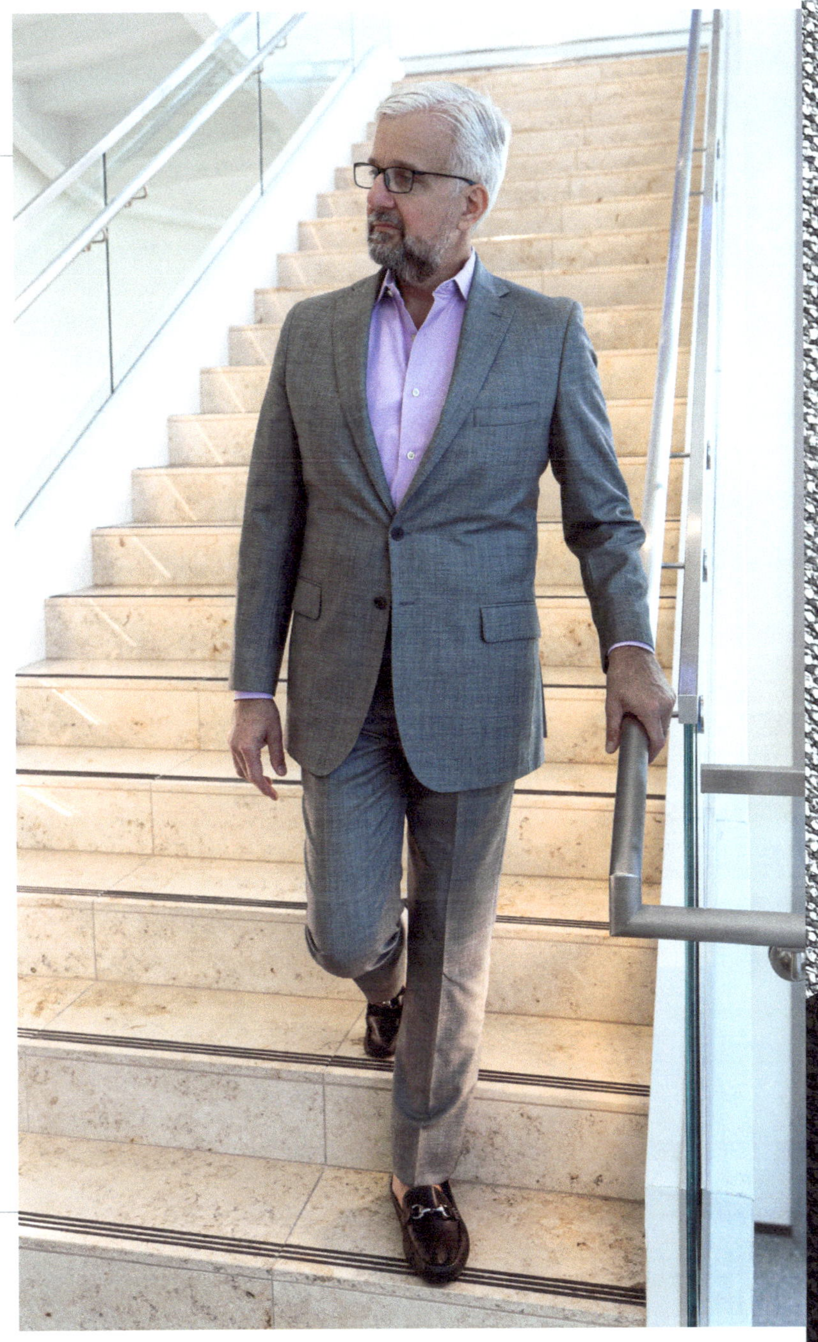

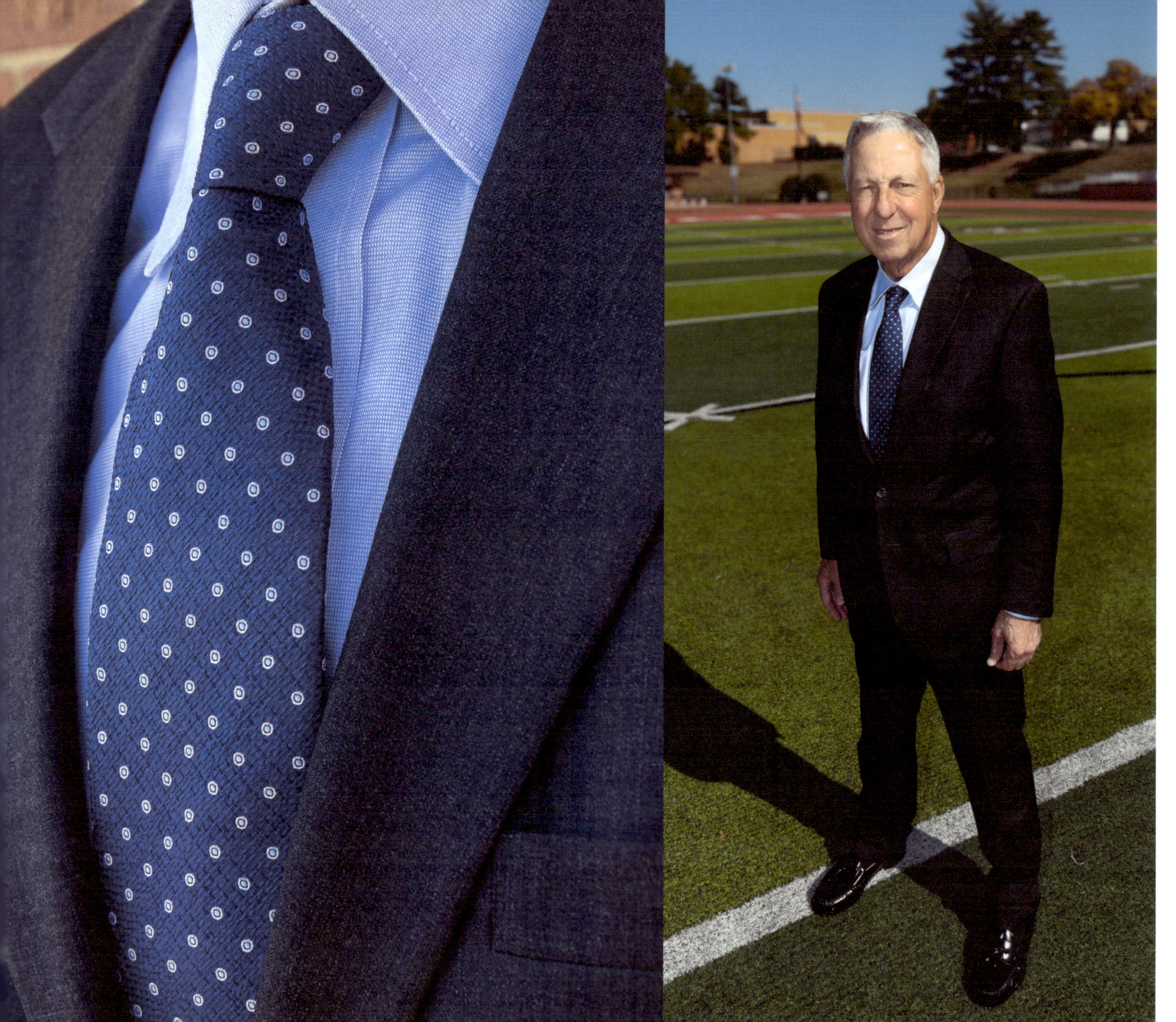

Joe Larrew

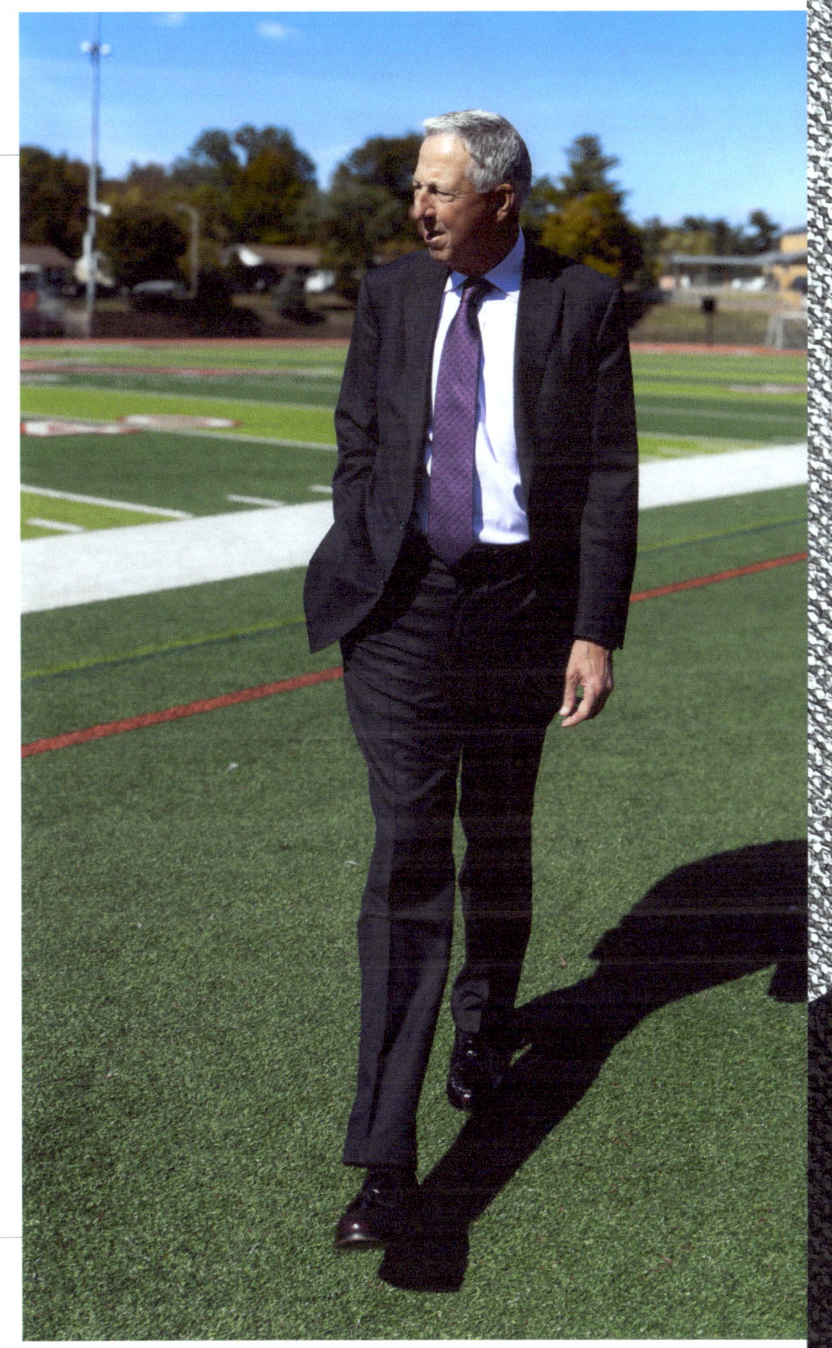

WHAT IS YOUR OCCUPATION?

Attorney

WHAT ARE YOUR HOBBIES AND INTERESTS?

Playing golf, spending time with my grandchildren, cigars, and football.

WHAT IS A FUN FACT ABOUT YOU?

I was a football official in the NFL for 20 years and officiated Super Bowl XLVII between San Fransisco and Baltimore, when the Harbaugh brothers coached against each other.

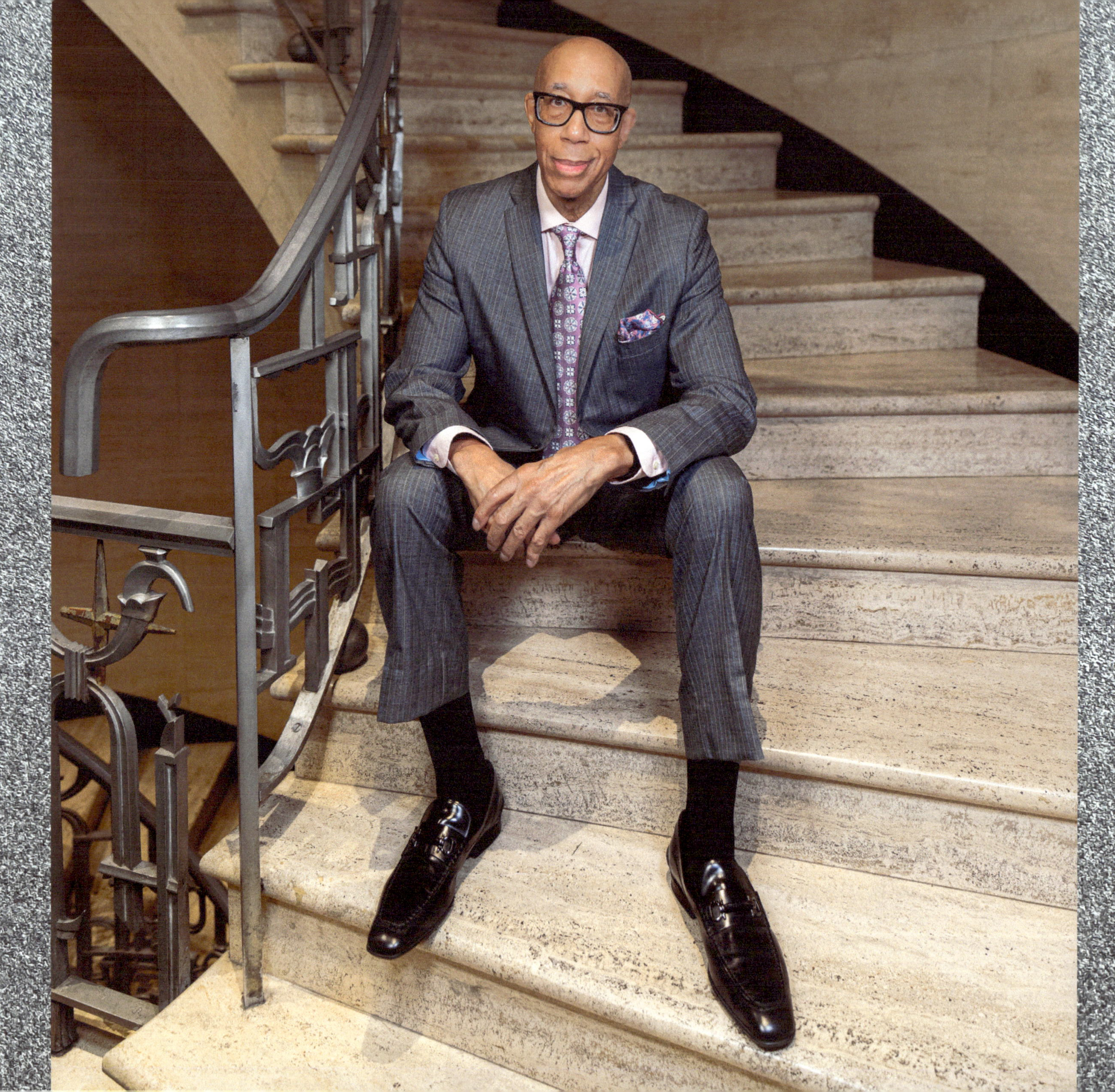

GREY & BLUE-GREY STRIPE

PROFESSIONAL • CLASSIC • RESPECTABLE • TIMELESS

Conservative and traditional, grey and blue-grey stripe suits are simply a must-have for professional men. They produce a sense of invincibility that many men gravitate towards depending on their profession and audience. Depending on the shade of grey and the boldness of the stripe, the grey stripe can be intimidating, so be conscious of your audience and what your nonverbal messaging should be.

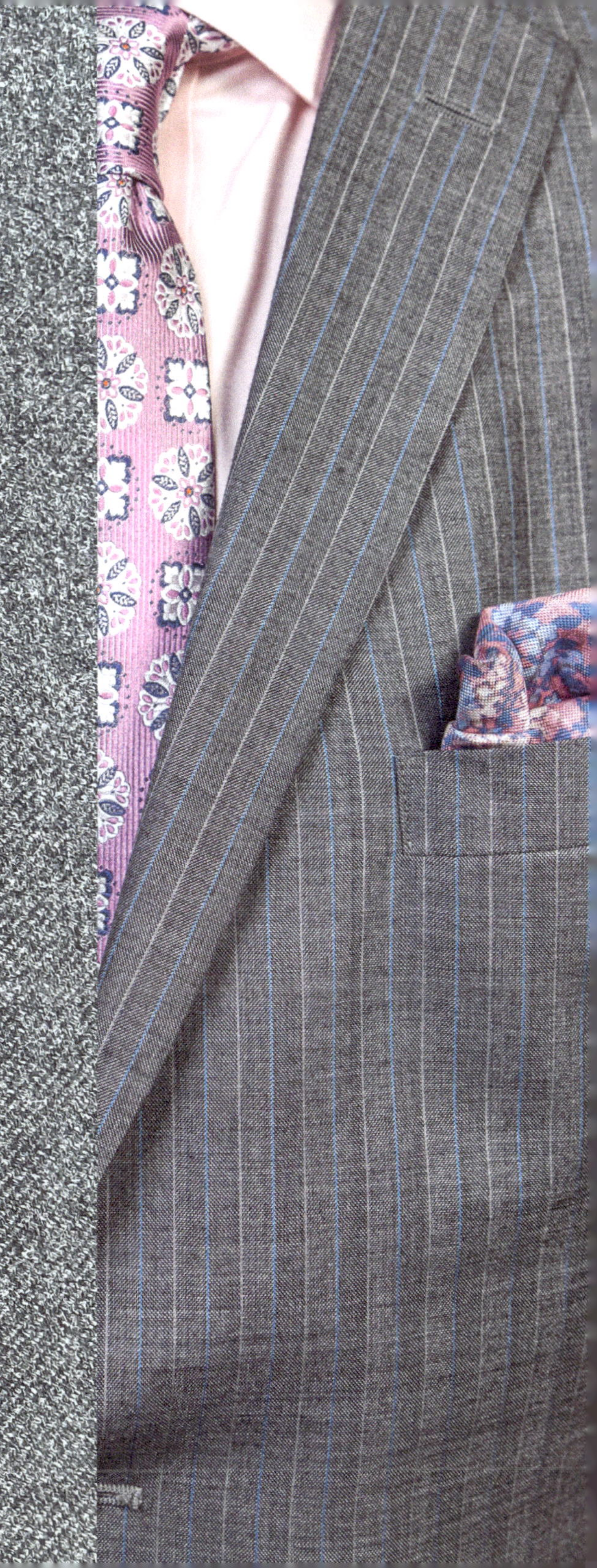

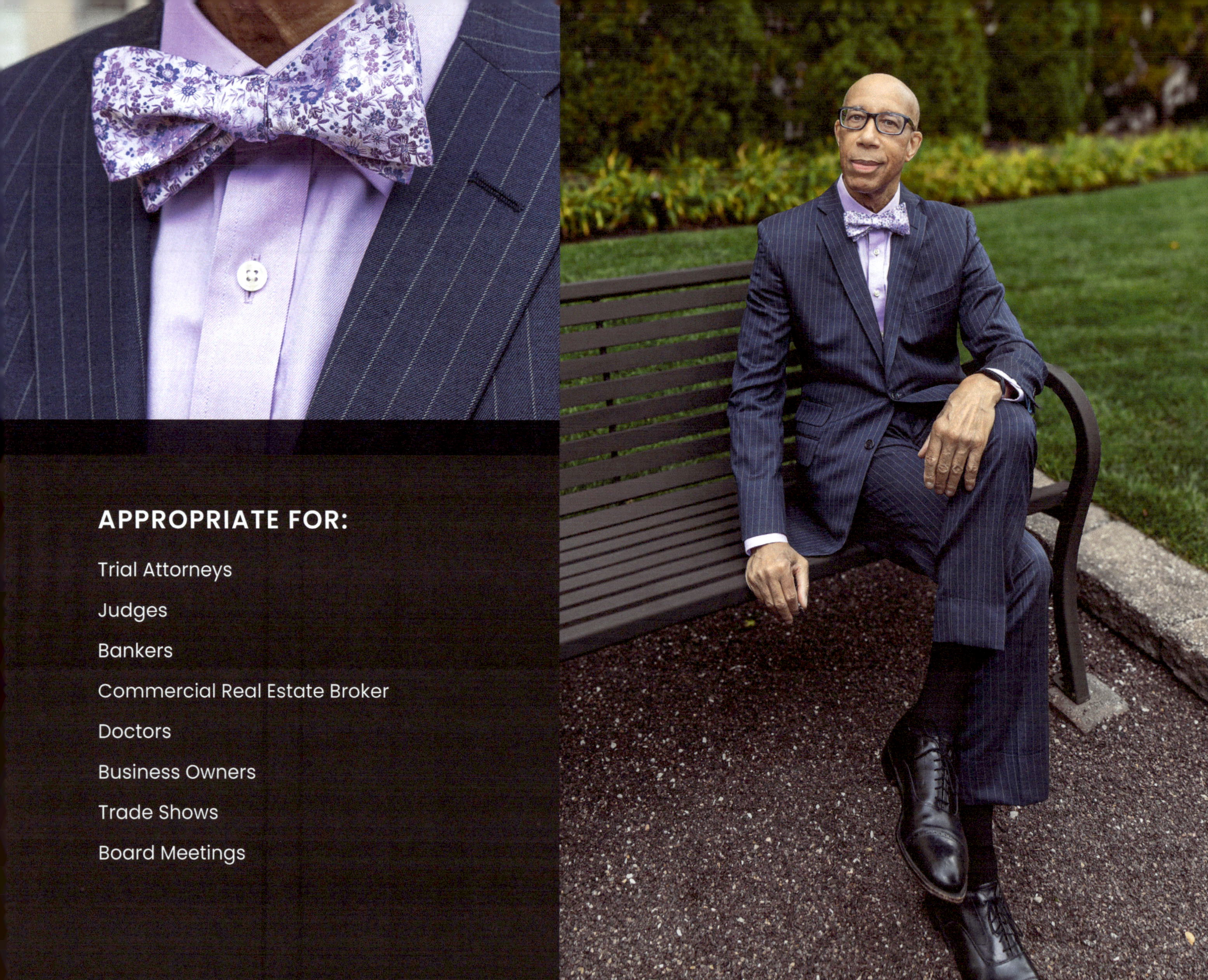
APPROPRIATE FOR:

Trial Attorneys

Judges

Bankers

Commercial Real Estate Broker

Doctors

Business Owners

Trade Shows

Board Meetings

GREY & BLUE-GREY STRIPE SUIT

SHIRTS TO MATCH

Solid Colors

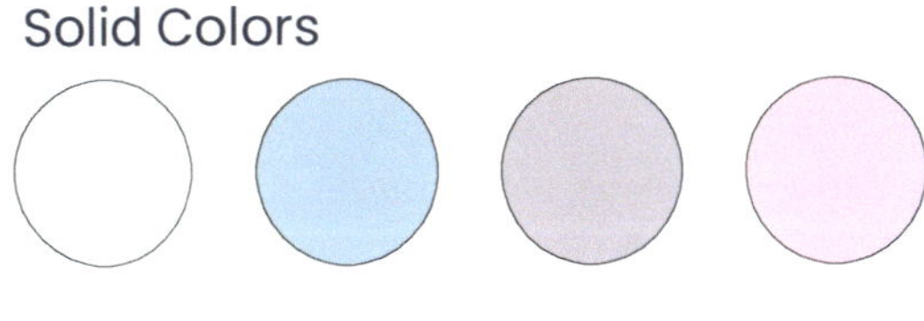

White – Color Stripe or Pattern

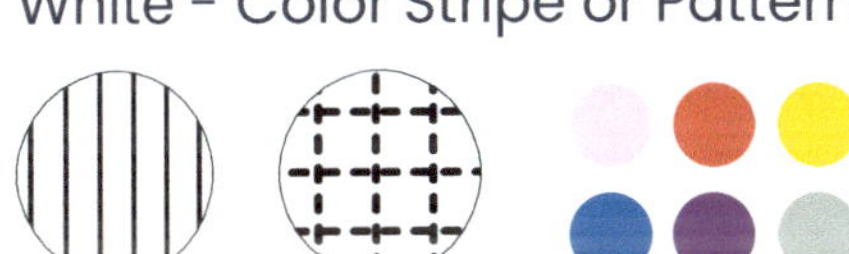

Blue – Color Stripe or Pattern

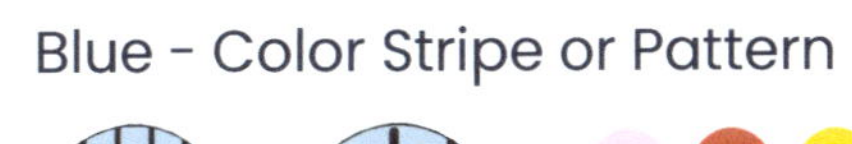
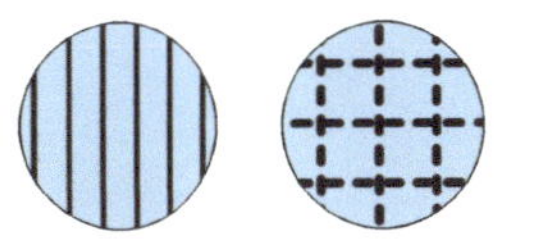
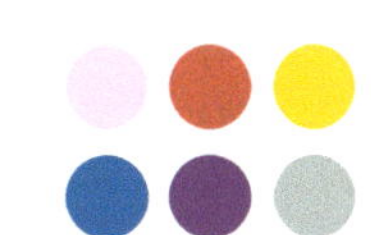

TIE COLORS

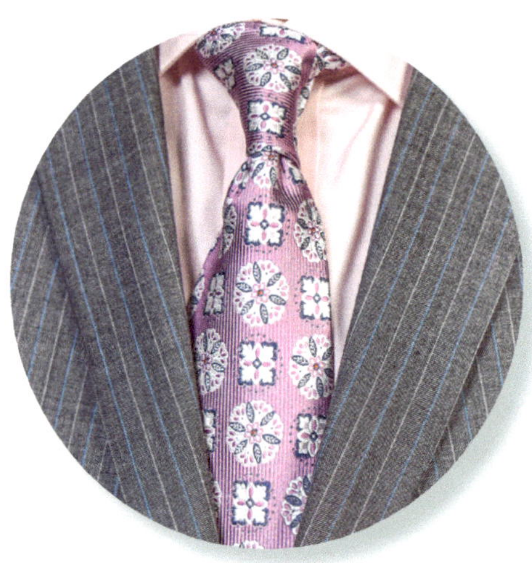

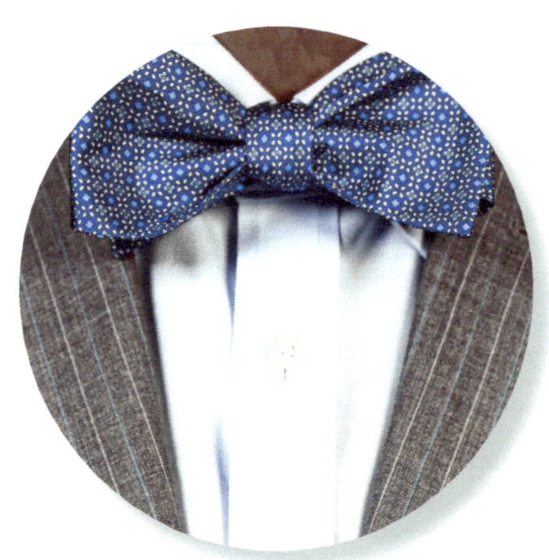

FOOTWEAR

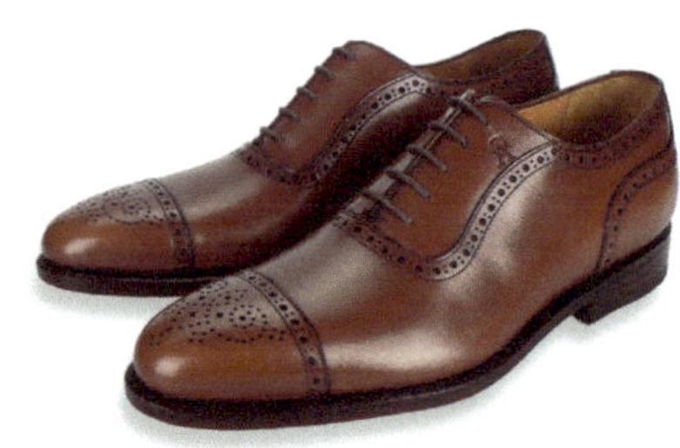

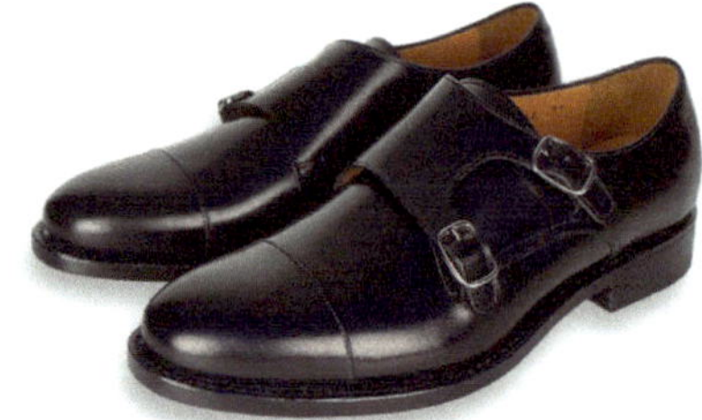

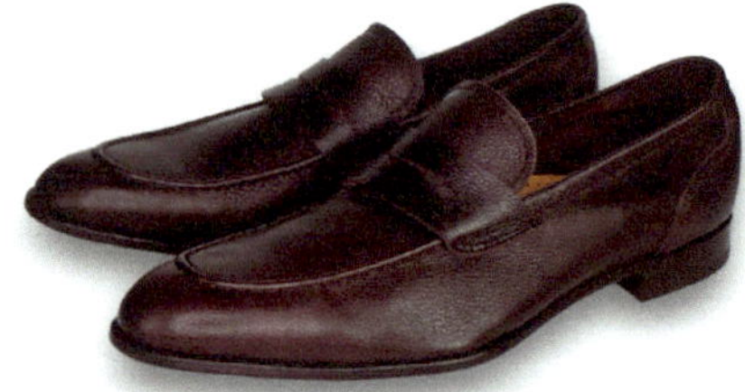

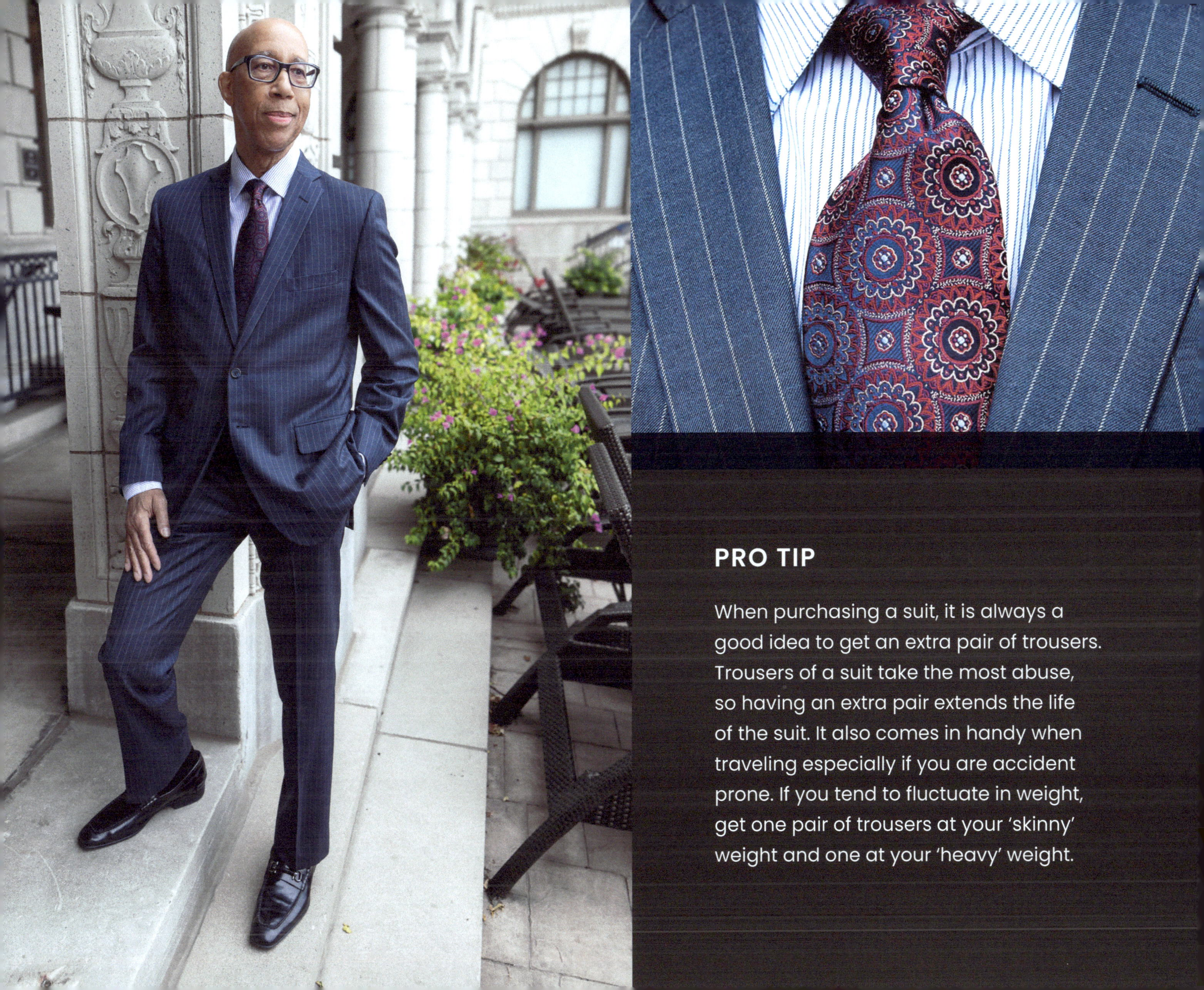

PRO TIP

When purchasing a suit, it is always a good idea to get an extra pair of trousers. Trousers of a suit take the most abuse, so having an extra pair extends the life of the suit. It also comes in handy when traveling especially if you are accident prone. If you tend to fluctuate in weight, get one pair of trousers at your 'skinny' weight and one at your 'heavy' weight.

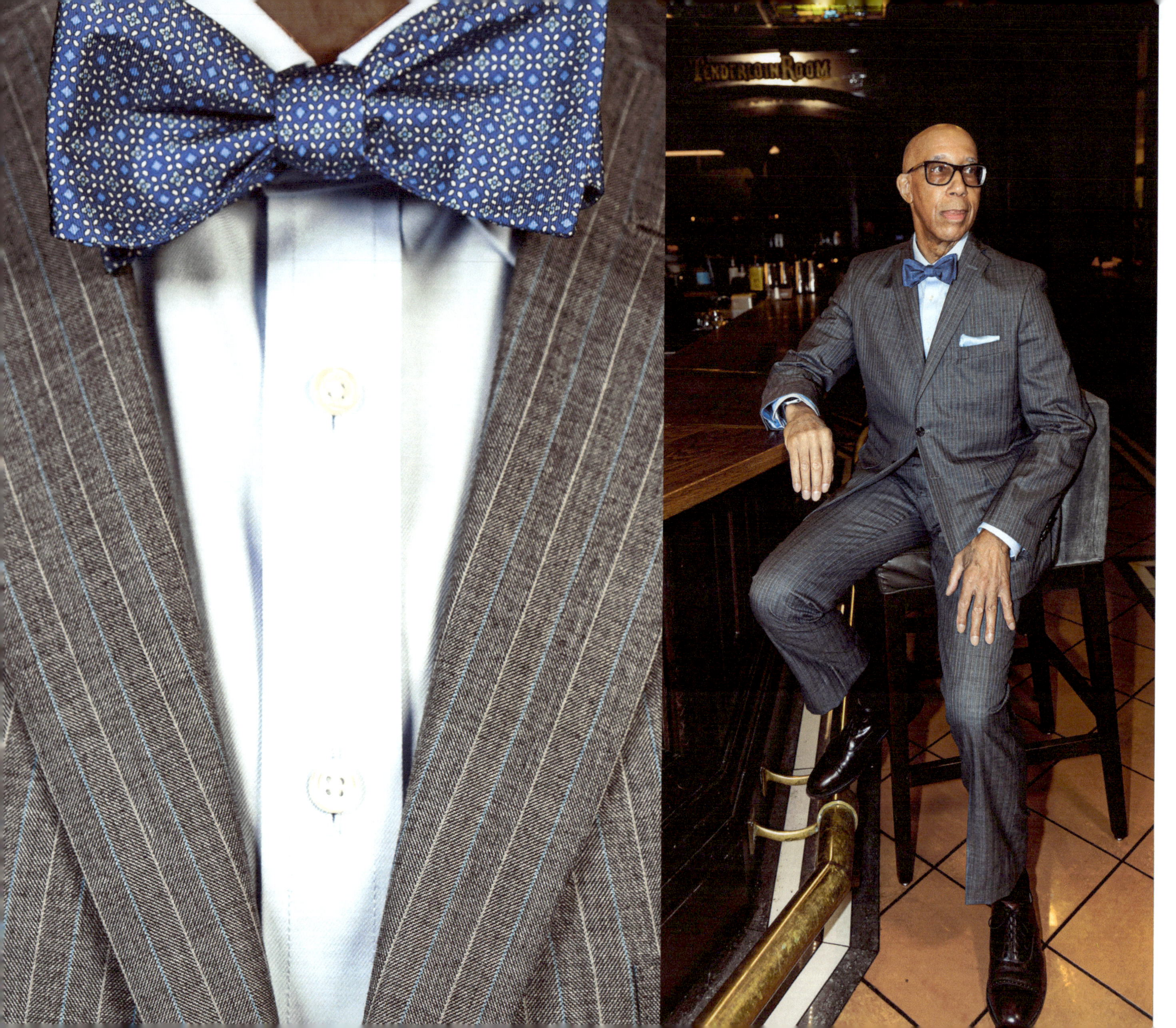

Keith Williamson

WHAT IS YOUR OCCUPATION?

President of Centene Foundation

WHAT ARE YOUR HOBBIES AND INTERESTS?

I enjoy working out, playing cards, and serving on the board of several nonprofits in the St. Louis community.

WHERE AND HOW DID YOU LEARN HOW TO DRESS?

My father was a great influence on me, and he appreciated the importance of dressing well. He loved wearing suits and looking his best, which I admired and wanted to prioritize in my life as well.

WHAT DO YOU BELIEVE IS THE MOST IMPORTANT PART OF YOUR SUCCESS JOURNEY?

How you feel about yourself is key, and looking good is part of that. It was Maya Angelou who said that success is liking yourself, liking what you do, and liking how you do it. It is important to me that I have enjoyed the jobs I have had and the people I have worked with during my career. It feels particularly good to know that I have helped others along the way.

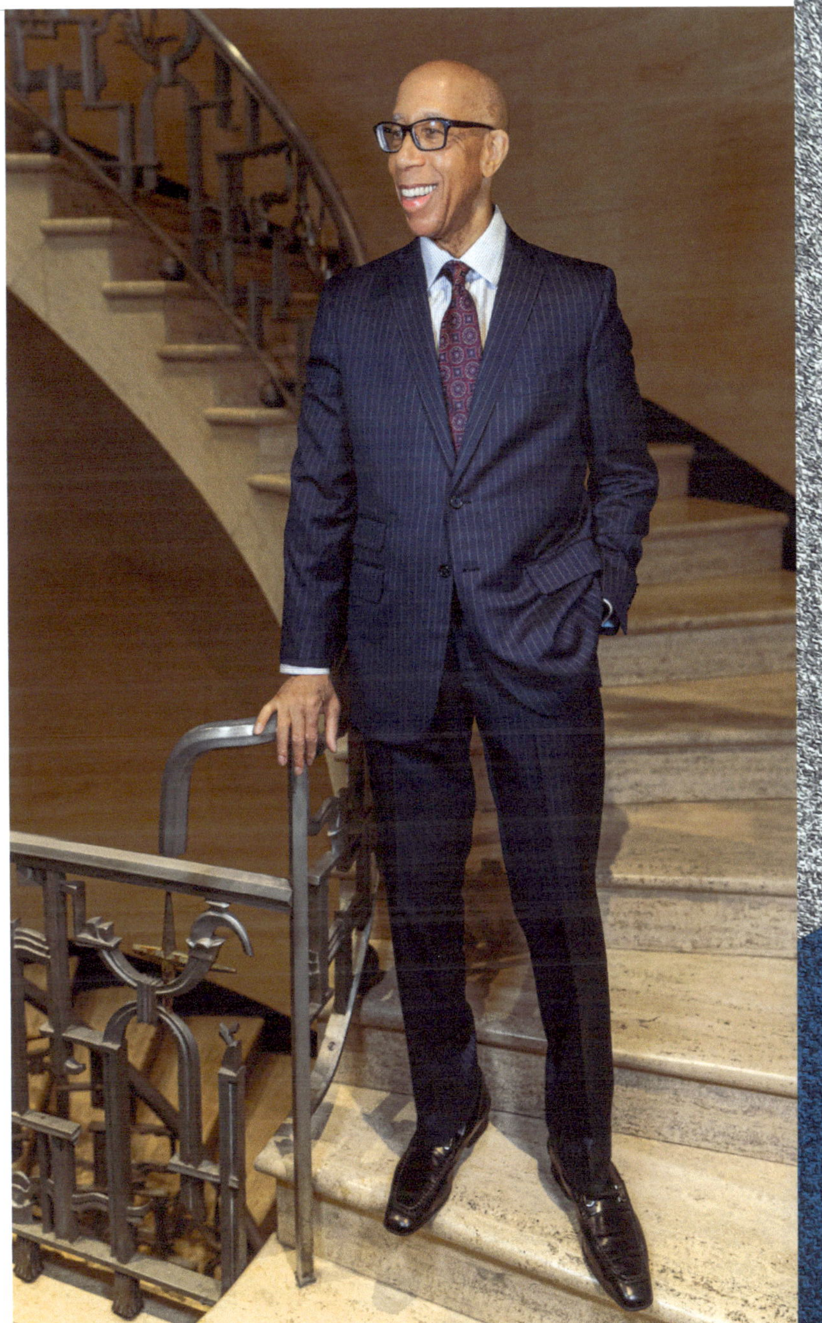

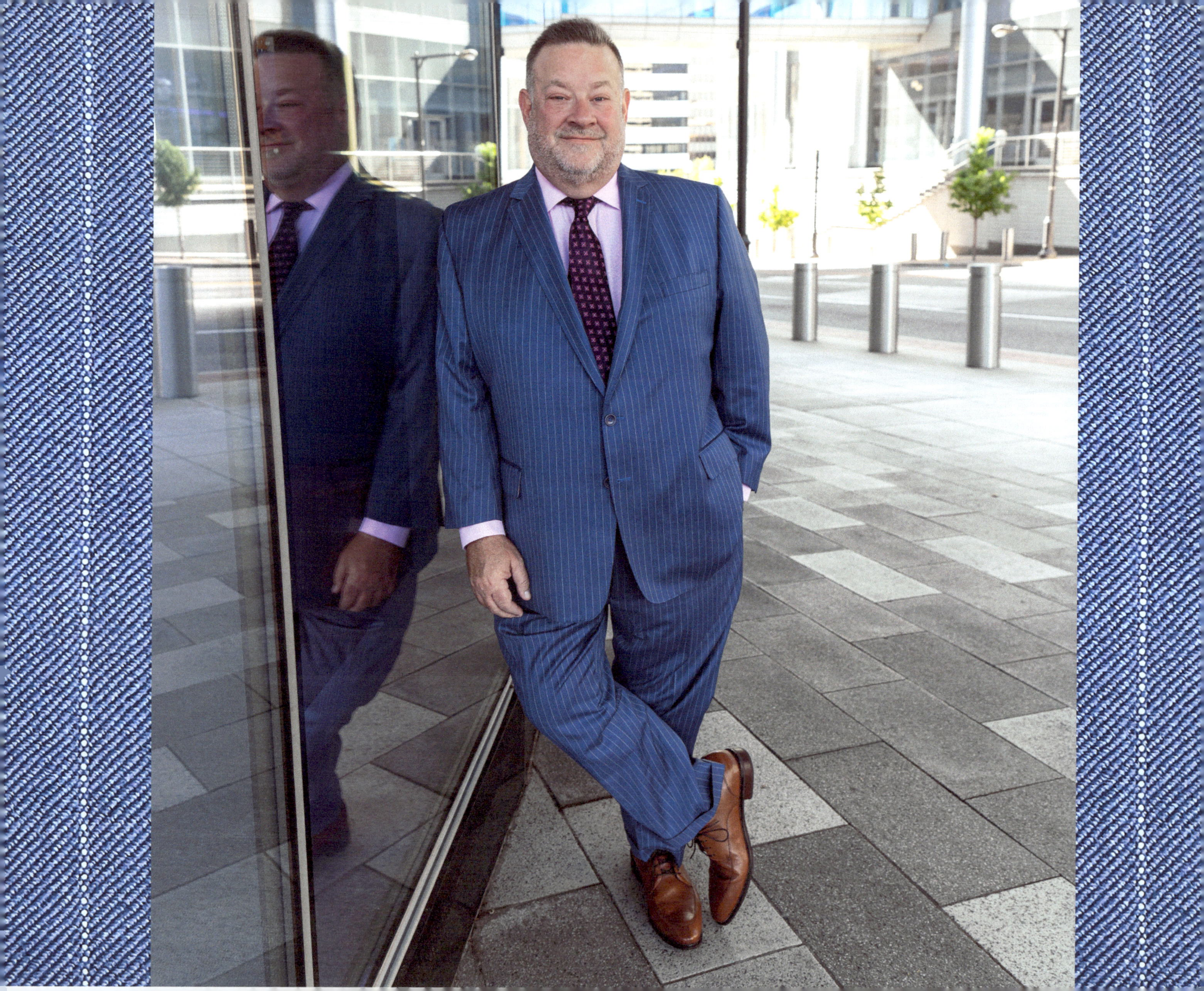

BLUE STRIPE

REFINED • DIGNIFIED • GENTLEMANLY • SERIOUS • CONFIDENT

The gentleman wearing a blue striped suit exudes authority and demands respect. The blue stripe instills a sense of mastery and makes you feel and look powerful, making it a perfect choice for a pro athlete before a game, or the CEO of a company walking into an investor meeting. Depending on the aggressiveness of the stripe, it may also appear intimidating, so consider your audience carefully.

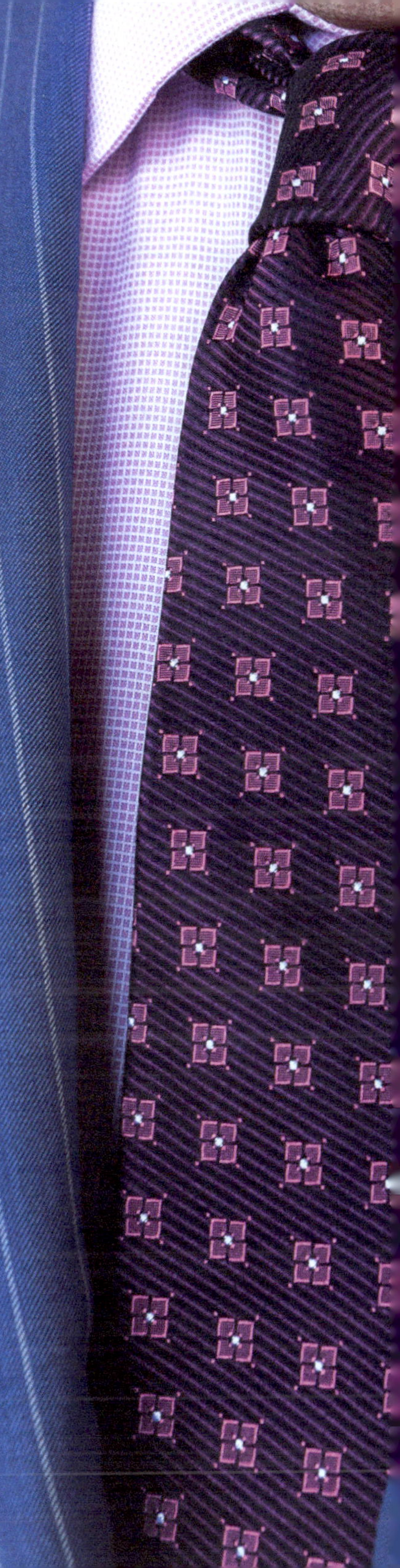

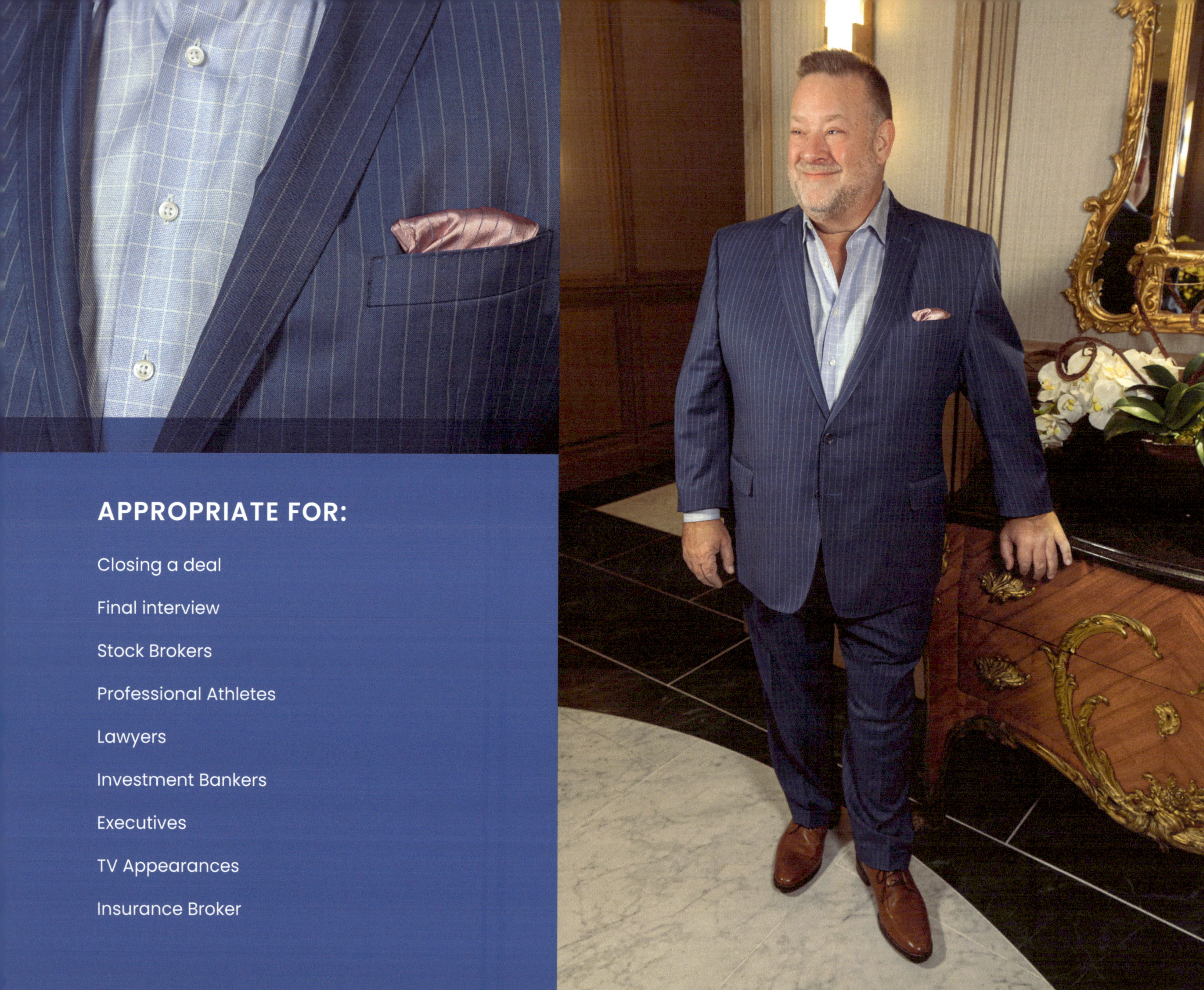
APPROPRIATE FOR:

Closing a deal

Final interview

Stock Brokers

Professional Athletes

Lawyers

Investment Bankers

Executives

TV Appearances

Insurance Broker

BLUE STRIPE SUIT

SHIRTS TO MATCH

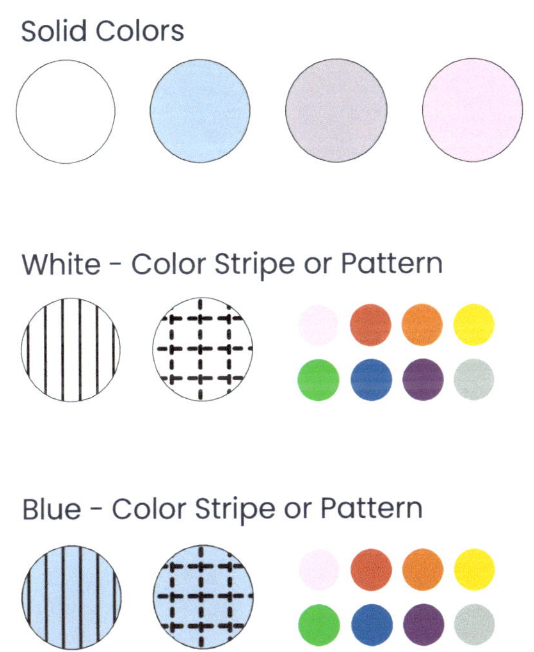

TIE COLORS

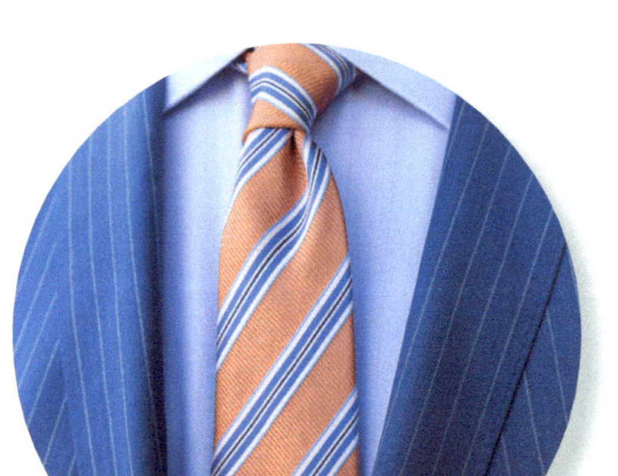

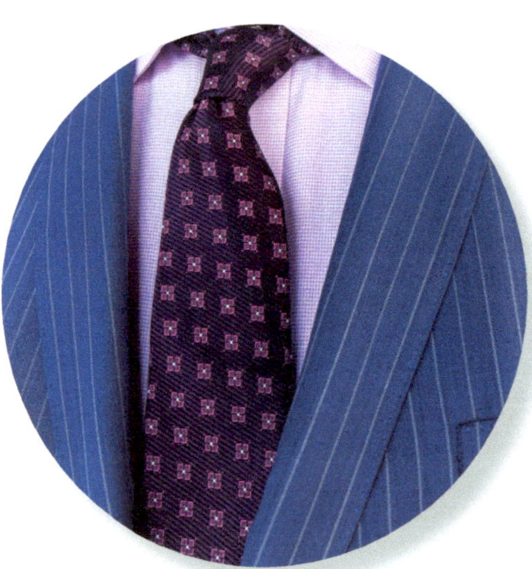

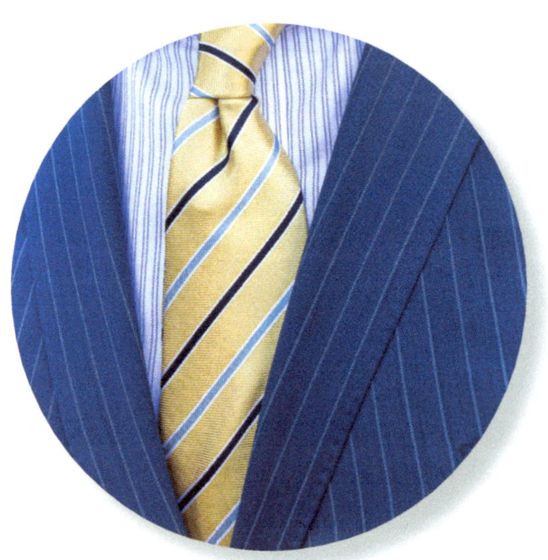

FOOTWEAR

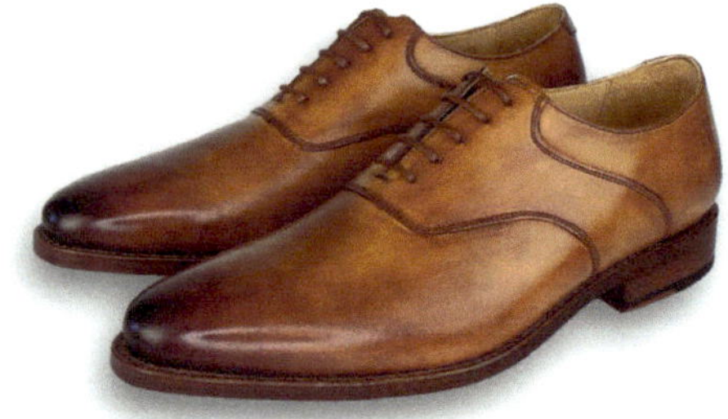

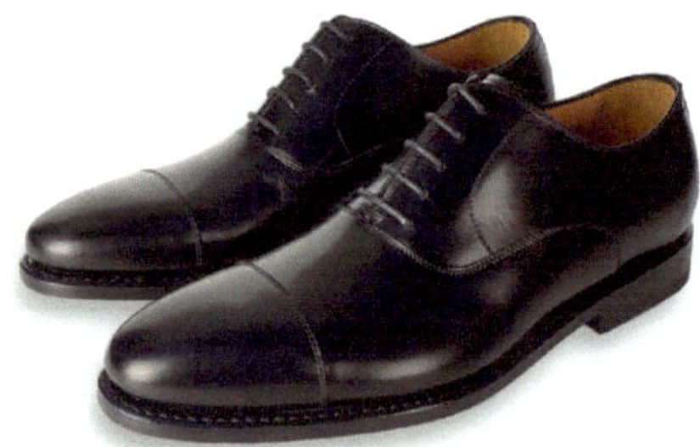

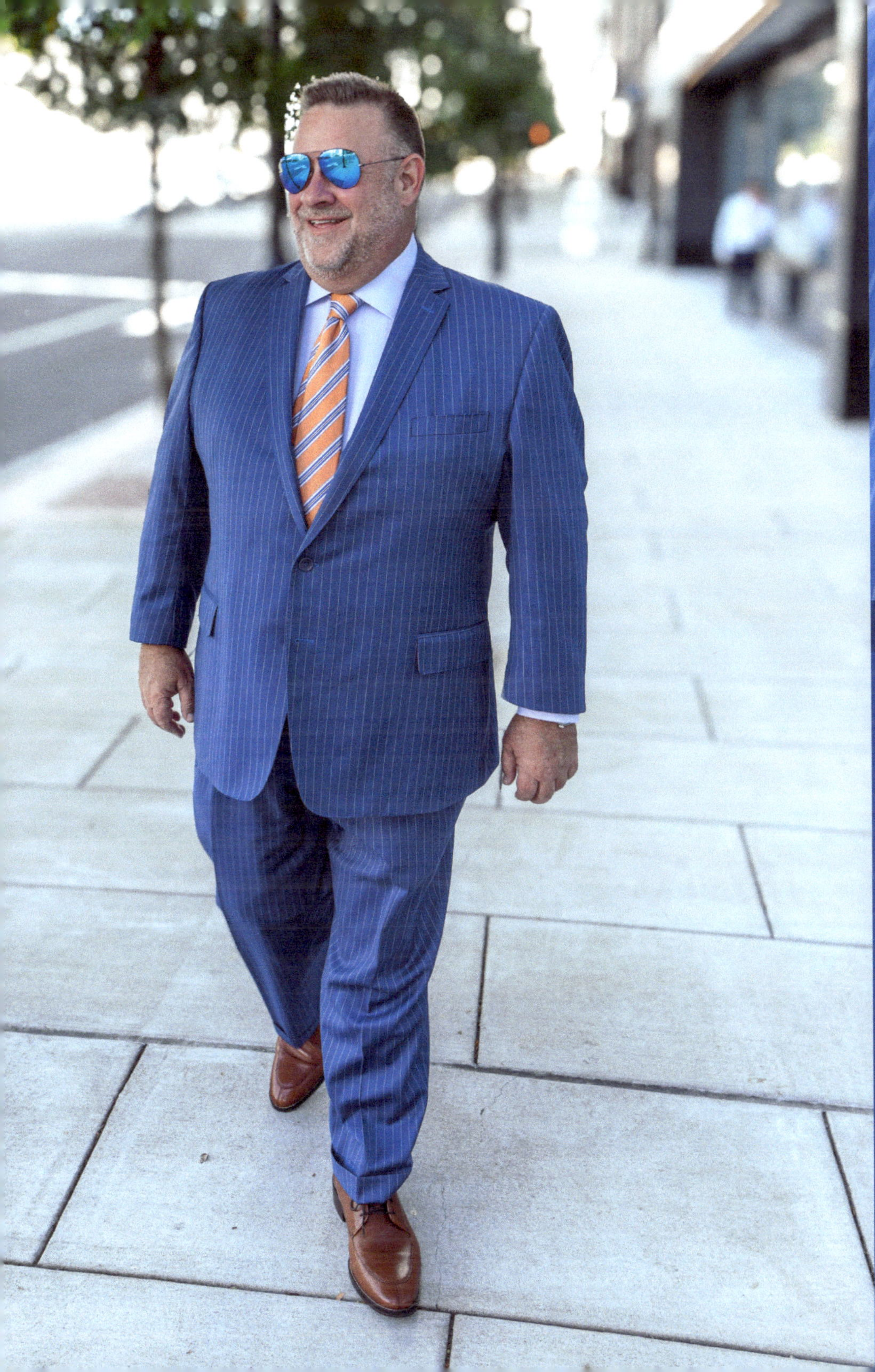

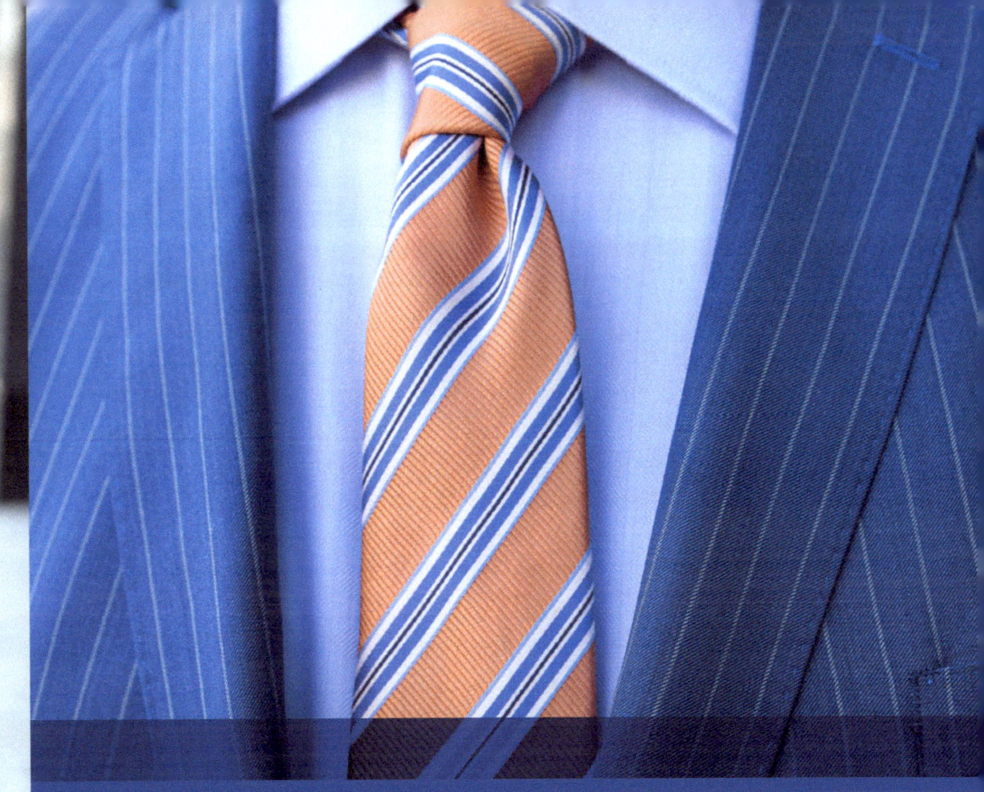

PRO TIP

Always fasten the top button on your jacket, and always leave the bottom one unfastened (for a two-button jacket). Unbutton the jacket only when you sit to avoid creases, and immediately fasten the button again when you stand unless you are going for a more casual look.

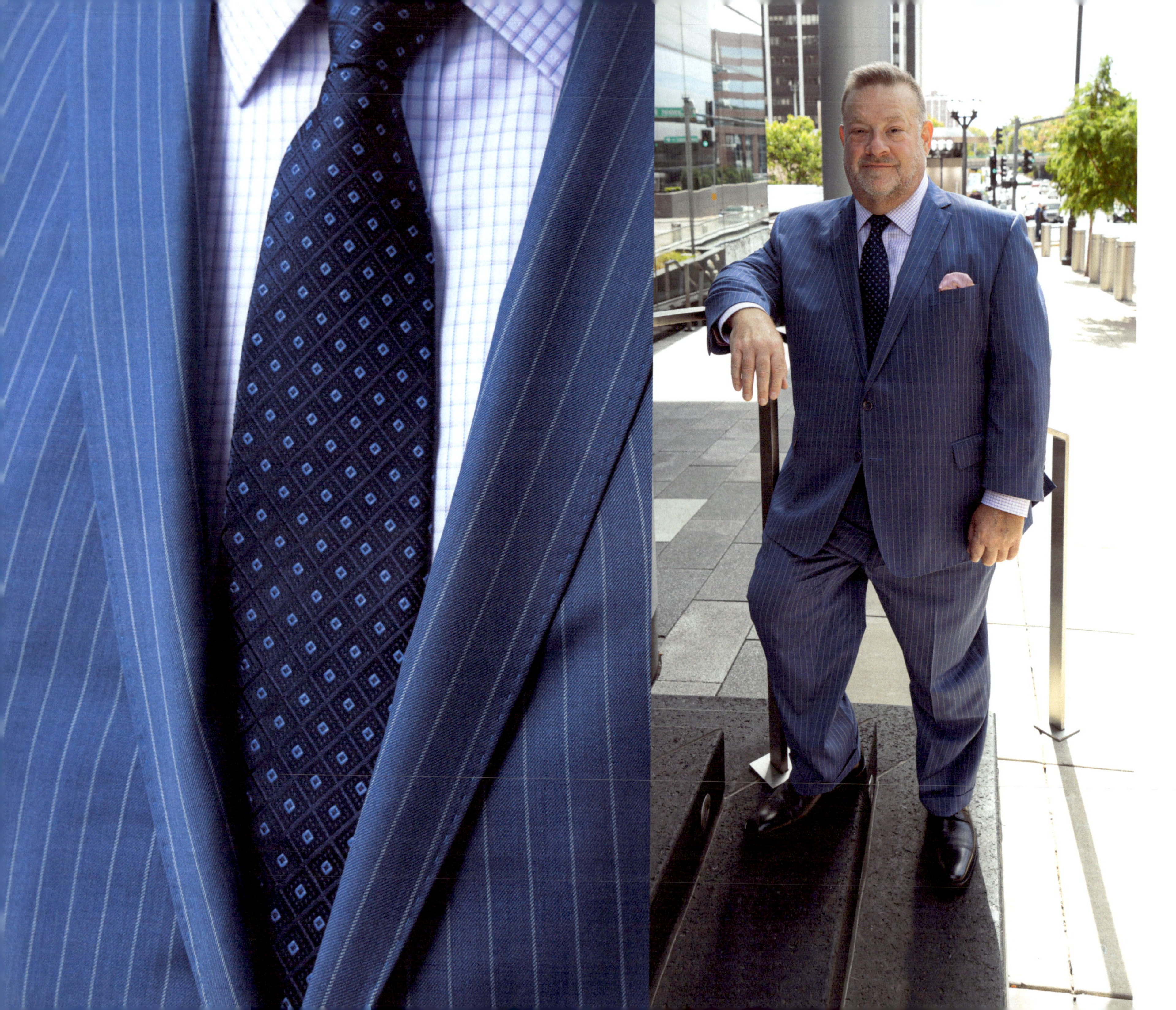

Kent Heintz

WHAT IS YOUR OCCUPATION?

Vice President at BMO Bank Commercial Lending

WHAT ARE YOUR HOBBIES AND INTERESTS?

I enjoy spending time scuba diving, spending time with my daughters, lacrosse, golfing, traveling, and charity work.

WHAT IS A FUN FACT ABOUT YOU?

I played semi-pro lacrosse.

WHAT DO YOU LIKE IN COLOR AND PATTERN IN YOUR CLOTHES?

I gravitate towards blues and plaids. I also enjoy colorful clothes and lean towards lighter colors.

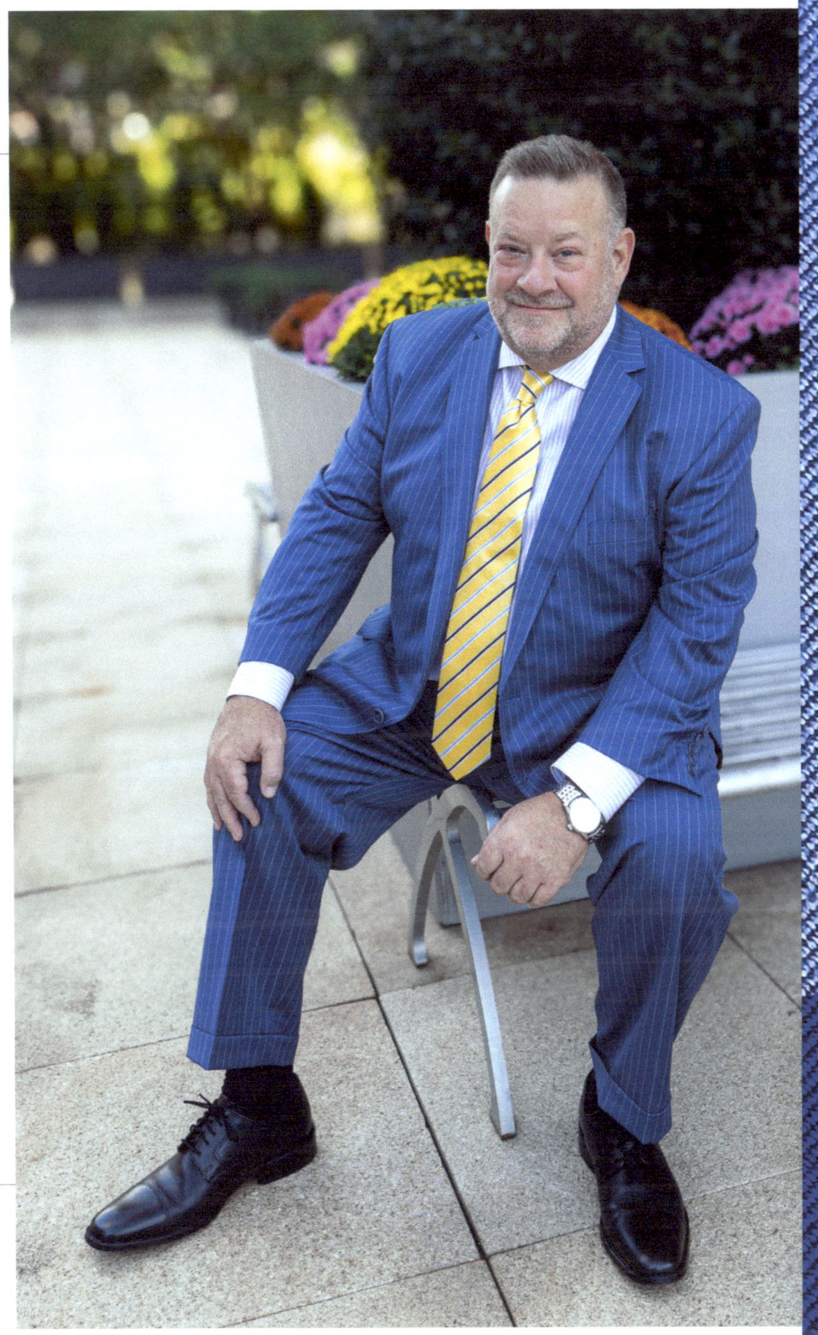

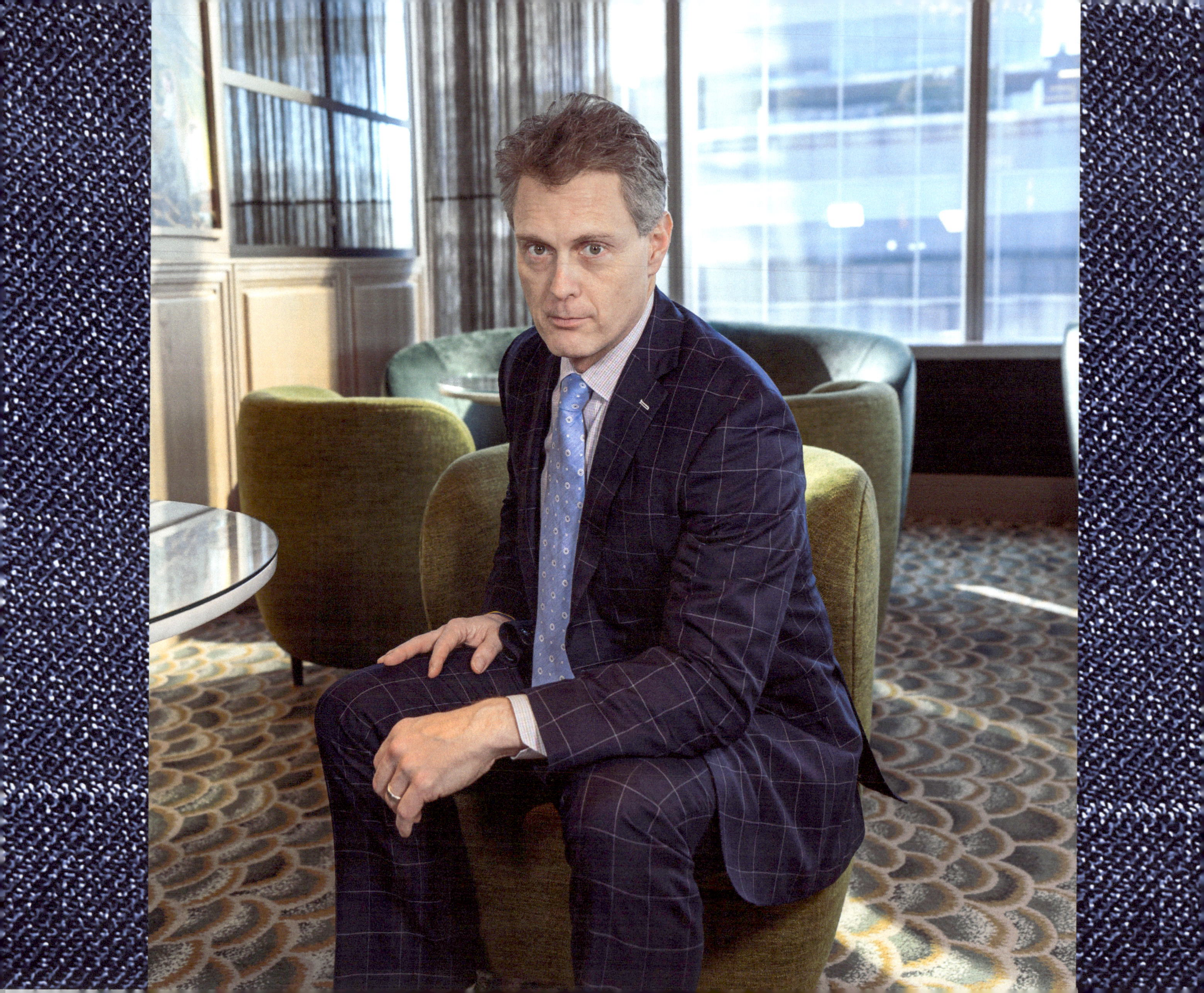

NAVY PATTERN

CONFIDENT • FUN • ADVENTUROUS • RISK TAKER • MODERN

Once a gentleman feels comfortable and confident wearing the basic rotation of suits, he should consider adding more patterns to his suit rotation. A navy pattern suit serves as a great starting point. When a man wears a suit with a pattern, it signals sophistication and open-mindedness, indicating that he has a healthy rotation of basics covered. A navy pattern suit provides a modern option for the gentleman who wants to have a lively and professional or social appearance. It is a great choice for those who enjoy receiving compliments and don't mind being the center of attention.

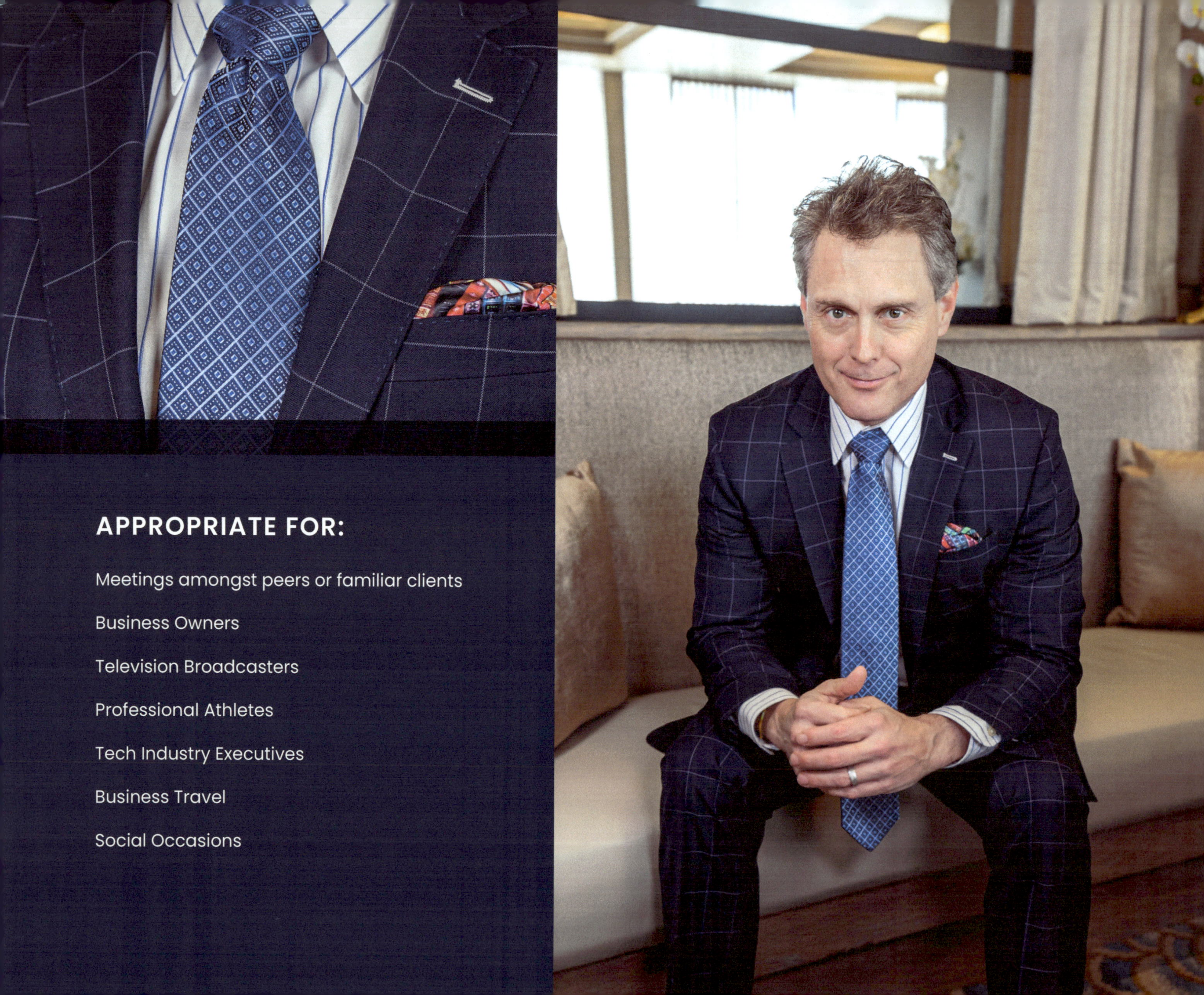
APPROPRIATE FOR:

Meetings amongst peers or familiar clients

Business Owners

Television Broadcasters

Professional Athletes

Tech Industry Executives

Business Travel

Social Occasions

NAVY PATTERN SUIT

SHIRTS TO MATCH

Solid Colors

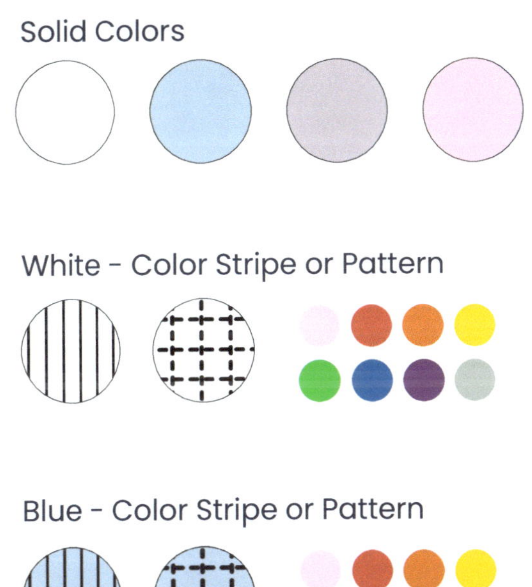

White - Color Stripe or Pattern

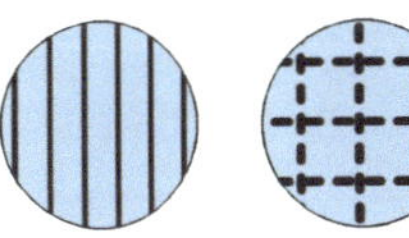

Blue - Color Stripe or Pattern

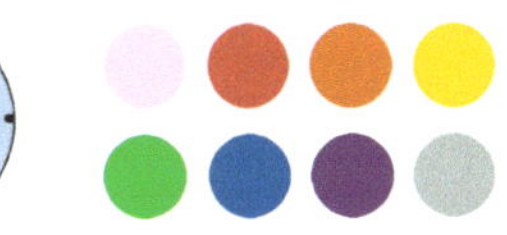

TIE COLORS

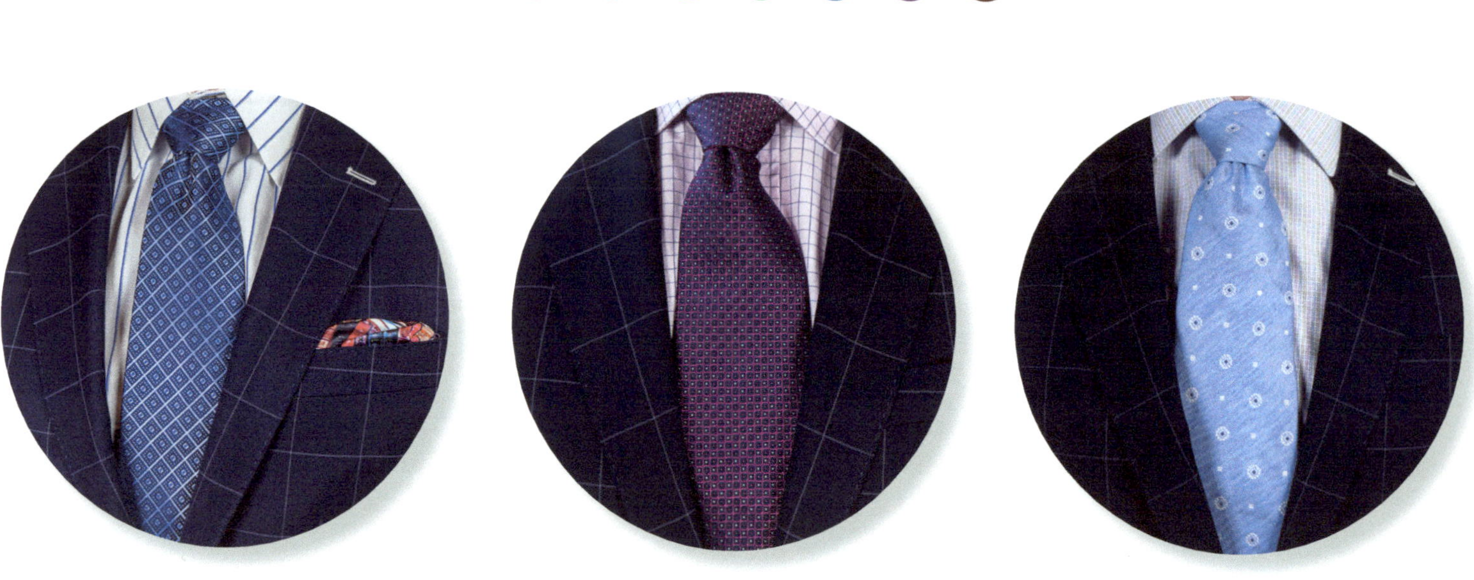

FOOTWEAR

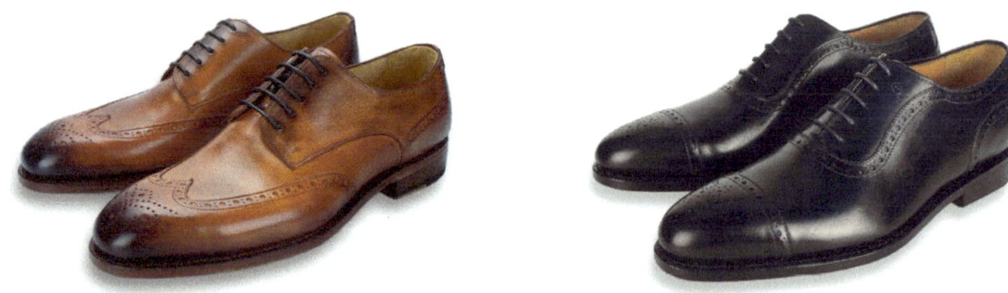

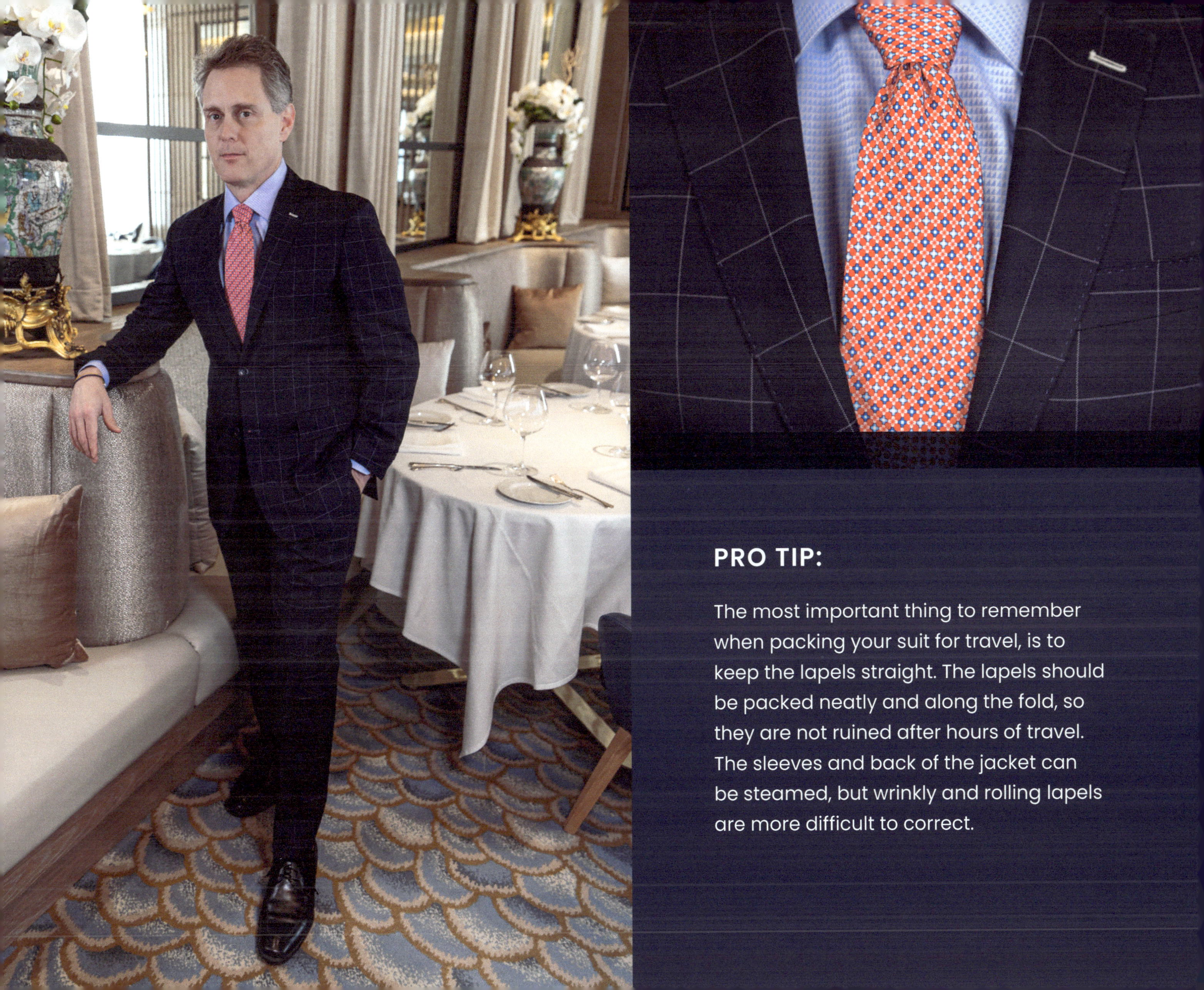

PRO TIP:

The most important thing to remember when packing your suit for travel, is to keep the lapels straight. The lapels should be packed neatly and along the fold, so they are not ruined after hours of travel. The sleeves and back of the jacket can be steamed, but wrinkly and rolling lapels are more difficult to correct.

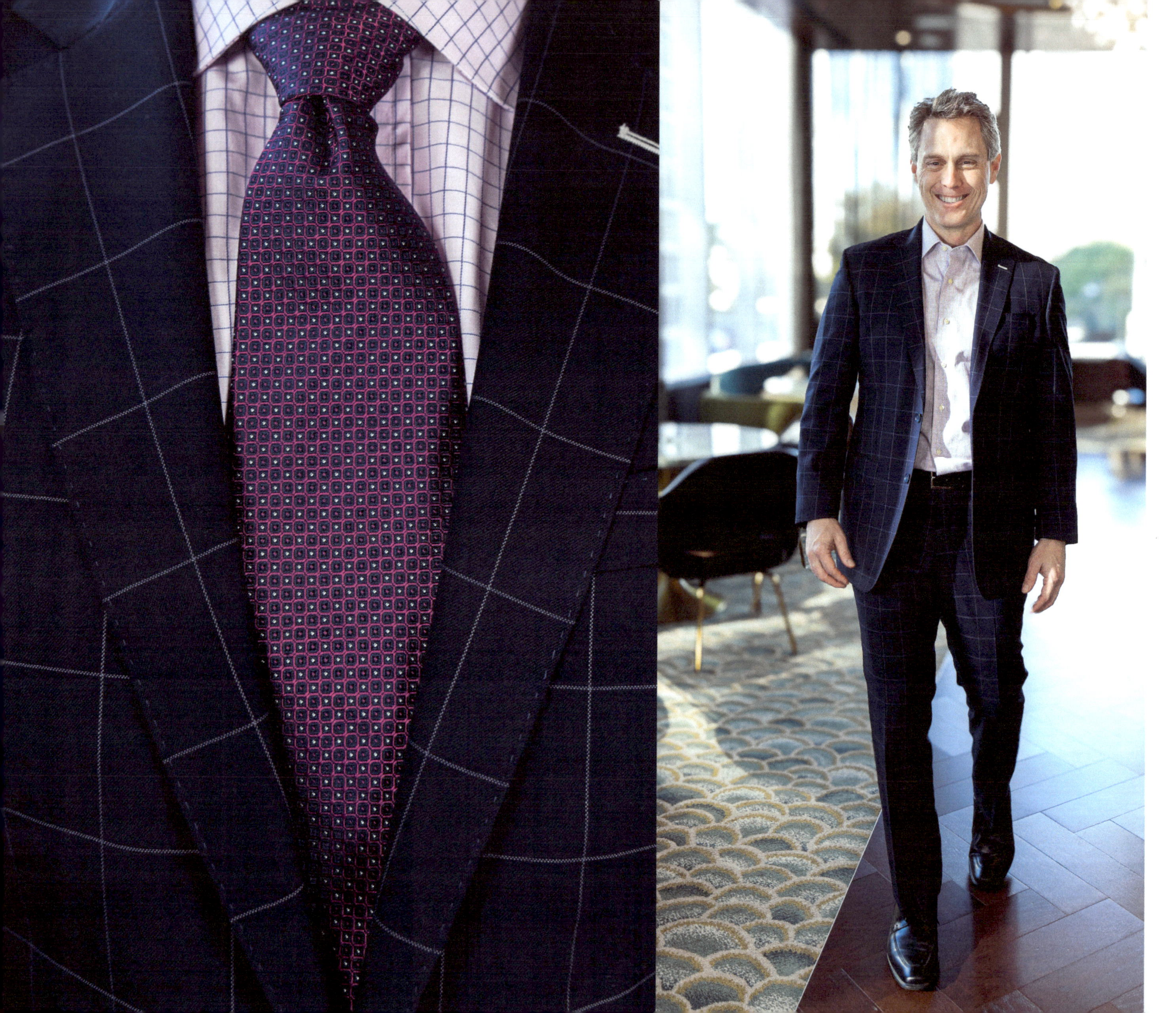

John Jennings

WHAT IS YOUR OCCUPATION?

President and Chief Strategist
at St. Louis Trust and Family Office

WHAT ARE YOUR HOBBIES AND INTERESTS?

Writing, public speaking, adjunct professor, reading,
and exercising.

WHAT IS A FUN FACT ABOUT YOU?

I lost my academic scholarship to a private college due to a
1.8 GPA (but I redeemed myself later!) I am the author of
"The Uncertainty Solution" and frequently write for Forbes.

WHAT ARE YOUR TIPS FOR PACKING
AND TRAVELING?

I travel a ton for business and personal reasons. As a rule,
you probably don't need to pack as many clothes as you think
you do. If you need to wear it twice that's fine. Pro Tip: get
yourself some dry fit underwear, and wash it in the hotel sink!

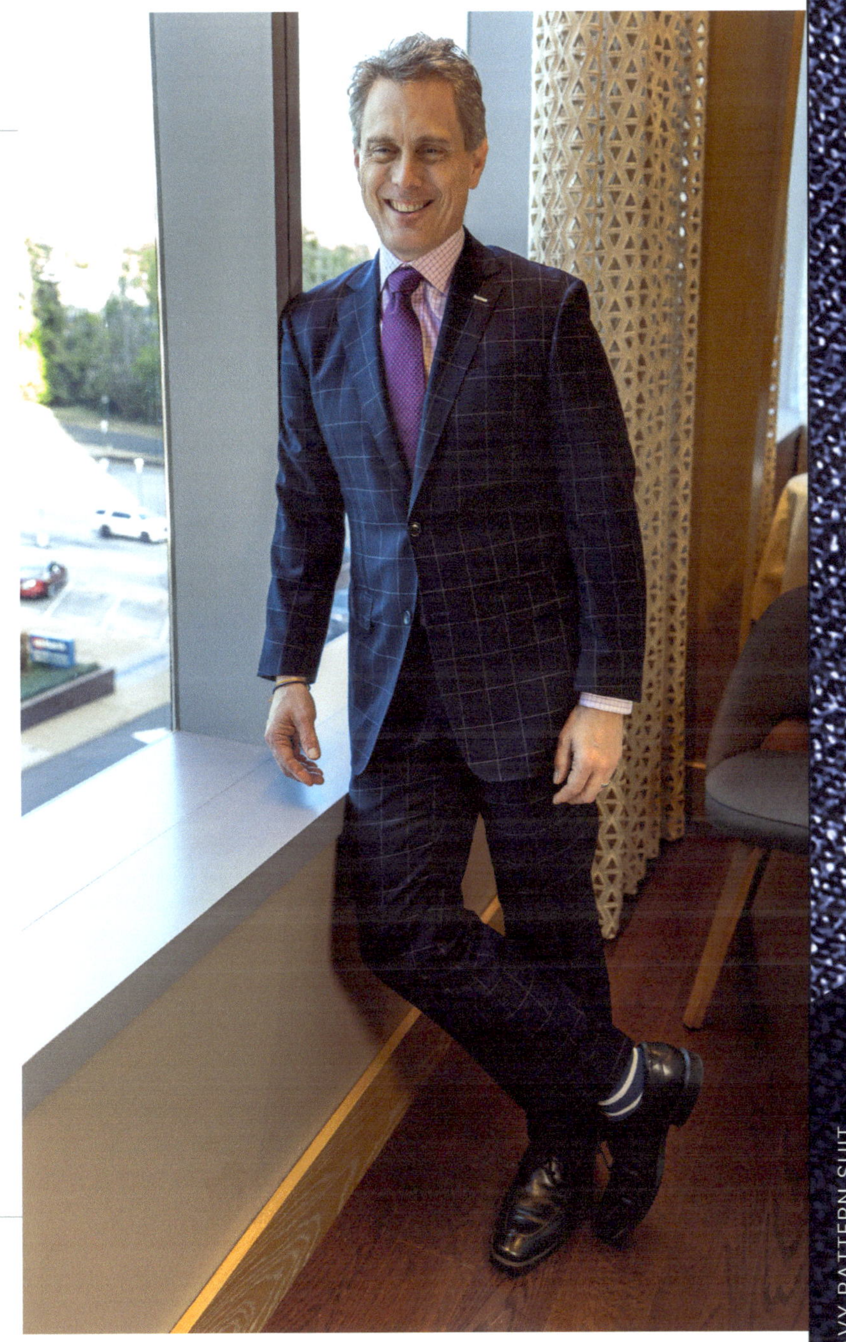

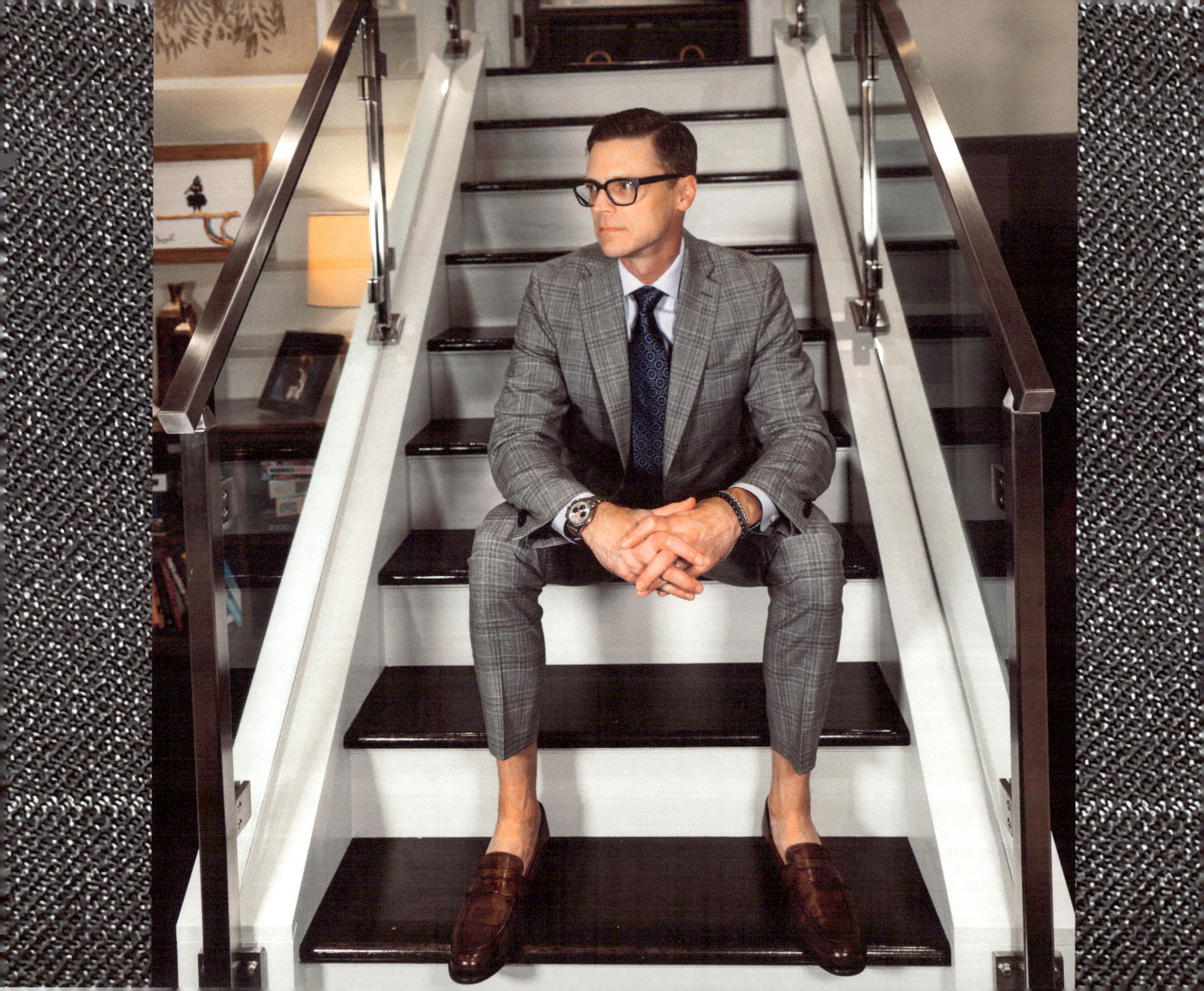

GREY PATTERN

SOPHISTICATED • APPROACHABLE • PROGRESSIVE • POSITIVE

Carefree and confident about your life choices, the grey suit with a pattern shows others you are not afraid to step out of your comfort zone and you are certain of the decisions you make with nothing to prove. Colleagues and business partners will feel comfortable confiding in you and discussing difficult or contentious topics. Grey pattern suits can easily range from more muted patterns to more aggressive, so choose a pattern that feels like 'you' and one appropriate for the occasion. The contemporary grey patterned suit can be worn for business or casual purposes, and with or without a tie.

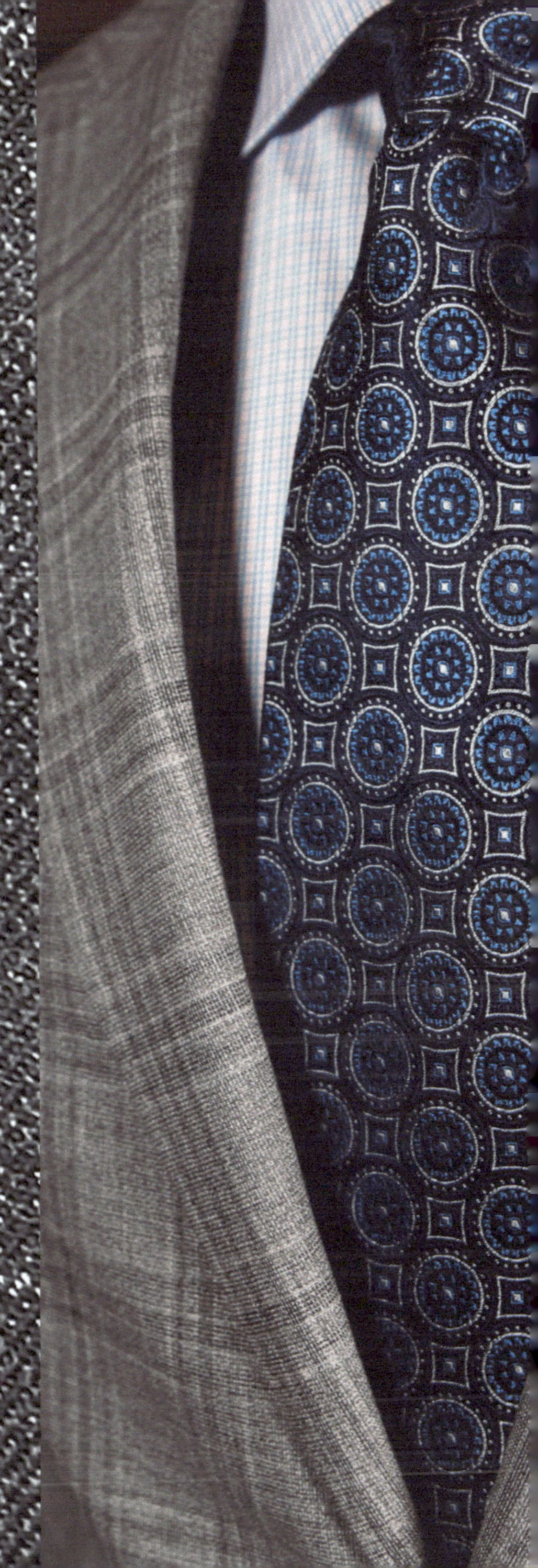

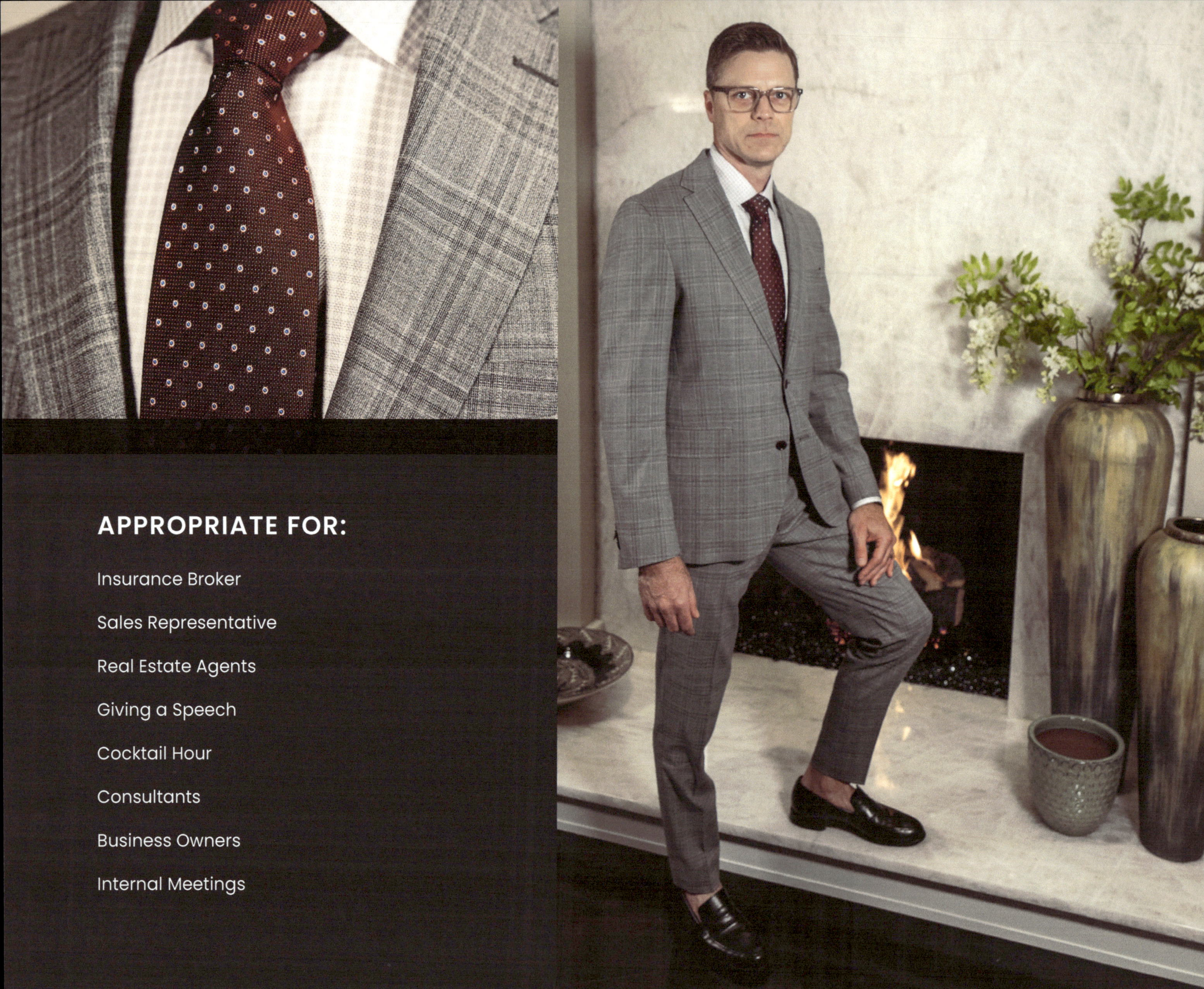
APPROPRIATE FOR:

Insurance Broker

Sales Representative

Real Estate Agents

Giving a Speech

Cocktail Hour

Consultants

Business Owners

Internal Meetings

GREY PATTERN SUIT

SHIRTS TO MATCH

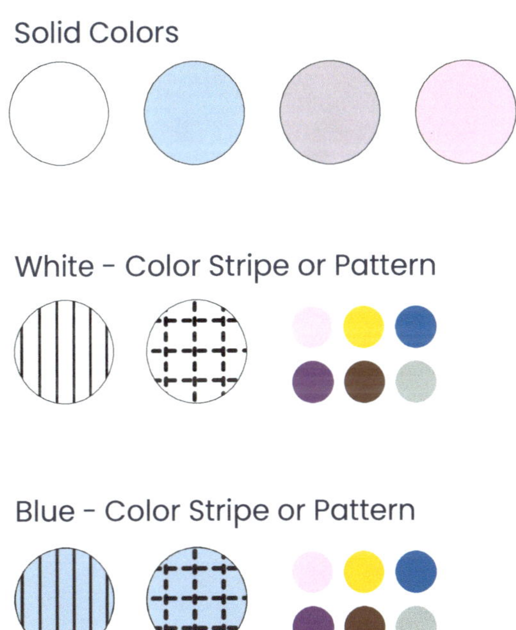

Solid Colors

White – Color Stripe or Pattern

Blue – Color Stripe or Pattern

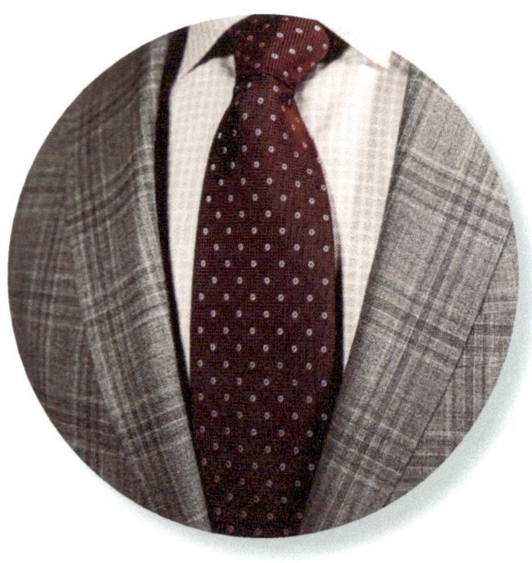 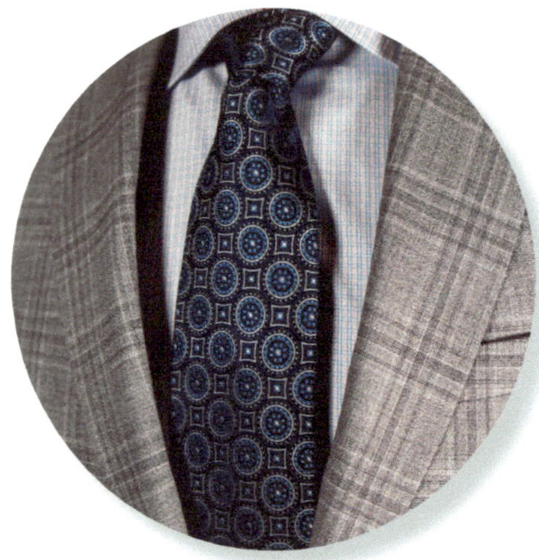 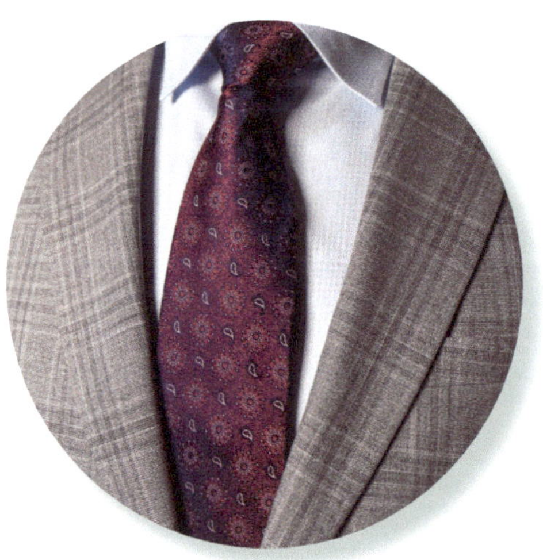

FOOTWEAR

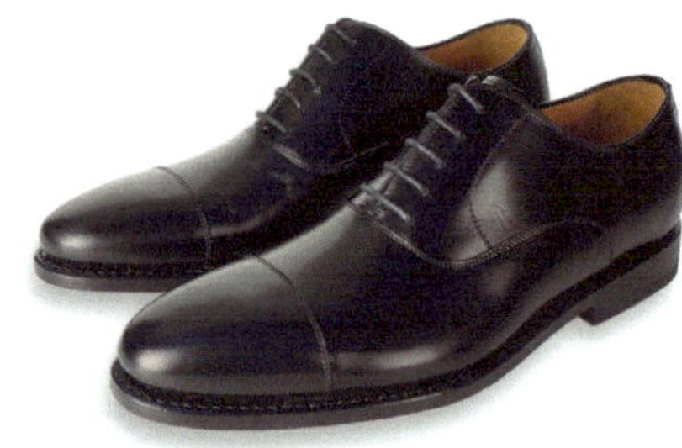 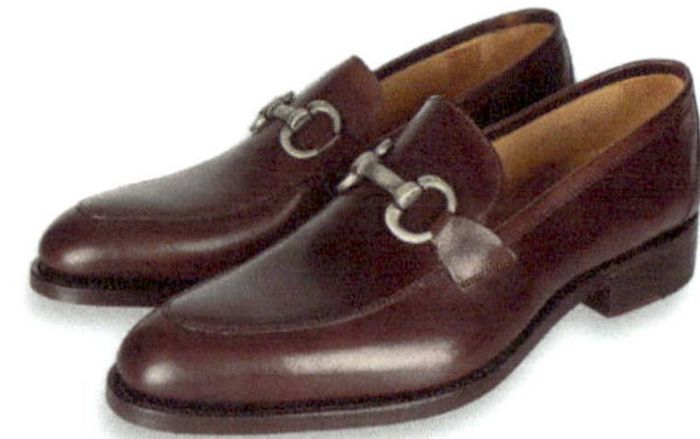 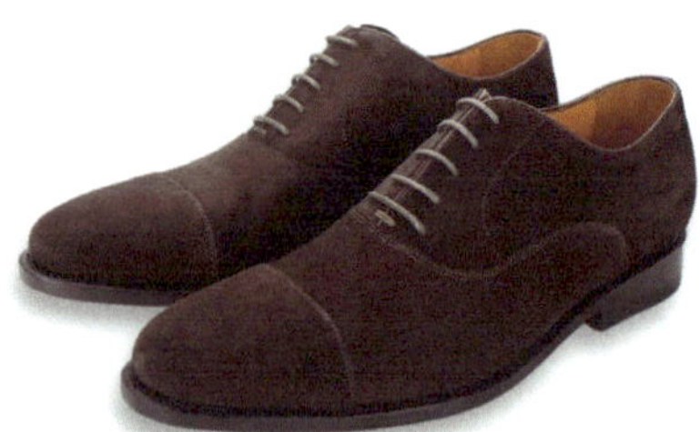

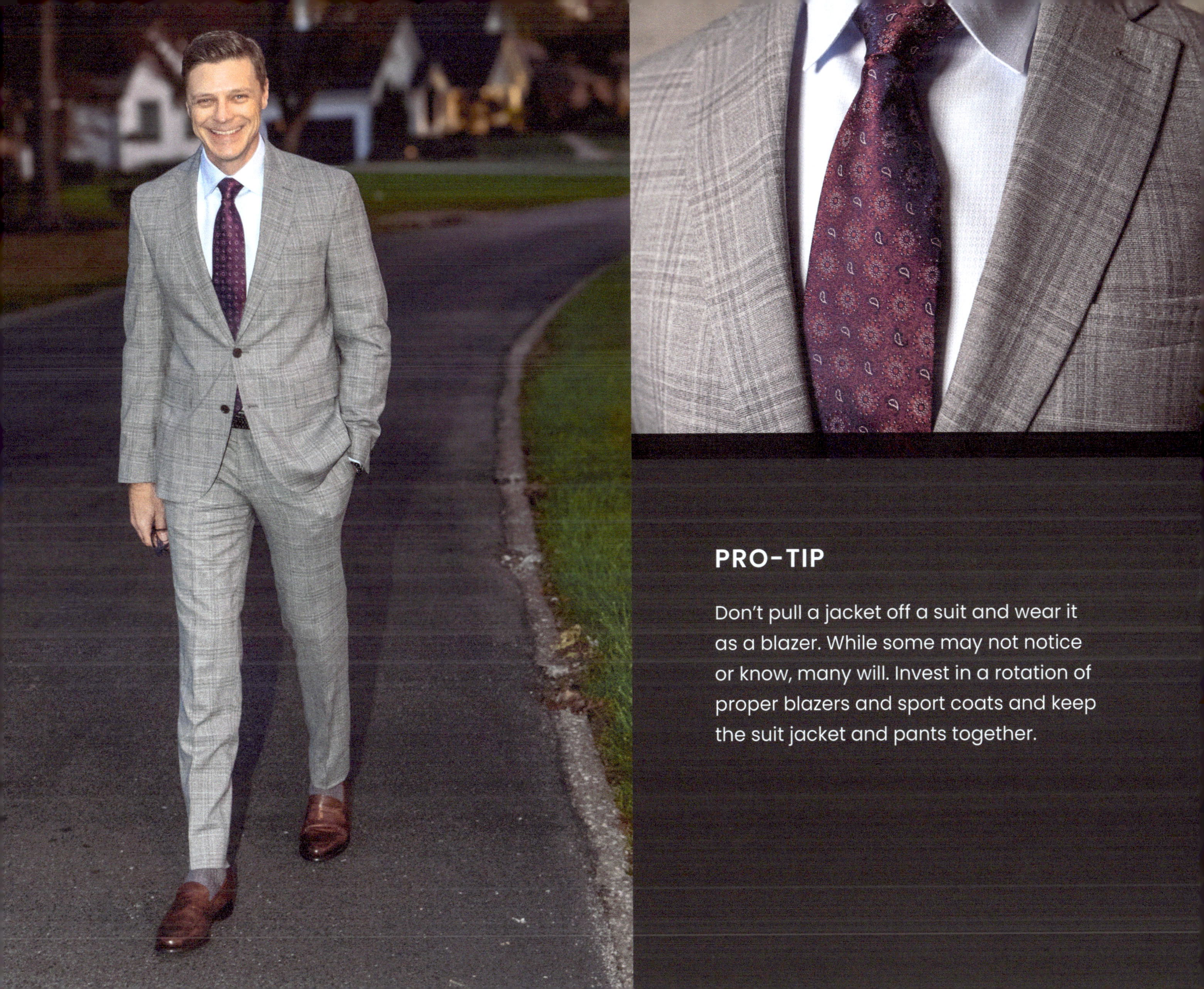

PRO-TIP

Don't pull a jacket off a suit and wear it as a blazer. While some may not notice or know, many will. Invest in a rotation of proper blazers and sport coats and keep the suit jacket and pants together.

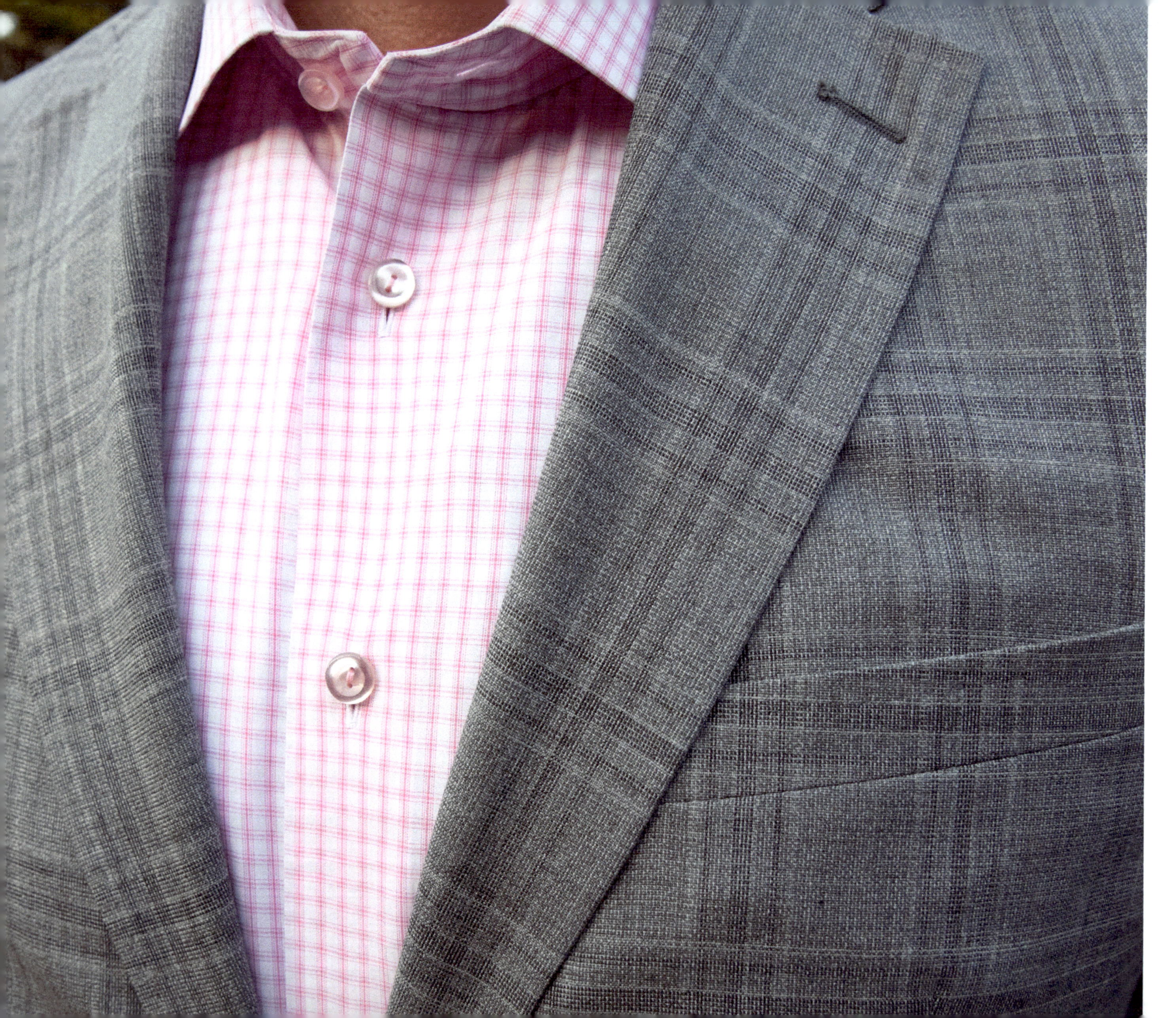

Andy Bagnall

WHAT IS YOUR OCCUPATION?

President and CEO of St. Luke's Hospital St. Louis

WHAT ARE YOUR HOBBIES AND INTERESTS?

I enjoy golfing, mixology, traveling, football, baseball, and exercising.

WHAT DO YOU BELIEVE HAS BEEN THE KEY TO YOUR SUCCESS IN YOUR CAREER?

It has been important for me to be uncomfortable and vulnerable at different times in my career in order to achieve and advance to the next level. Being put in difficult situations to work through the problem, find the solution, handle the pressure, and execute the plan has been the number one driver of my success.

WHAT DO YOU DRAW FROM IN YOUR PAST THAT MAKES DRESSING WELL A PRIORITY FOR YOU?

I played baseball in college and whenever I was dressed well, I played well. The same principle applies in business. When I show up dressed my best, I feel ready to take on any challenge I may face that day. No matter the setting - business or baseball - going into the environment you work in dressed your best gives you the confidence to do the job well.

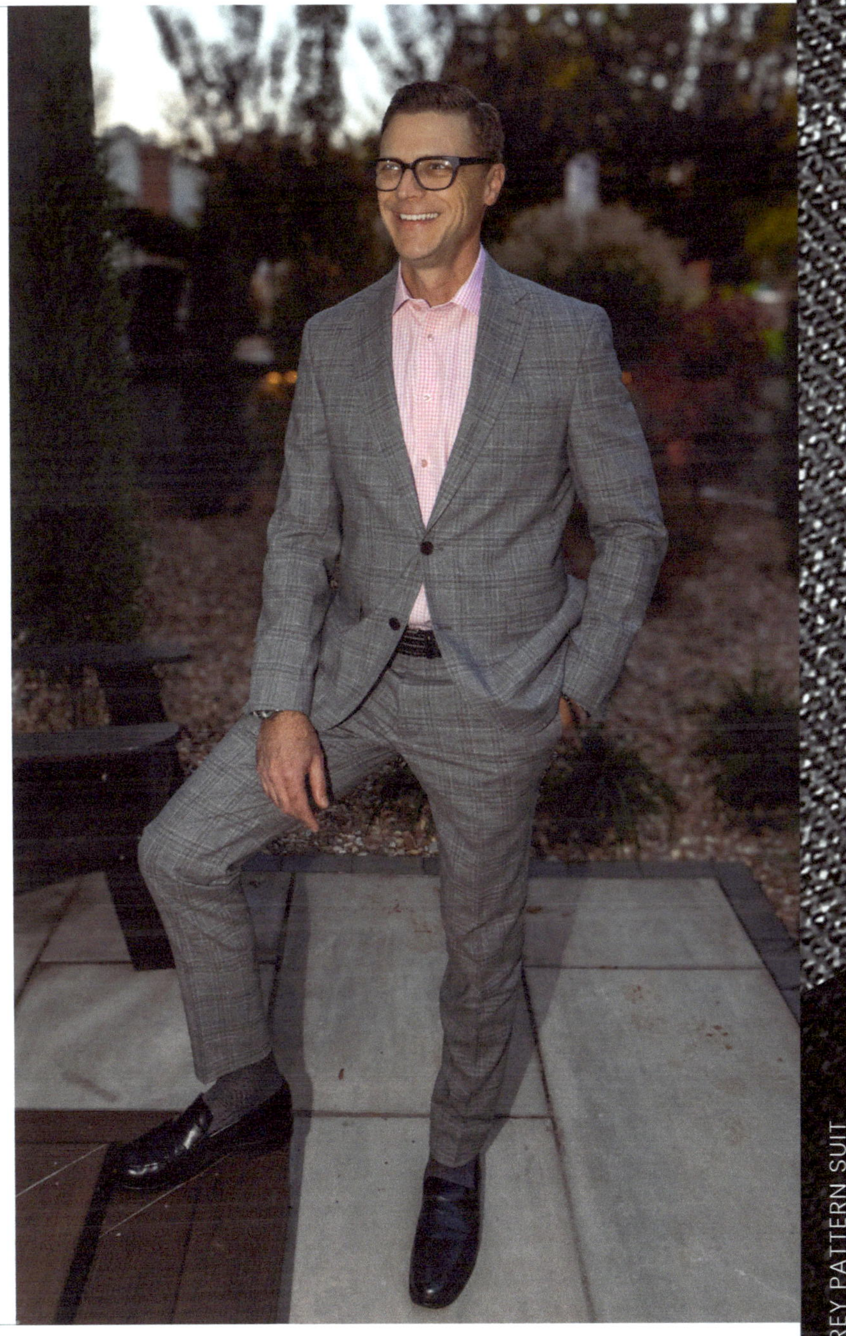

SPORT COATS

It is both delusional and stupid to think that clothes don't really matter and we should all wear whatever we want. Most people don't take clothing seriously enough, but whether we should or not, clothes do talk to us and we make decisions based on people's appearances.

– G. BRUCE BOYER

Sport coats are a crowd favorite and often steal the spotlight as statement pieces. In contrast to blazers, which have a solid color, sport coats have a pattern. They are worn with a trouser of a different fabric, typically a solid color, which brings sport coats to the top of the list when choosing versatile pieces to add to your wardrobe. The patterns in jackets can include plaid, windowpane, checks, houndstooth or stripes. Sport coats have become very common and provide great diversity of color and pattern to a man's rotation. They are typically worn for a normal business day, social outings, vacations, and business trips. Client meetings and other professional settings are appropriate occasions for sport coats, provided the colors and patterns are appropriate for your audience.

Business trips and vacations are a great opportunity to wear a sport coat because of the diversity of outfits it can provide. When the occasion and audience permits, sport coats are a great way to minimize the amount of outfits to pack and can typically provide you with at least three different outfit changes.

It is important to remember that when pairing with a trouser, the color of the trouser should not be too similar to the jacket. For example, avoid wearing a navy sport coat with a navy trouser. Choose a light or medium grey trouser instead for contrast between the trouser and jacket.

If you are wearing a bold plaid sport coat, choose a micro pattern in your shirt with a complementary or monochromatic color. If you are wearing a minor patterned jacket, such as houndstooth, do not be afraid to pair an alternative pattern with similar intensity (like a simple stripe). I would not advise a bold colorful pattern shirt with either jacket. For ties, coordinate with a color from the jacket to create a cohesive outfit.

For those looking to get started with sport coats, start with navy and grey. Keep the colors simple, and choose jackets that you can confidently pair with trousers. Next, try incorporating bolder and more colorful patterns, like a blue sport coat with an orange pattern or a grey sport coat with a lavender pattern.

For those who have a diverse selection of options for sport coats and are looking for inspiration, try different shades of green or purple color schemes, or take a leap into the earth tones for a warm and more casual look.

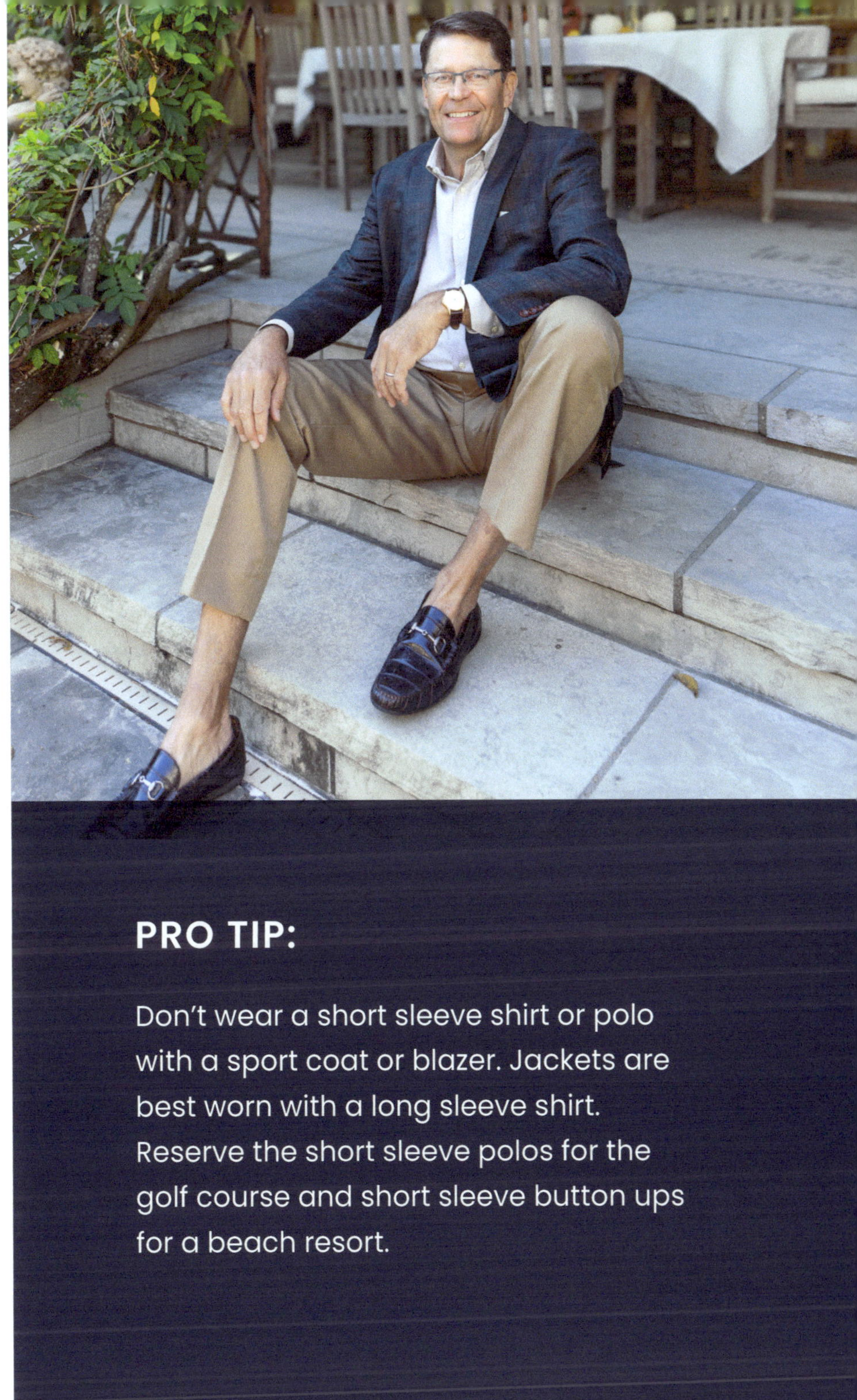

PRO TIP:

Don't wear a short sleeve shirt or polo with a sport coat or blazer. Jackets are best worn with a long sleeve shirt. Reserve the short sleeve polos for the golf course and short sleeve button ups for a beach resort.

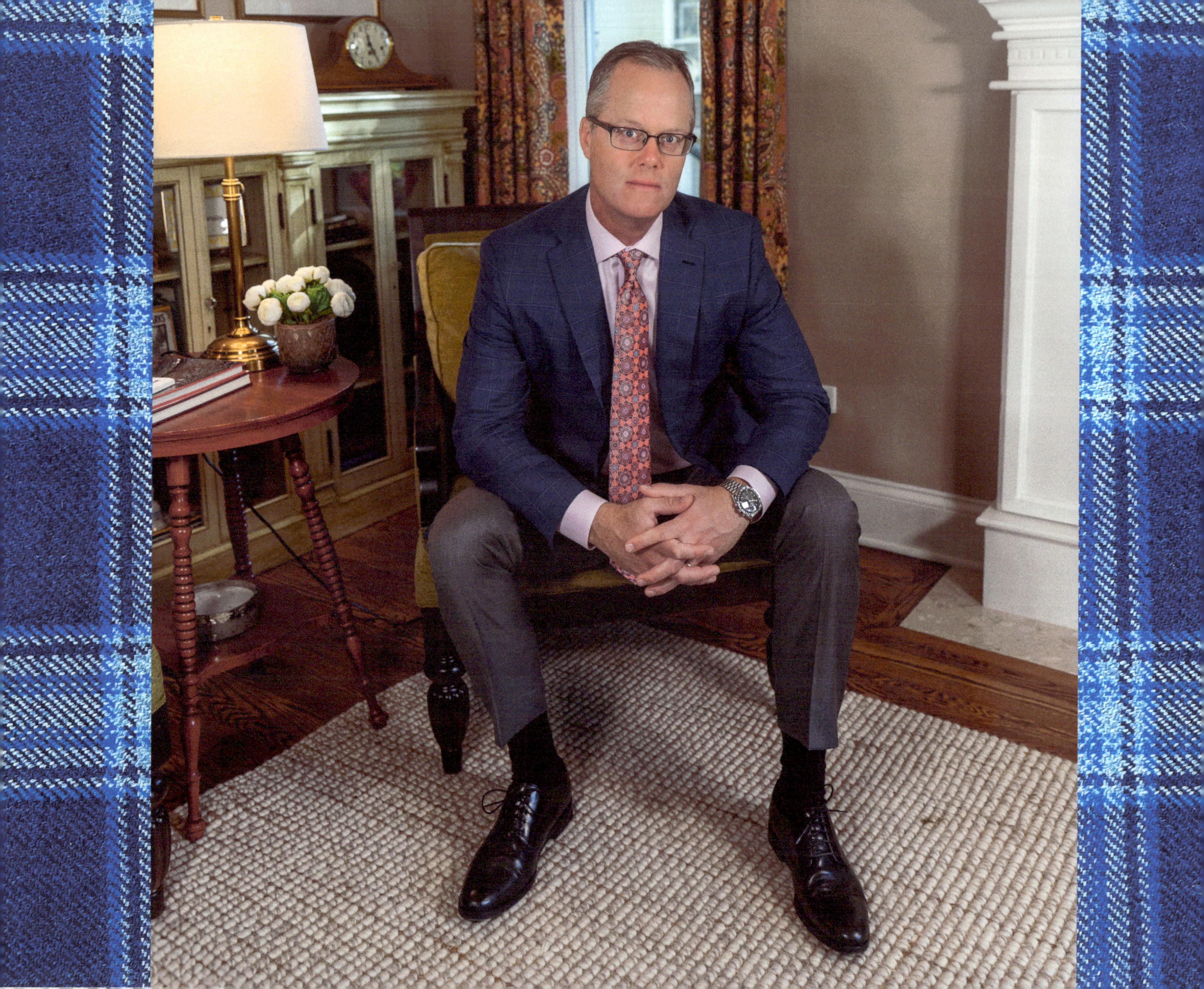

BLUE

ELECTRIC • MASCULINE • OPTIMISTIC • VERSATILE

Blue sport coats are the most common for gentlemen who find themselves wearing a jacket in both social and professional settings. They can be dark blue or light blue. Choose a dark blue or navy hue for a rich and low key look, or a turquoise or light blue for a brighter more exciting vibe.

The same rule for blazers and trousers applies to sport coats. Always wear a contrasting color pant to your jacket. With a navy sport coat, wear light grey, medium grey, light blue or tan trousers and jeans for more casual wear. For a lighter brighter blue sport coat, wear navy, dark blue, medium grey, dark grey, or jeans. If the sport coat has a pattern with a contrasting color in it, say, red, pink, lavender, or yellow, match the trouser with that color in the jacket for a more fashion-forward and exciting outfit.

Matching a shirt depends on the size and intensity of the pattern in the jacket. Complement a big patterned jacket like a plaid or windowpane with a shirt choice of a micro pattern, stripe, or check. Herringbone, houndstooth or tweed sport coats have a more subtle pattern, which allows more expression in shirt choice.

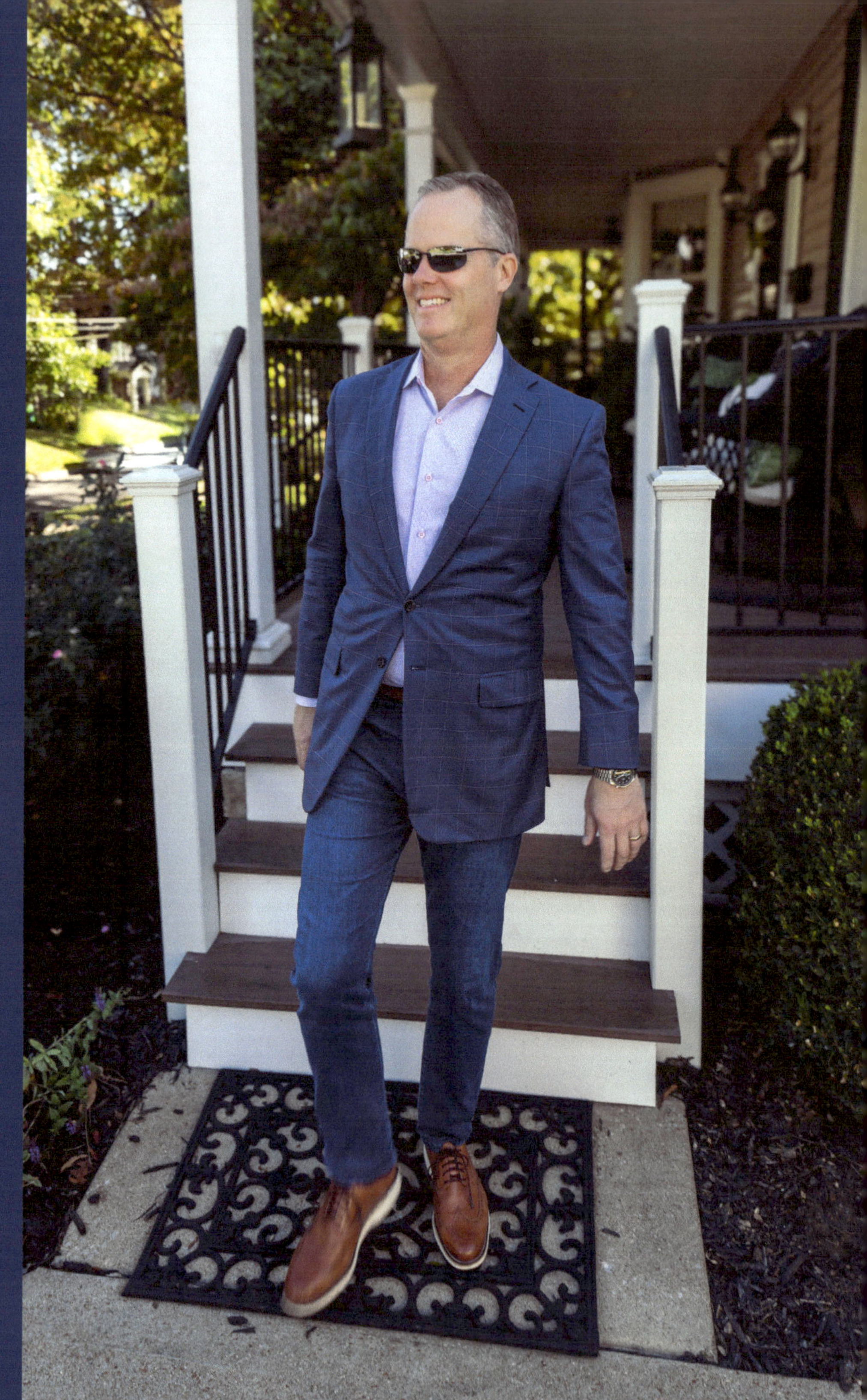

BLUE SPORT COAT

SHIRTS TO MATCH

Solid Colors

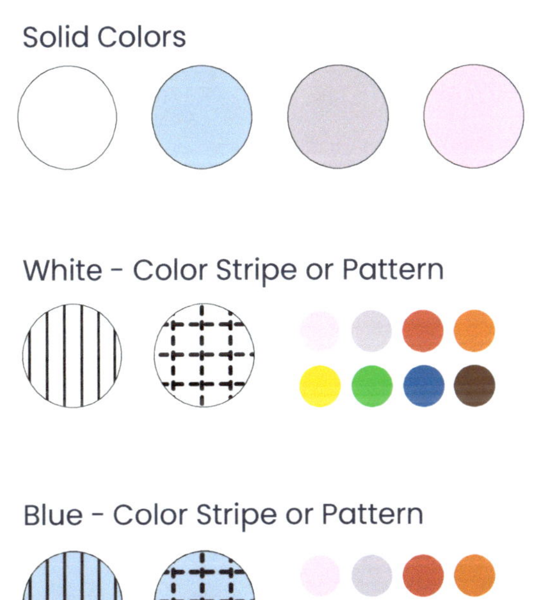

White - Color Stripe or Pattern

Blue - Color Stripe or Pattern

TROUSERS

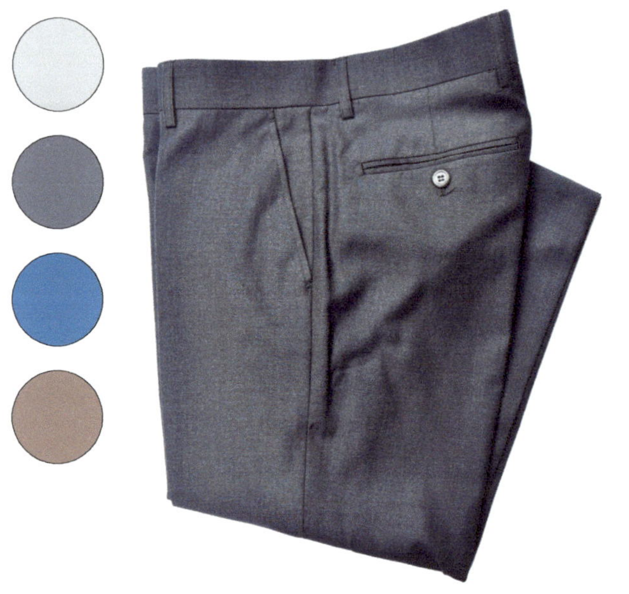

JEANS

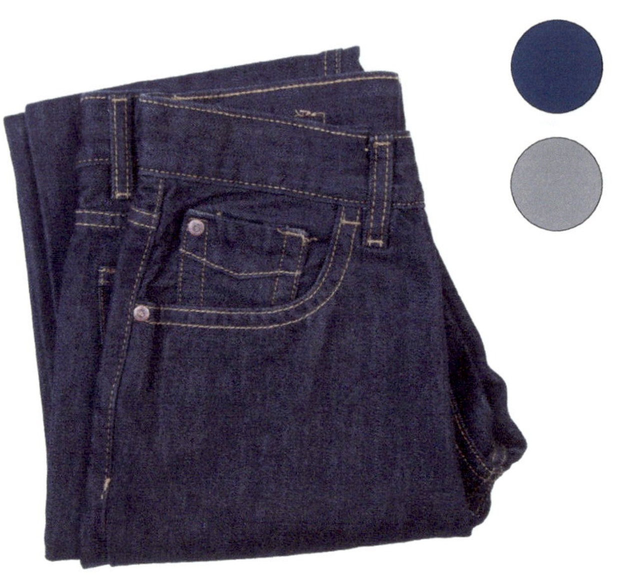

FOOTWEAR

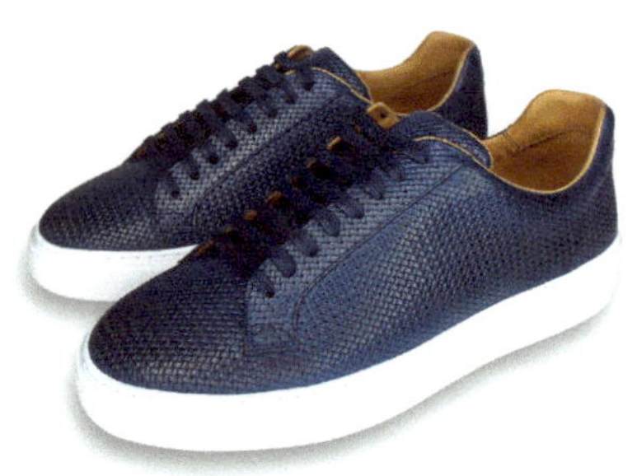

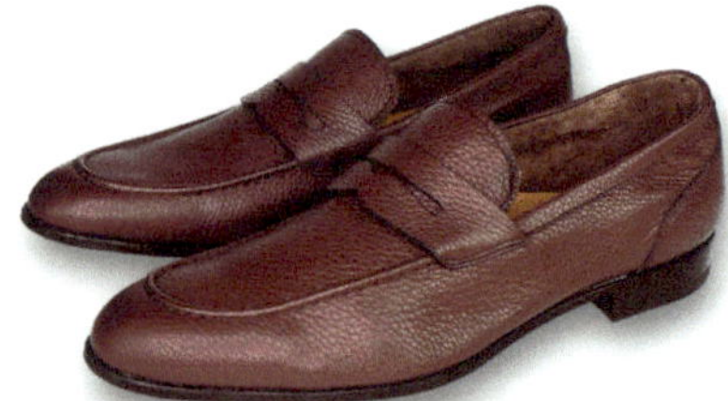

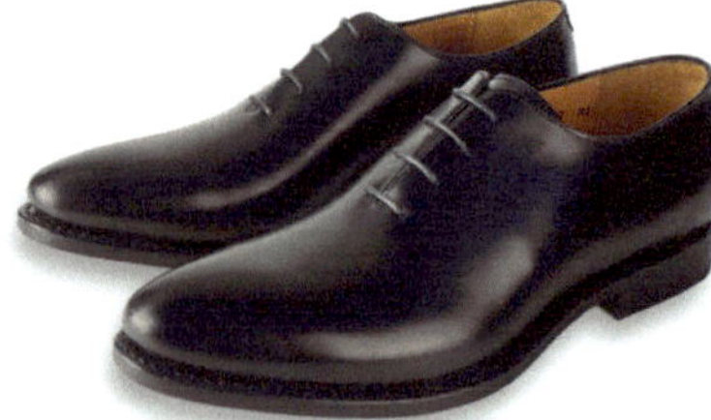

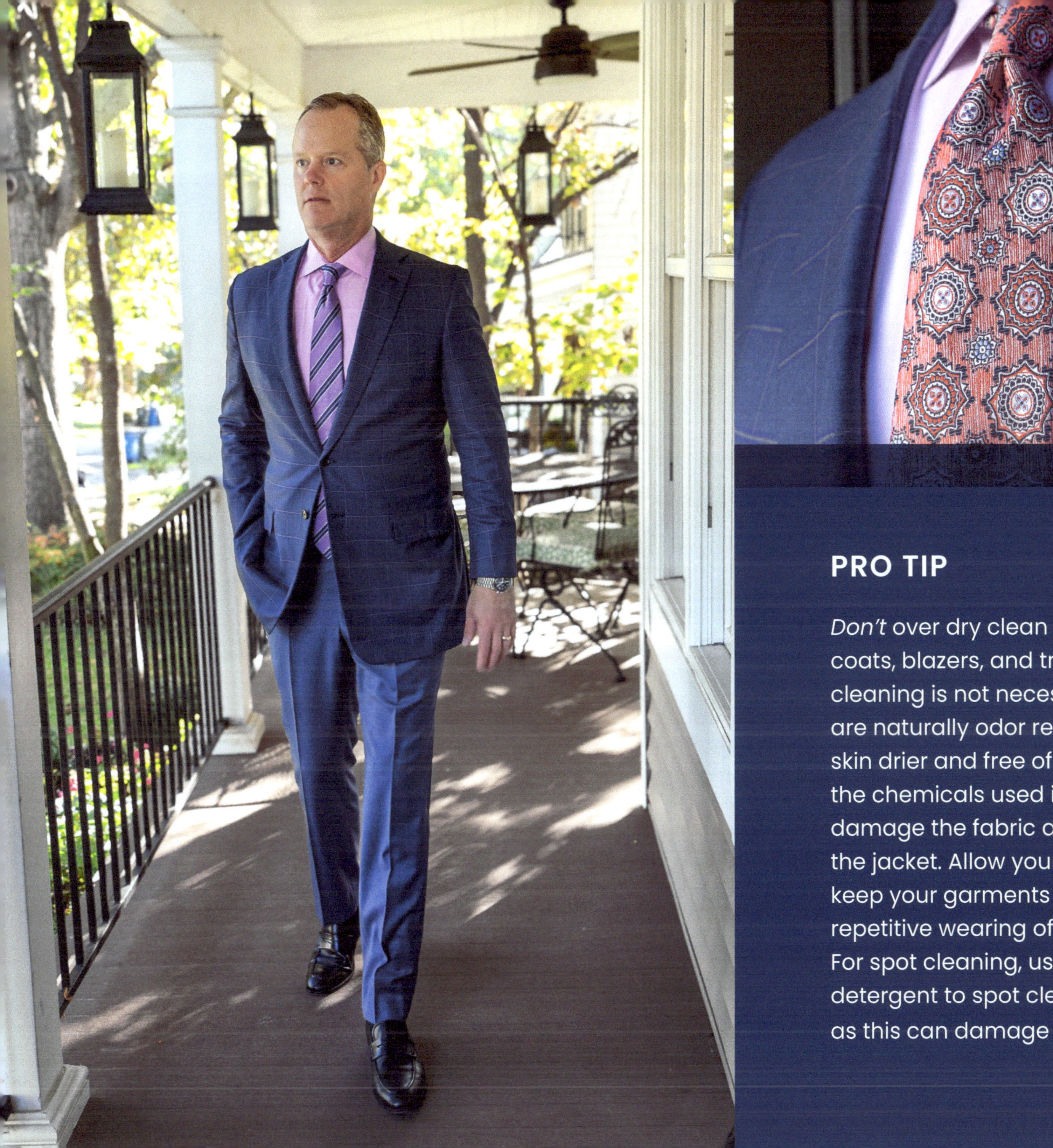

PRO TIP

Don't over dry clean your suits, sport coats, blazers, and trousers. Excessive dry cleaning is not necessary, as wool fibers are naturally odor resistant and keeps the skin drier and free of bacteria. Additionally, the chemicals used in dry cleaning can damage the fabric and the canvassing of the jacket. Allow your garment to hang and keep your garments in rotation to avoid repetitive wearing of the same garments. For spot cleaning, use a wool-specific detergent to spot clean and avoid rubbing, as this can damage the wool fibers.

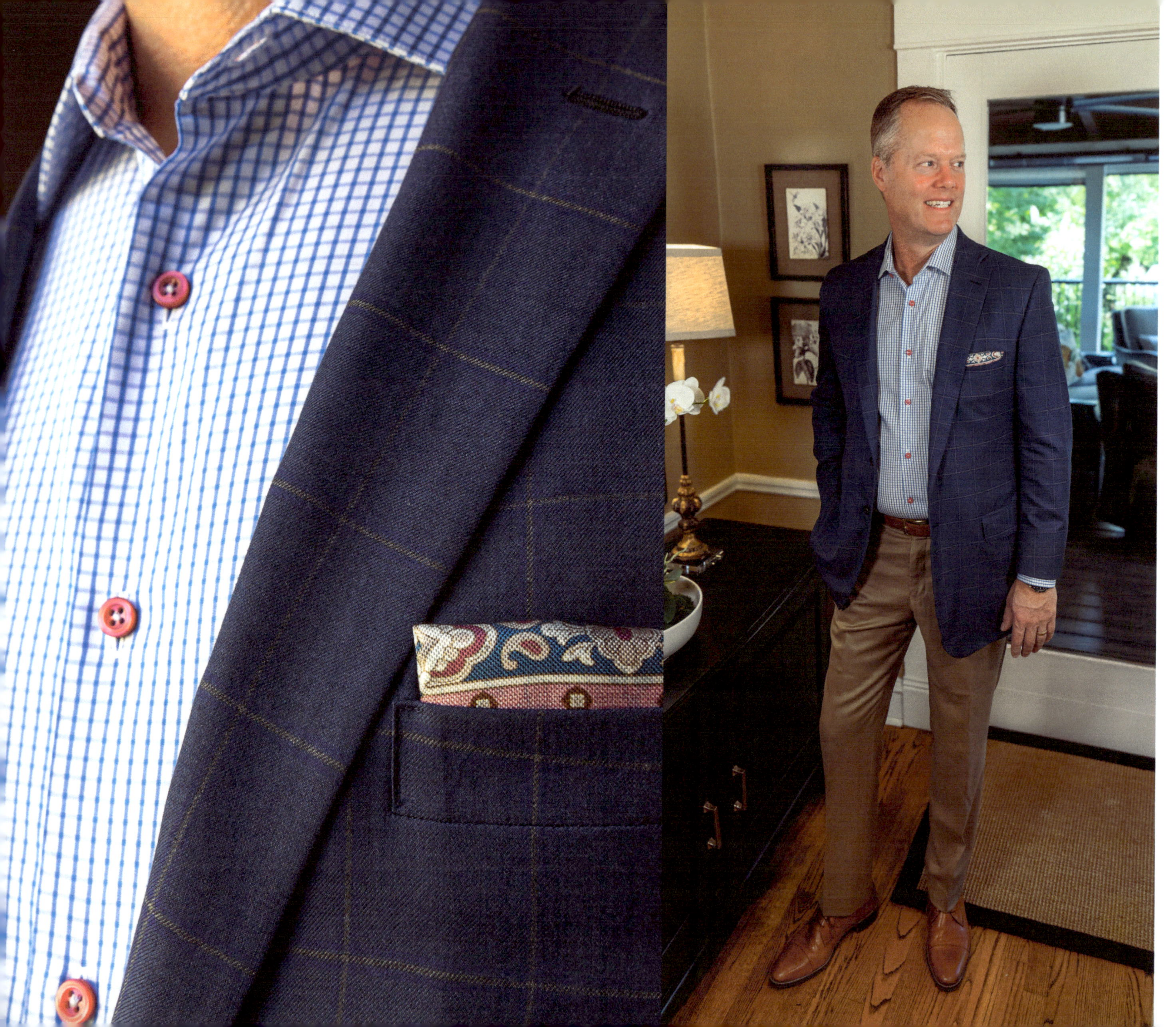

John Drexler

WHAT IS YOUR OCCUPATION?

Senior VP and Chief Operating Officer at Arch Resources

WHAT ARE YOUR HOBBIES AND INTERESTS?

I enjoy hockey, golf, scuba diving, theater, and traveling.

WHAT DO YOU BELIEVE IS THE MOST IMPORTANT PART OF YOUR SUCCESS JOURNEY?

I believe hard work, dedication, and passion for what I do has been my key contributor to success. I know I can outwork anyone else in the room!

WHAT TIPS DO YOU HAVE FOR PACKING FOR A BUSINESS TRIP?

Pack light and don't overthink it!

WHAT IS YOUR FAVORITE THING IN YOUR CLOSET TO WEAR?

Margo Jackets!

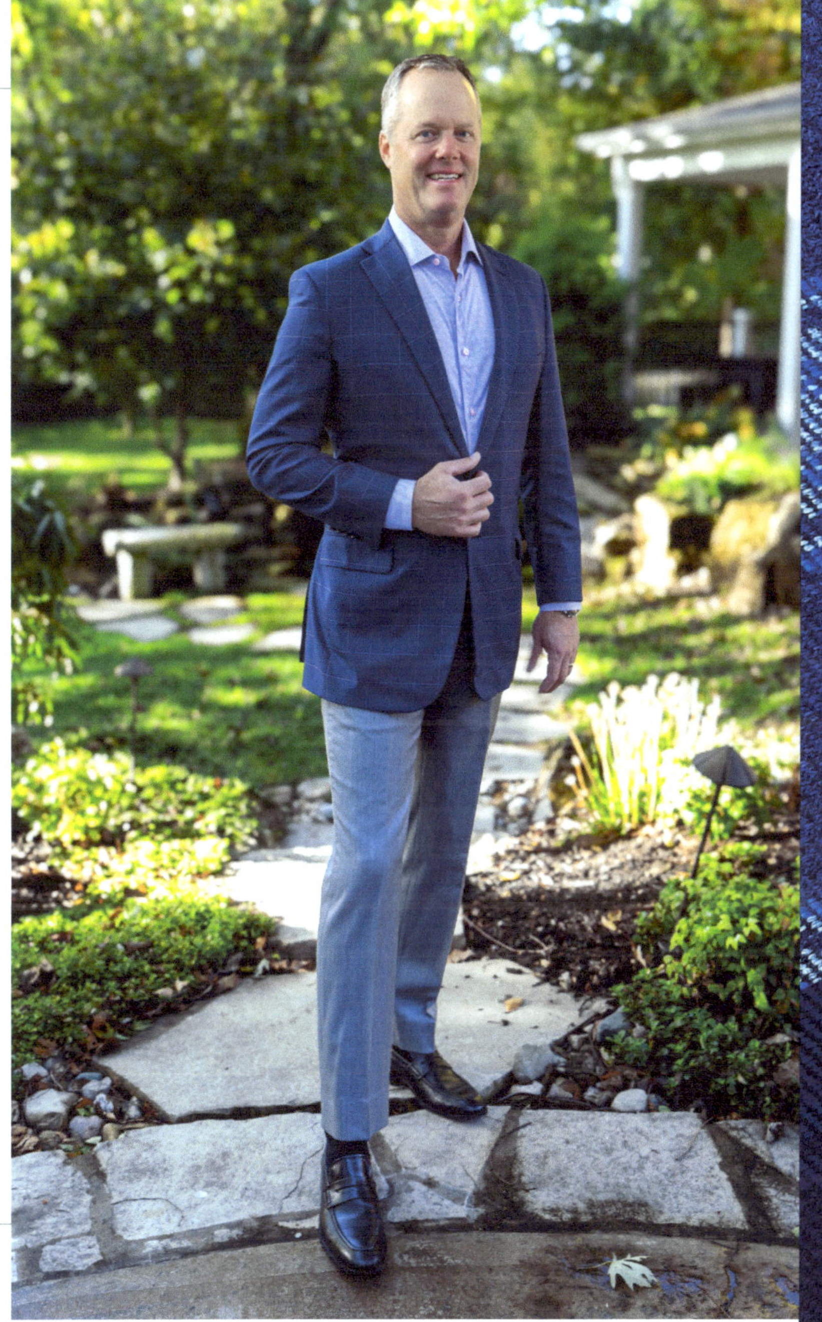

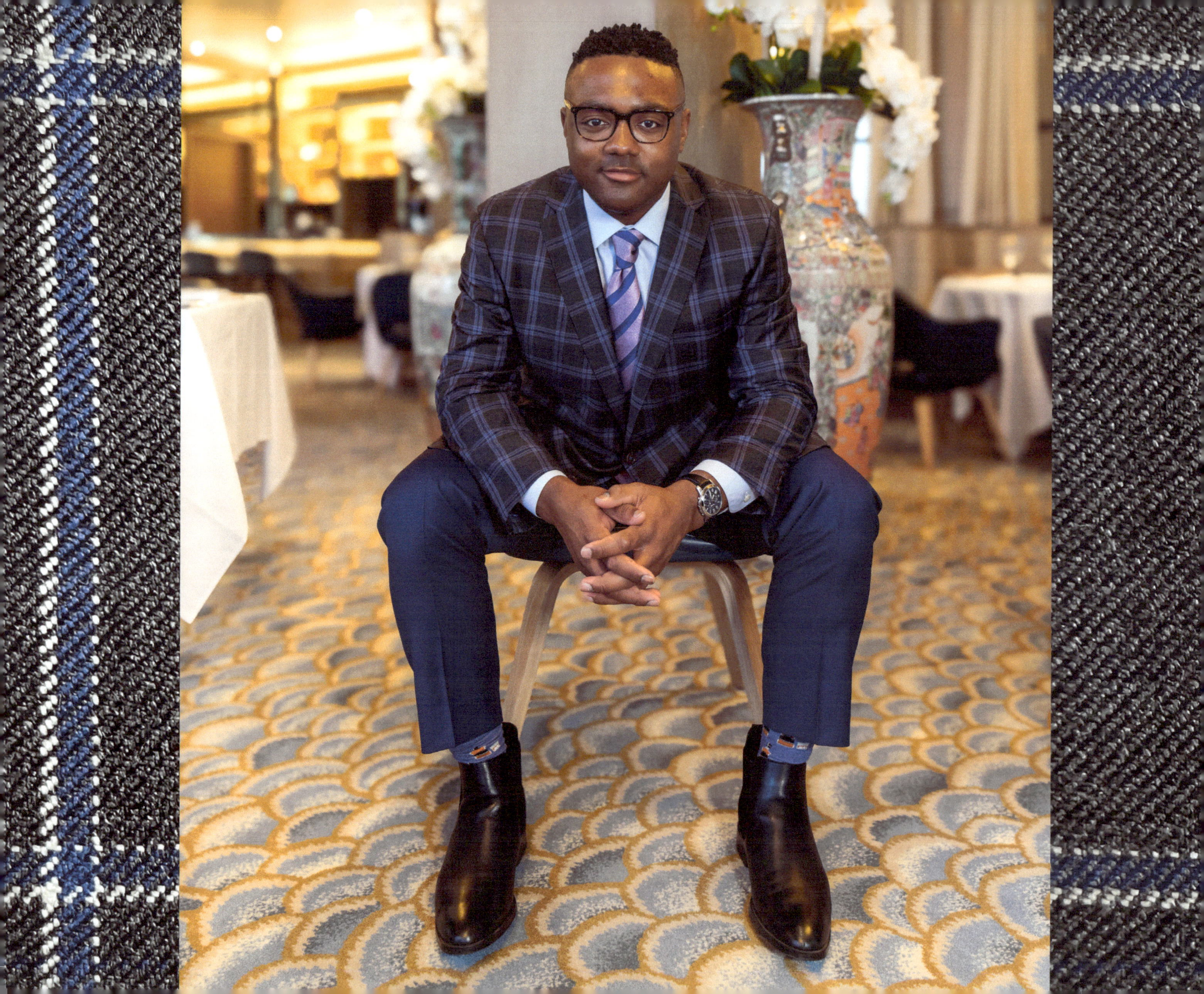

GREY

ASTUTE • REFINED • CONSISTENT

When selecting trousers, consider the shade of grey in your sport coat. For darker sport coats, opt for a lighter shade trouser. Alternatively, if it is lighter shade, wear a darker color trouser to achieve the required contrast. Jeans are appropriate for both!

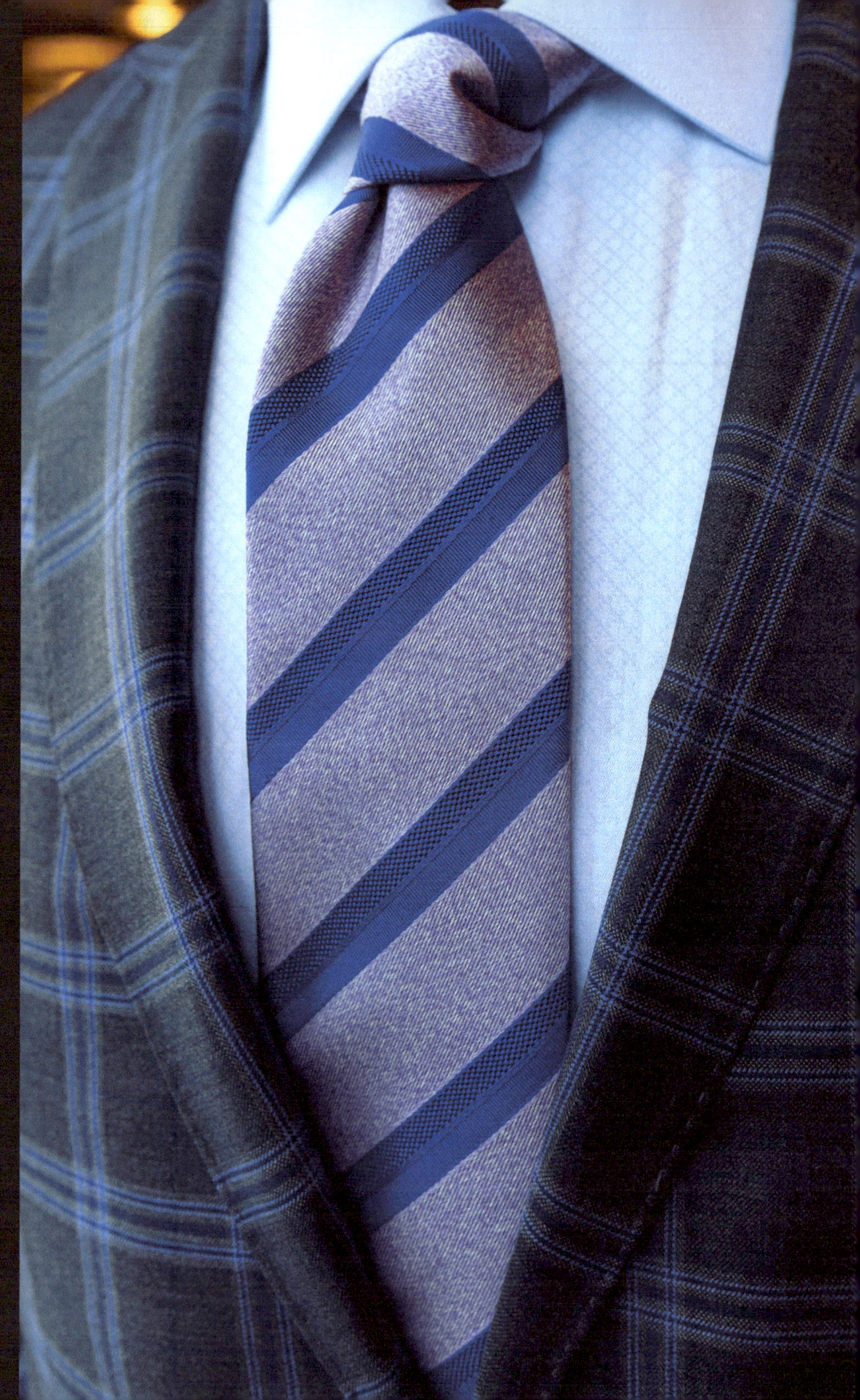

Sometimes sport coats have a color in the pattern like electric blue, purple, pink, or green. If you are looking to avoid navy or grey trousers, pick the color of that pattern as your trouser. Yes, I am recommending pink, purple, or green pants! It will elevate your look immediately from good to great, and make the color in the jacket pop.

Grey sport coats can easily range from muted patterns to bold, and this should guide your shirt selection. Complement bold patterns with minor patterned shirts. Make more muted jackets pop with an assertive shirt that includes colors from the pattern in the jacket. The shirt pattern you choose can include checks, stripes, prints, or windowpanes.

GREY SPORT COAT

SHIRTS TO MATCH

Solid Colors

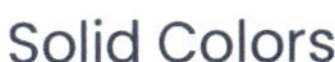
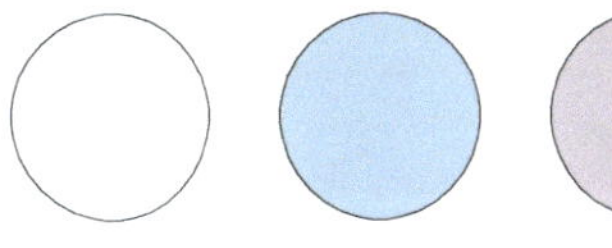
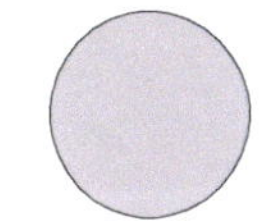

White - Color Stripe or Pattern

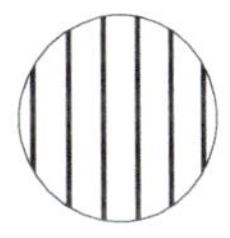
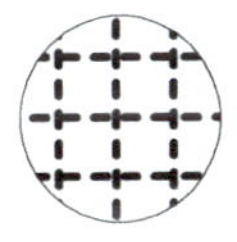
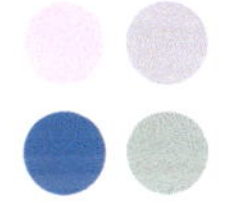

Blue - Color Stripe or Pattern

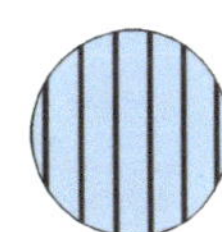
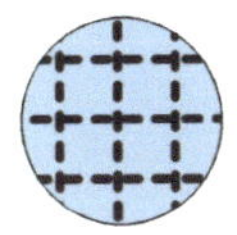
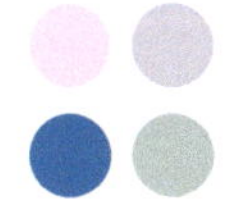

TROUSERS

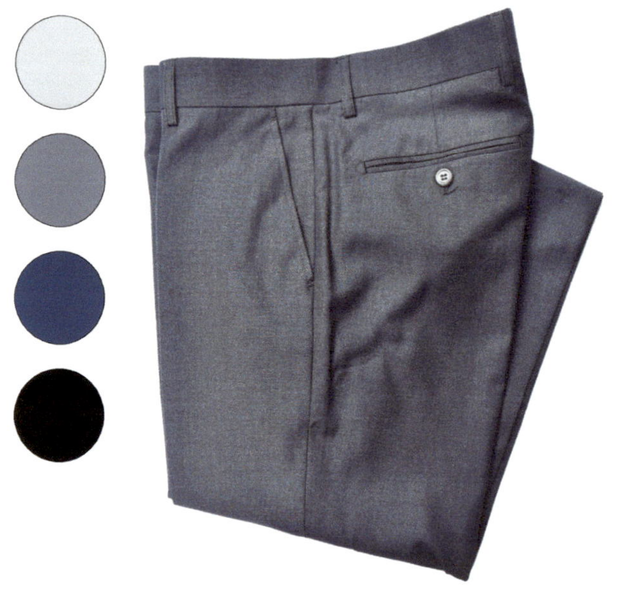

JEANS

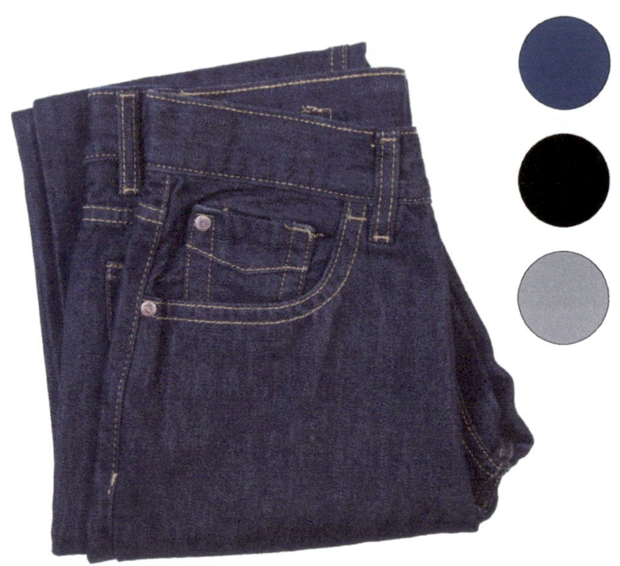

FOOTWEAR

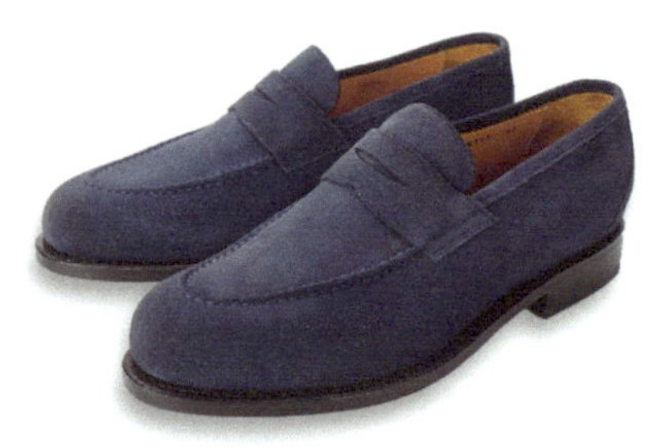

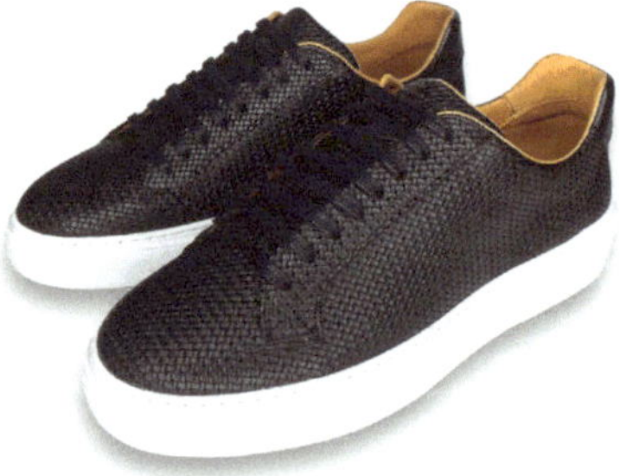

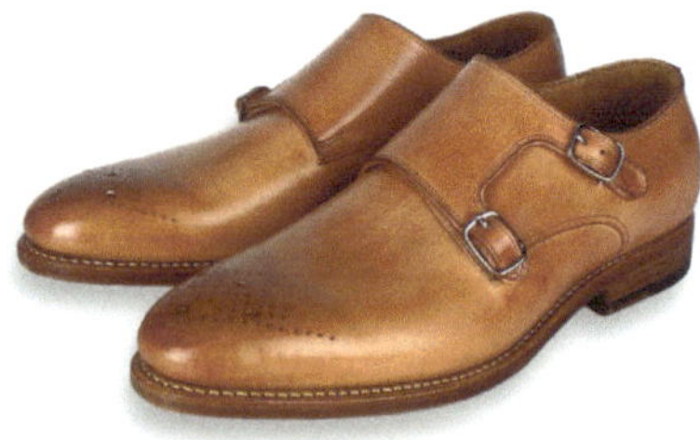

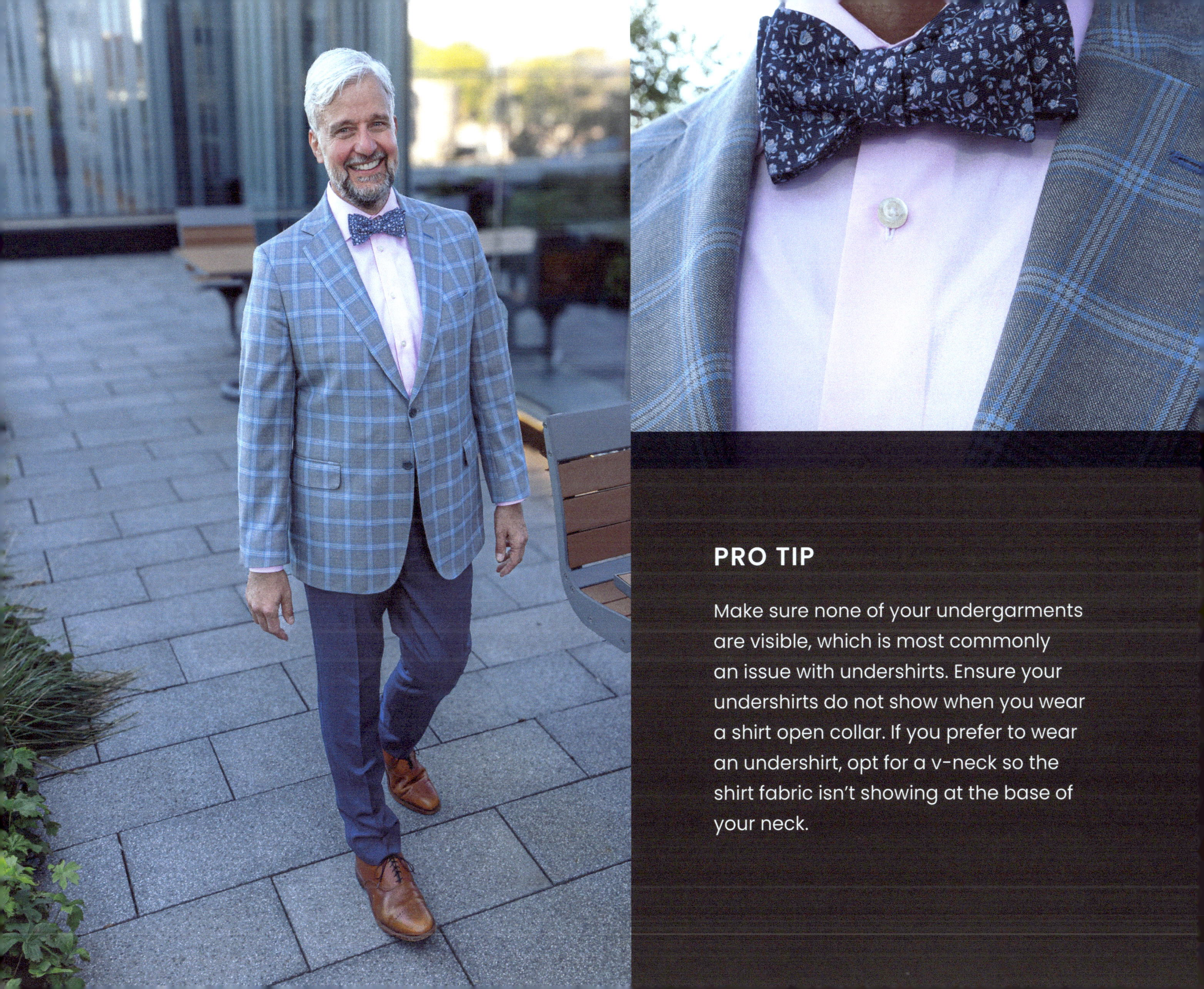

PRO TIP

Make sure none of your undergarments
are visible, which is most commonly
an issue with undershirts. Ensure your
undershirts do not show when you wear
a shirt open collar. If you prefer to wear
an undershirt, opt for a v-neck so the
shirt fabric isn't showing at the base of
your neck.

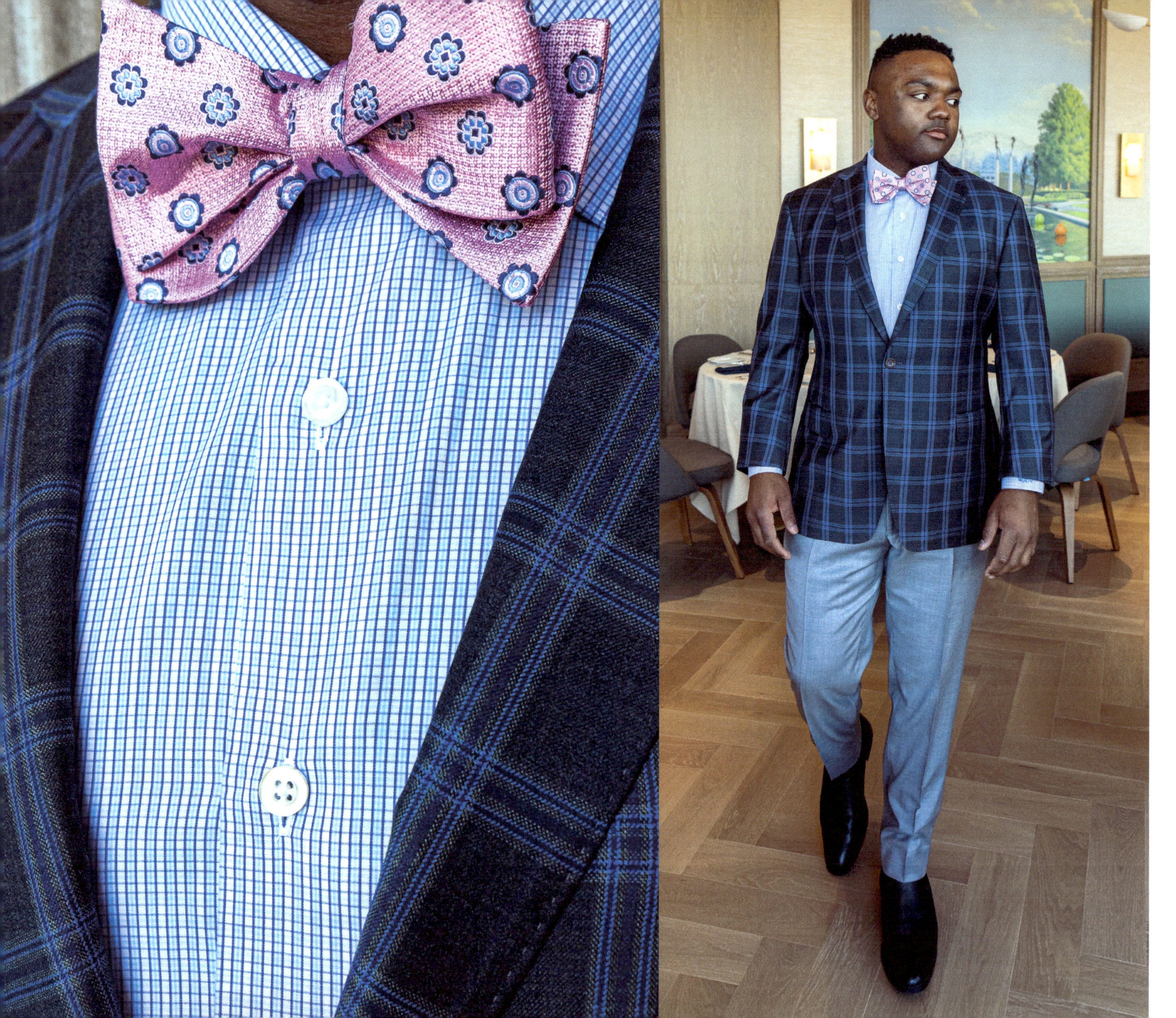

Willie Evans

WHAT IS YOUR OCCUPATION?

Operational Analysis Simulation SME

WHAT ARE YOUR HOBBIES AND INTERESTS?

I enjoy walks, meditating, yoga, pilates, chemistry, football, math, and electronic warfare.

WHAT IS A FUN FACT ABOUT YOU?

I am an Inferno Hot Pilates Instructor and my squat PR is 795 lbs.

WHAT IS MOST IMPORTANT TO YOU WHEN IT COMES TO THE FIT OF YOUR CLOTHING?

I have thick thighs so fit is important in legs, but will take style over comfort.

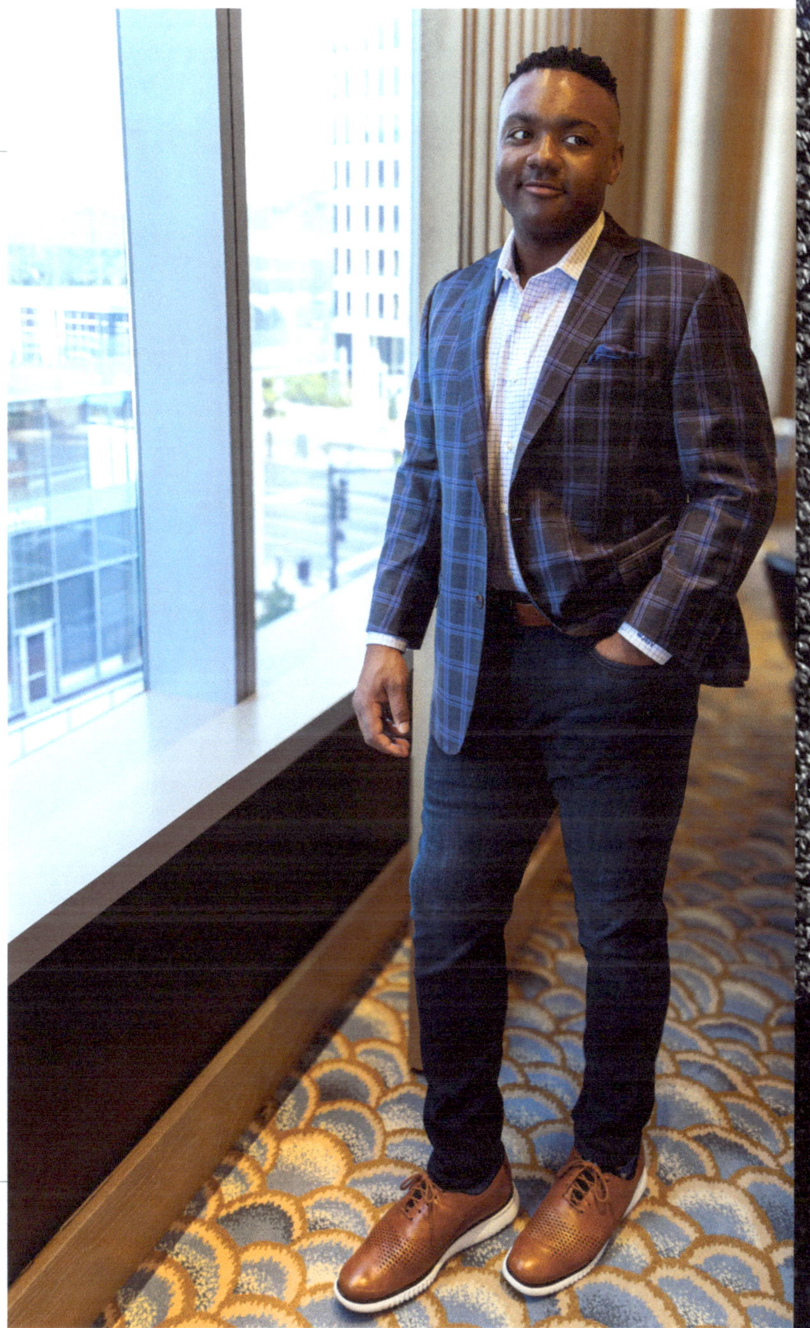

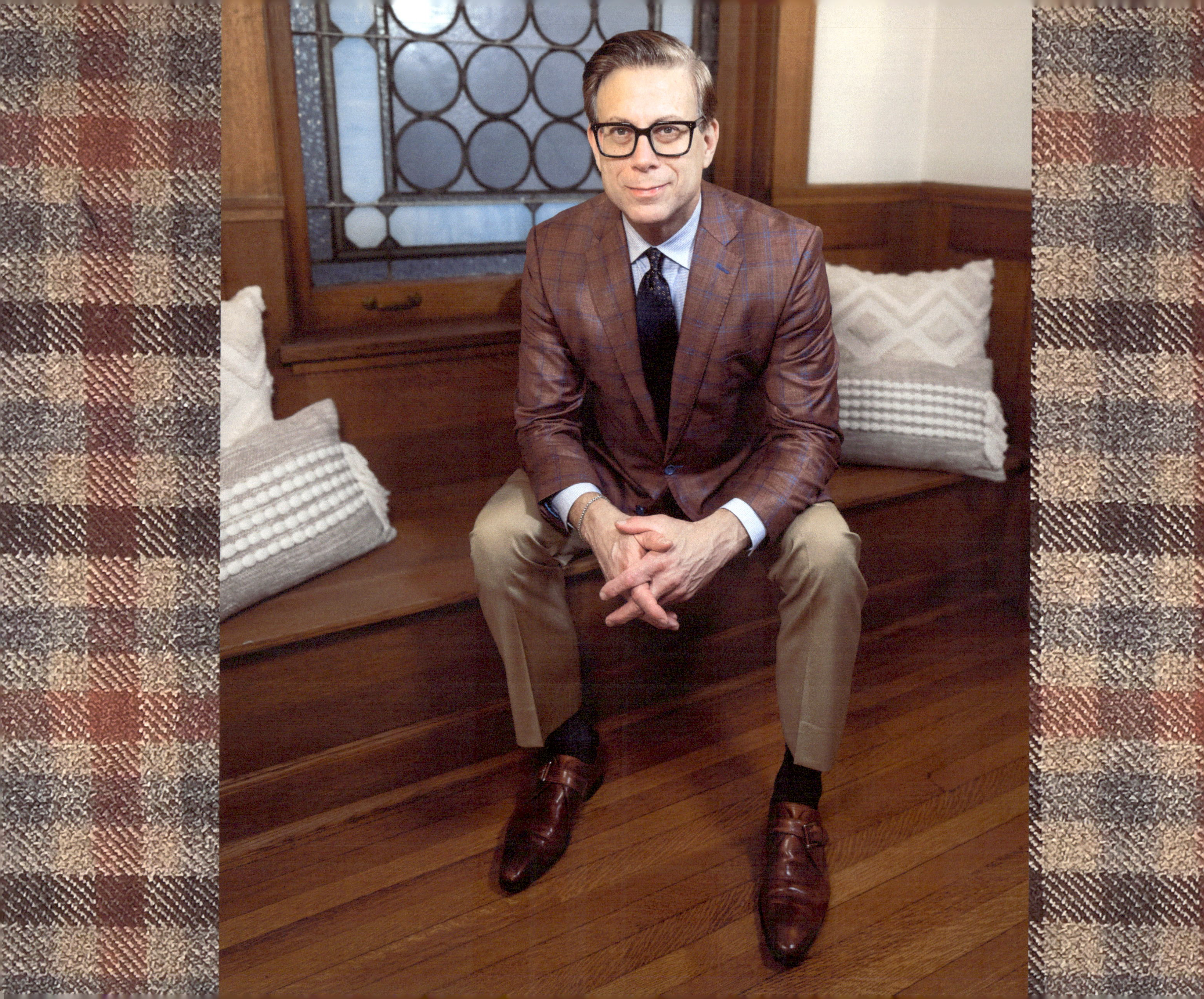

EARTH TONE

UNIVERSAL • APPROACHABLE • EXPERIENCED

After adding blue and grey sport coats to your wardrobe,
consider adding an earth tone to expand your repertoire.
Earth tones encompass a wide spectrum of colors including taupe,
tan, brown, khaki, olive, green, gold, terracotta, rust, and beige.
Choose earth tones that complement your coloring. If you have
dark skin, choose lighter shades of earth tones, and if you
have a lighter skin tone, opt for darker shades.

Warm and inviting earthy colors are great to wear casually with jeans or in more formal settings with slacks. If your jacket features a darker earth tone, wear a complementary lighter shade like tan, khaki, or beige. Conversely, for a lighter color jacket, opt for chocolate brown, olive, navy or dark taupe.

Avoid shirts that have pinks or purples. Incorporate blues, browns, rust, greens, golds, or reds for a better match with earth tone sport coats.

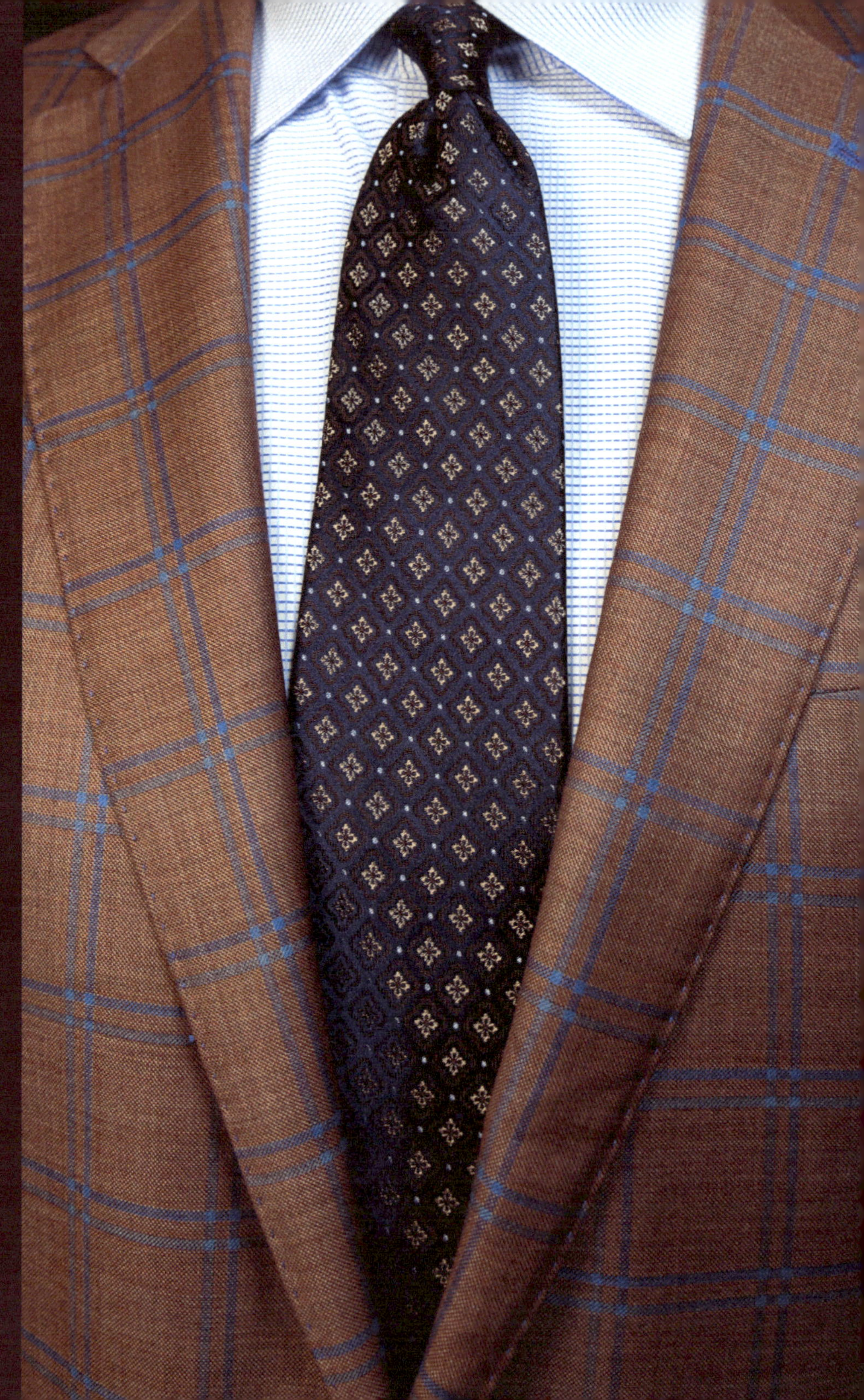

EARTH TONE SPORT COAT

SHIRTS TO MATCH

Solid Colors

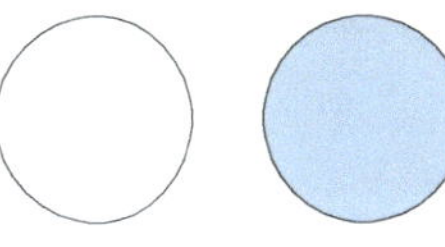

White - Color Stripe or Pattern

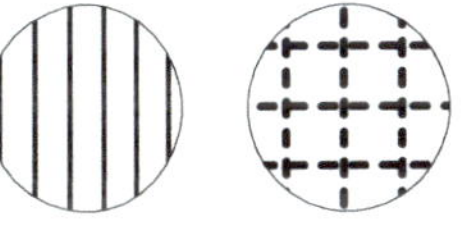
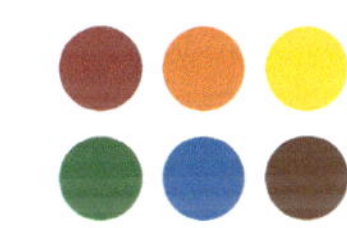

Blue - Color Stripe or Pattern

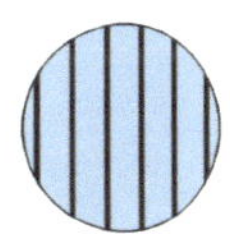
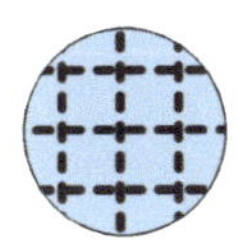
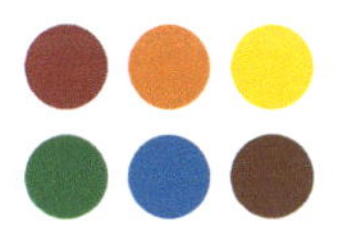

TROUSERS

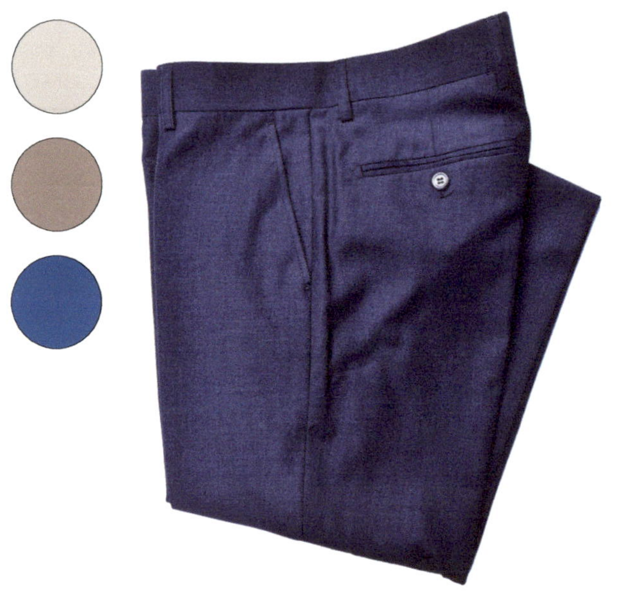

JEANS

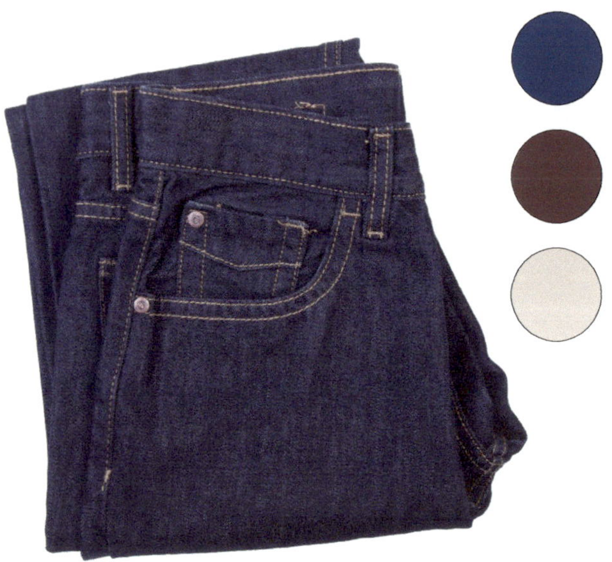

FOOTWEAR

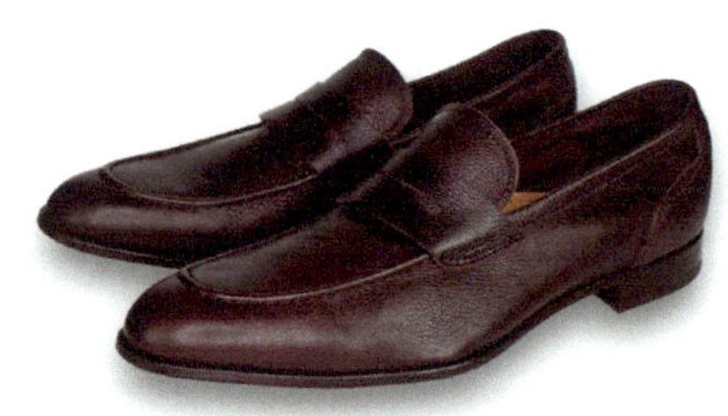

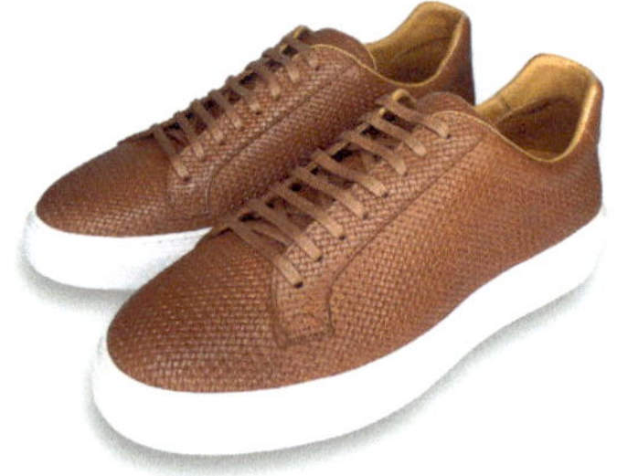

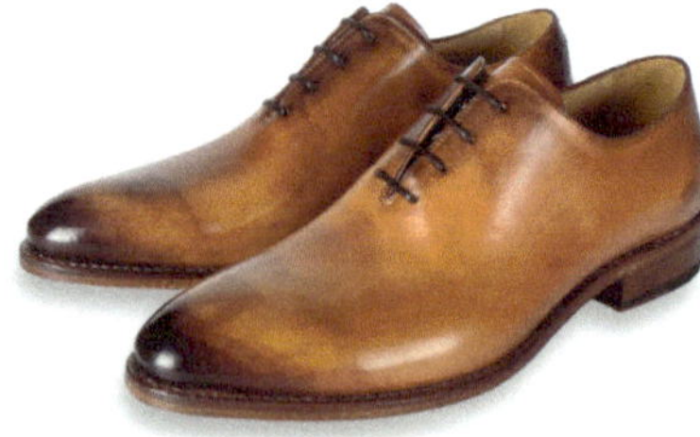

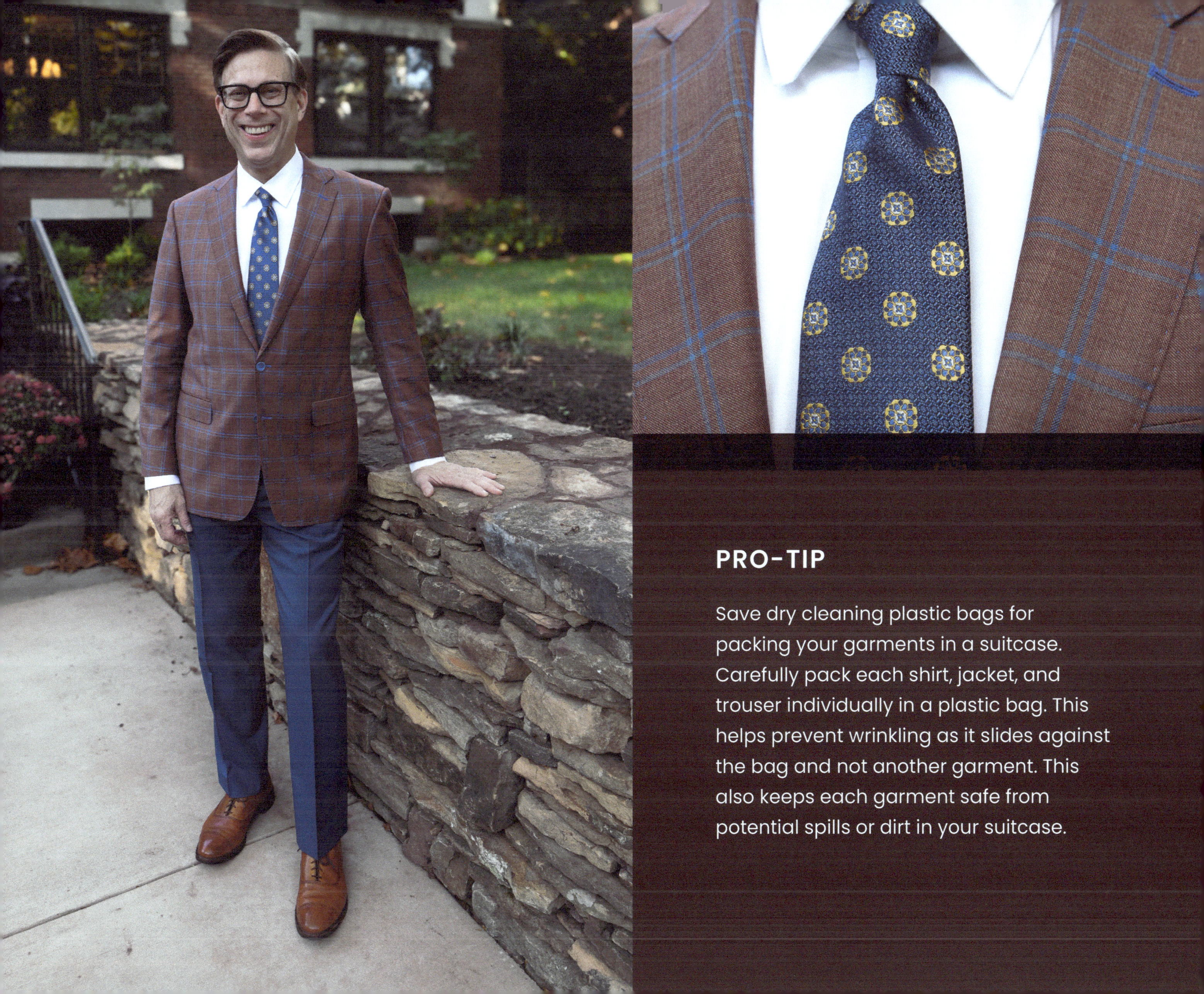

PRO-TIP

Save dry cleaning plastic bags for
packing your garments in a suitcase.
Carefully pack each shirt, jacket, and
trouser individually in a plastic bag. This
helps prevent wrinkling as it slides against
the bag and not another garment. This
also keeps each garment safe from
potential spills or dirt in your suitcase.

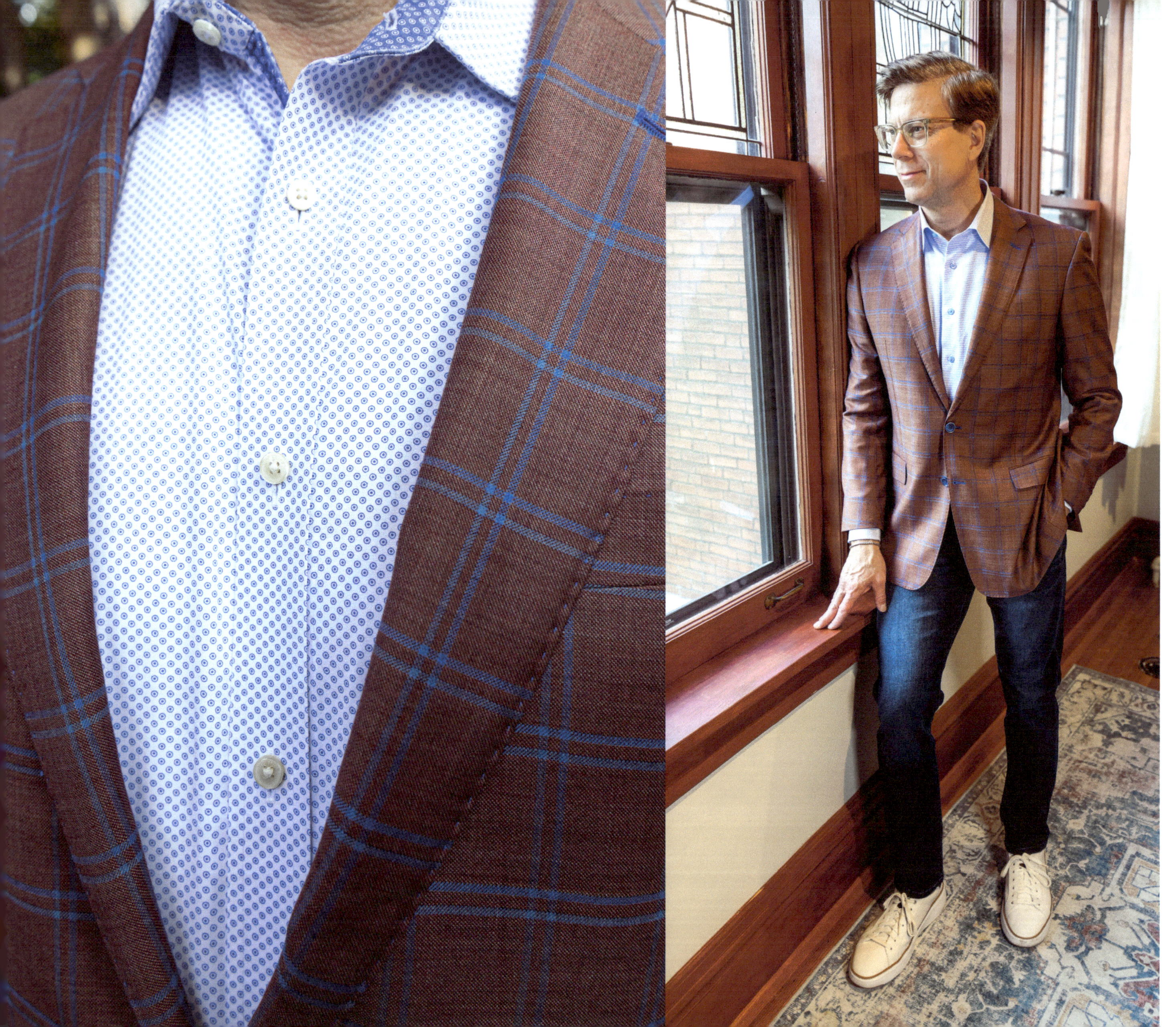

John Banjak

Principal & General Counsel for True Title Company

I enjoy yoga, traveling, exercising, and spending time with my kids.

I'm a yoga instructor.

Dressing well is so important. It makes me feel confident, focused, put together, and takes the distraction or worry off my mind so I can focus on my interaction with others. It's a confidence boost!

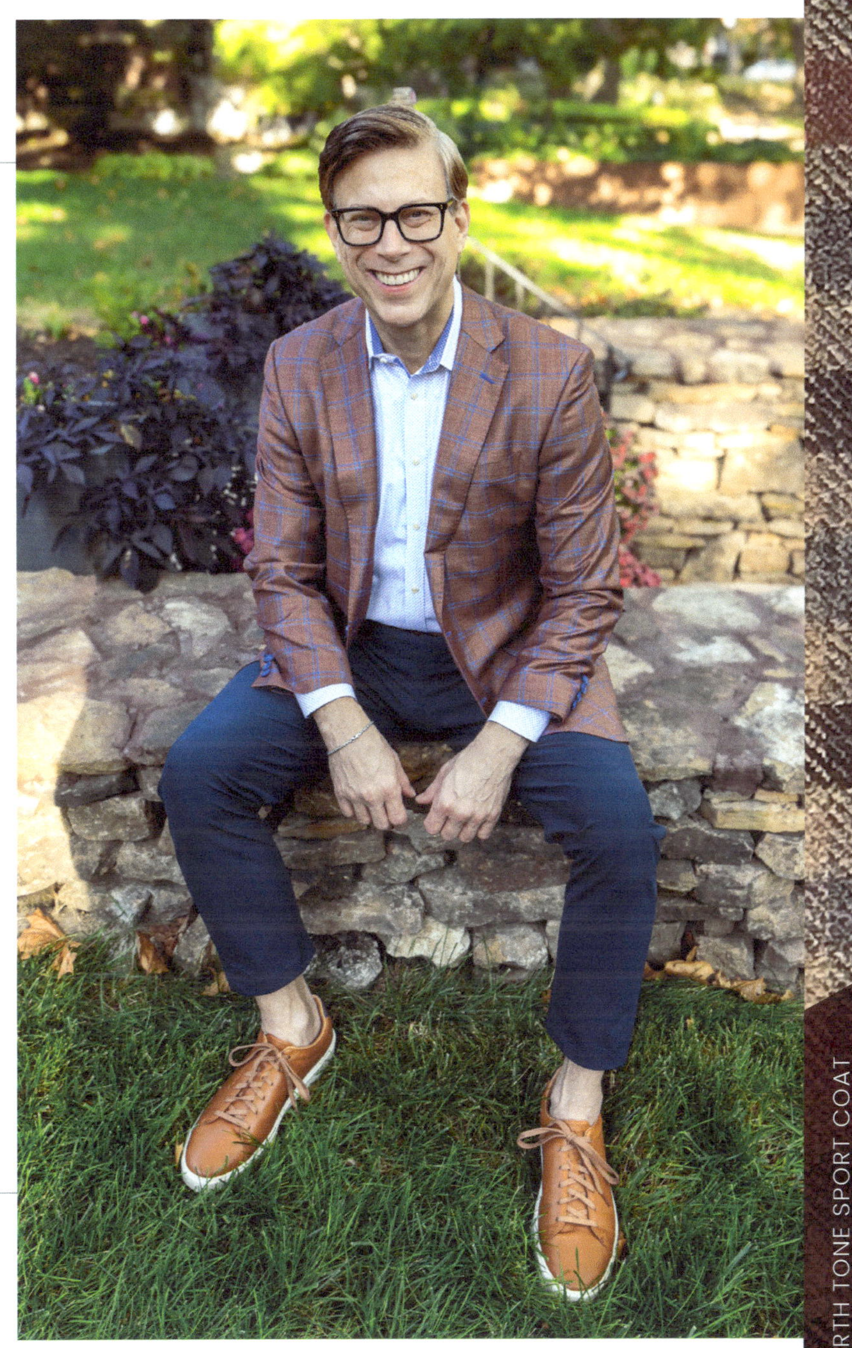

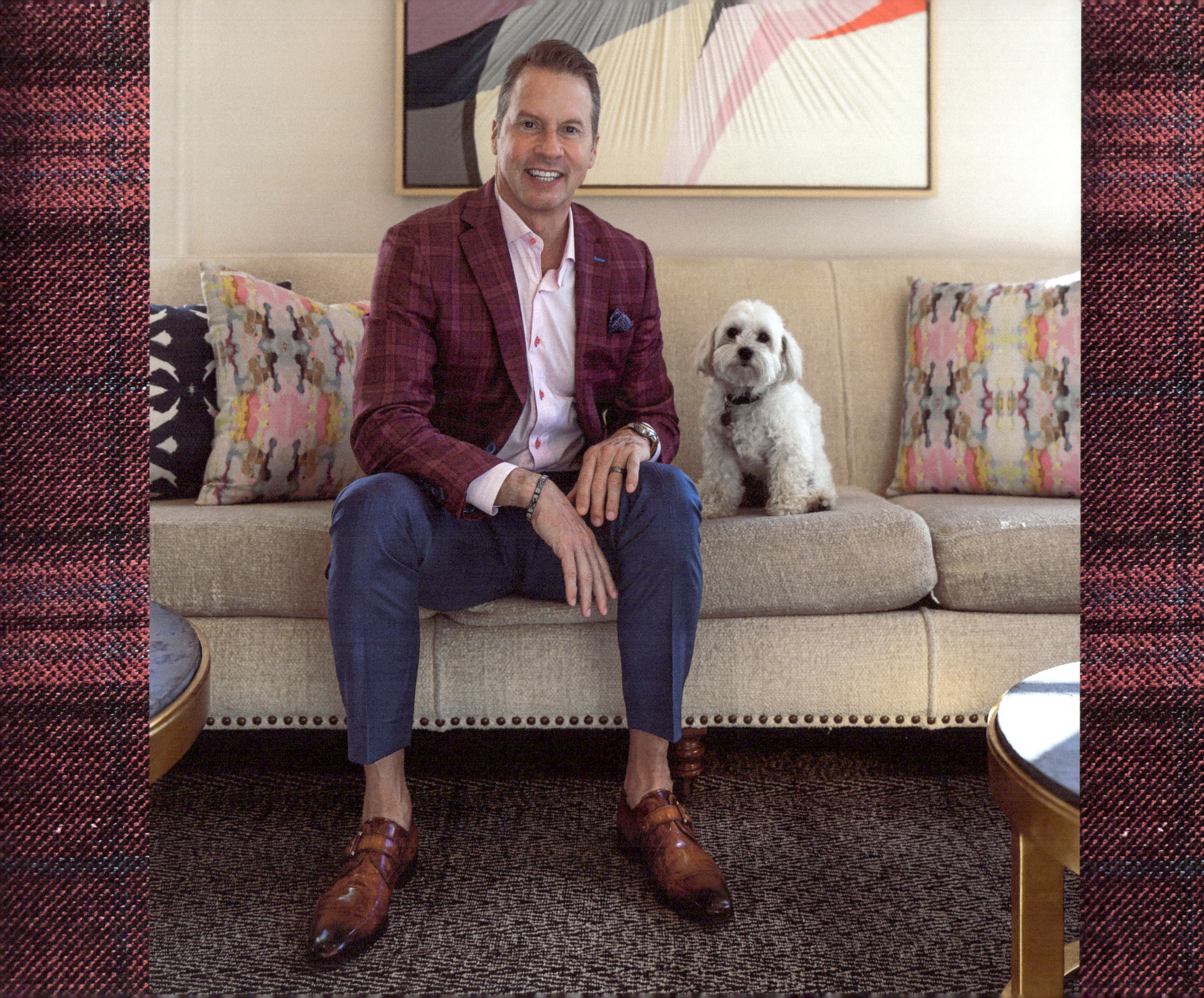

BERRY

EXCITING • FUN • OPEN • INTERESTING

A modern and colorful statement piece, berry sport coats
are sure to attract compliments and catch attention.
Surprisingly versatile, the berry family of jackets can be worn
with numerous pant and shirt combinations.

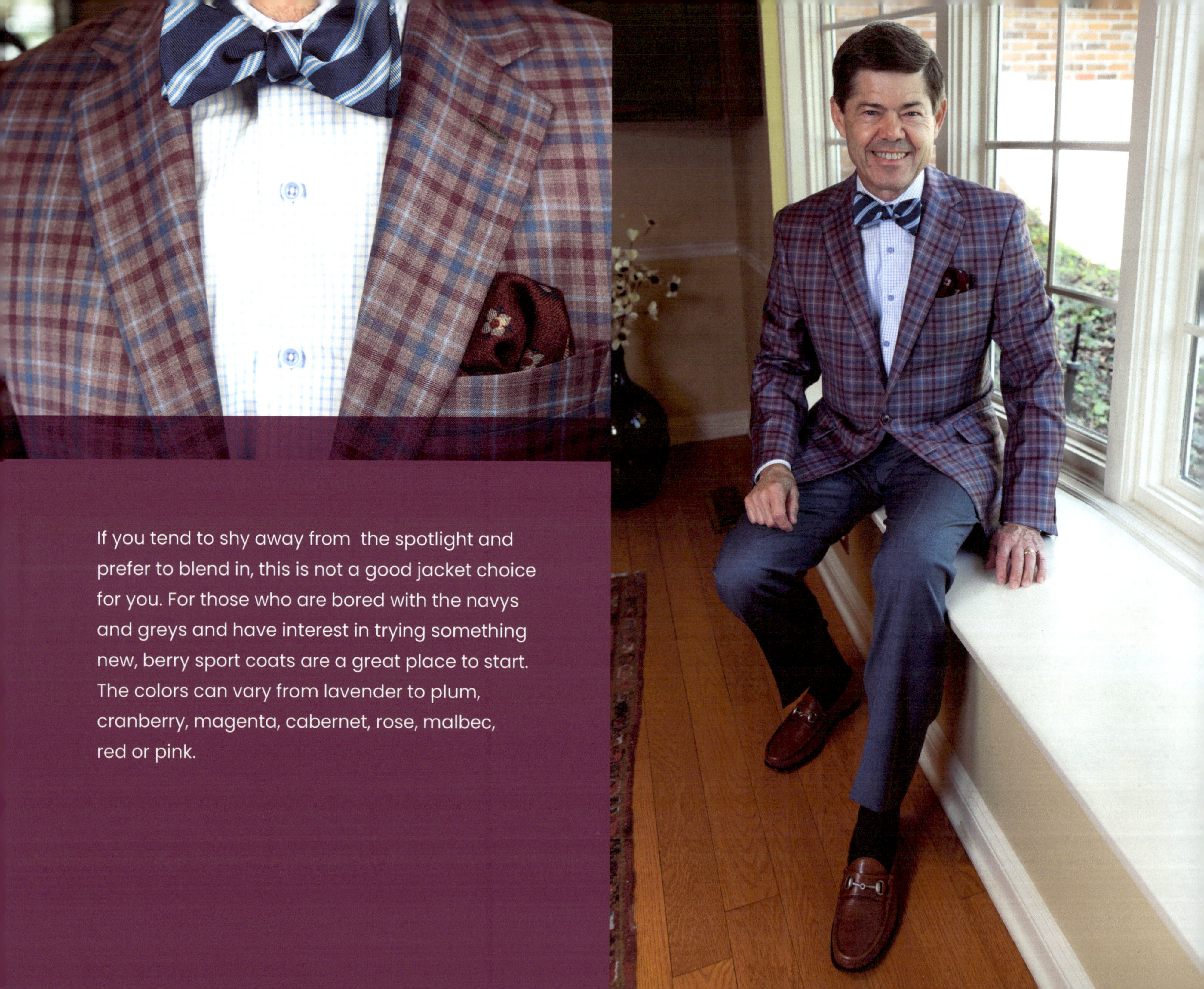

If you tend to shy away from the spotlight and prefer to blend in, this is not a good jacket choice for you. For those who are bored with the navys and greys and have interest in trying something new, berry sport coats are a great place to start. The colors can vary from lavender to plum, cranberry, magenta, cabernet, rose, malbec, red or pink.

SHIRTS TO MATCH

Solid Colors

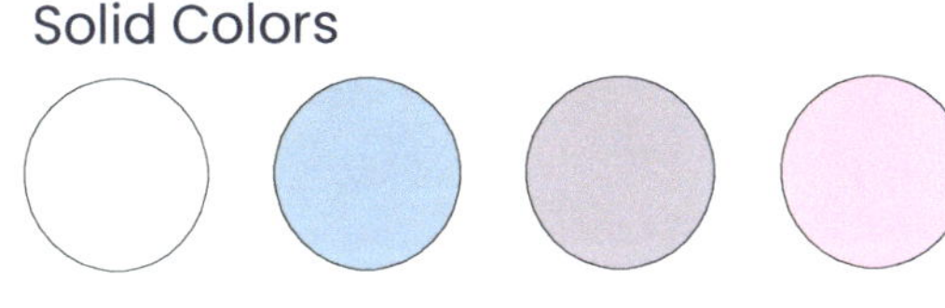

White – Color Stripe or Pattern

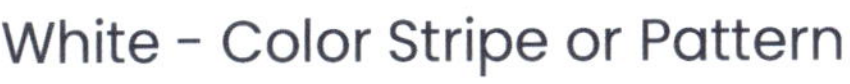

Blue – Color Stripe or Pattern

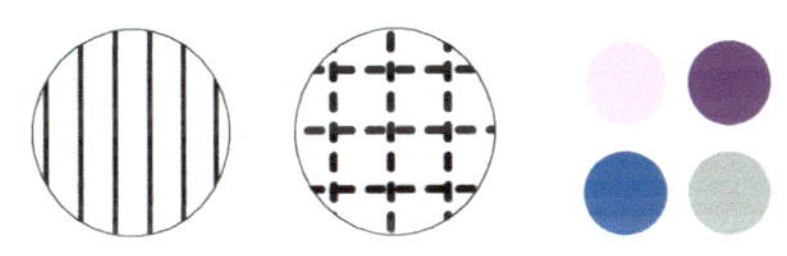

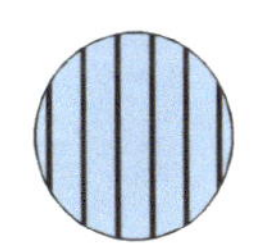

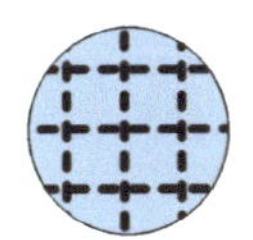

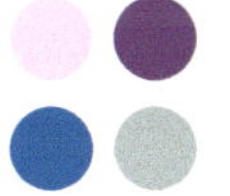

TROUSERS

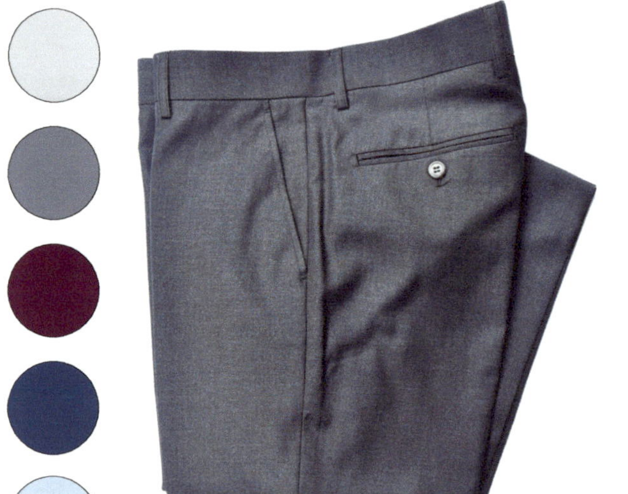

JEANS

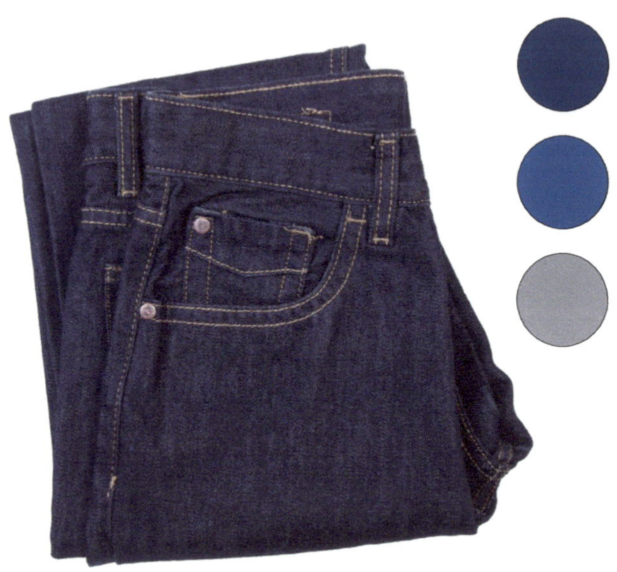

FOOTWEAR

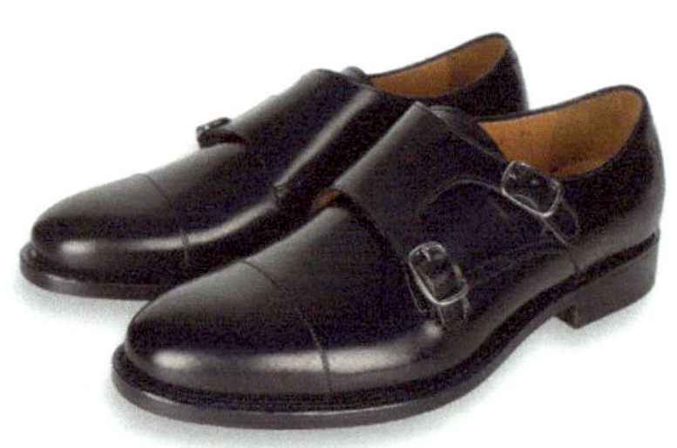

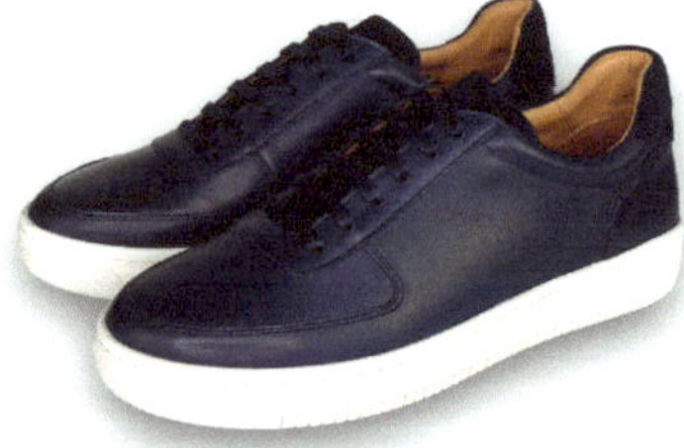

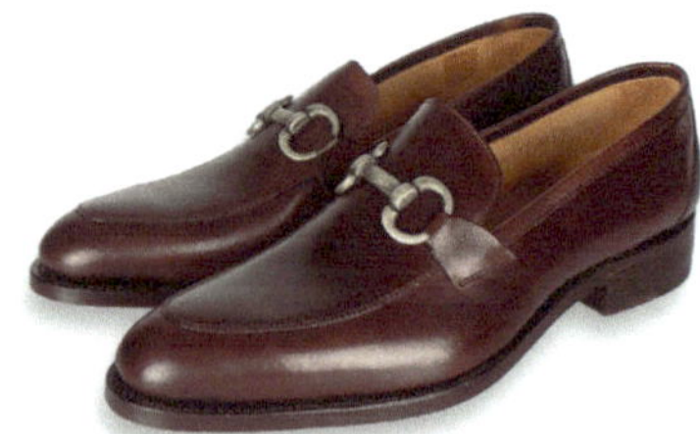

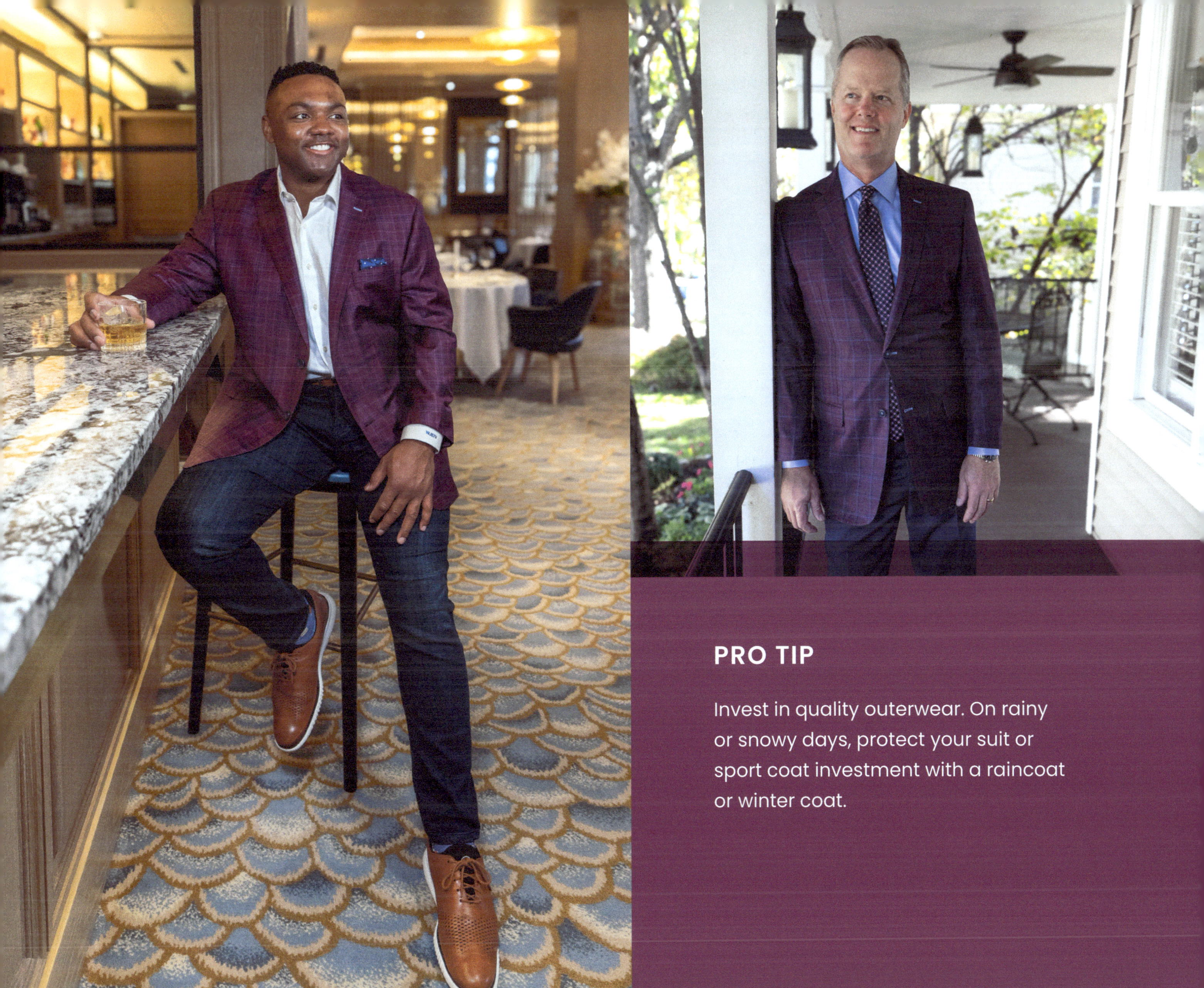

PRO TIP

Invest in quality outerwear. On rainy or snowy days, protect your suit or sport coat investment with a raincoat or winter coat.

BLAZERS

Clothes and manners do not make the man; but when he is made, they greatly improve his appearance.

HENRY WARD BEECHER

Blazers are a solid jacket of any color historically designed with metal buttons. Blazer colors can range from traditional navy, to black, olive, brown, grey, merlot, or even pink! Modern men shopping for blazers typically prefer to have brighter lighter colored blazers with a horn button, while mature men like the look of darker shades with metal buttons.

Selecting a trouser to complement blazers can be challenging as they require a contrasting shade to the jacket. For instance, wearing a navy trouser with a navy blazer is a definite faux pas. Instead, wear a light or medium grey trouser with a navy blazer to achieve the necessary contrast.

For the fashion forward gentleman, pair a blazer with a plaid, windowpane, check, or solid vibrant color trouser for a fun and exciting alternative. Yes, I am endorsing patterned pants!

Blazers are a more conservative option than a sport coat, and are suitable for social and professional occasions. They allow more creative expression in the shirt choice, as there is less concern about pairing patterns together. Overall, throwing on a blazer elevates your look no matter the occasion and proves itself as a reliable wardrobe staple to have in your wardrobe or hanging in your office for surprise client visits.

While many believe navy blazers are the best and most versatile option to add to their blazer selection, they prove difficult to coordinate with trousers due to the necessary contrast. Consider instead a wine, olive, mauve or light grey blazer, as they are much easier to pair with pants.

If you are looking to get started with blazers, start by considering what your preferences are when it comes to the color of your pants. If you wear mainly dark pants, a lighter shade of jacket may be a better choice for you. If you enjoy lighter colored pants or are open to adding them, a black or navy blazer would be suitable.

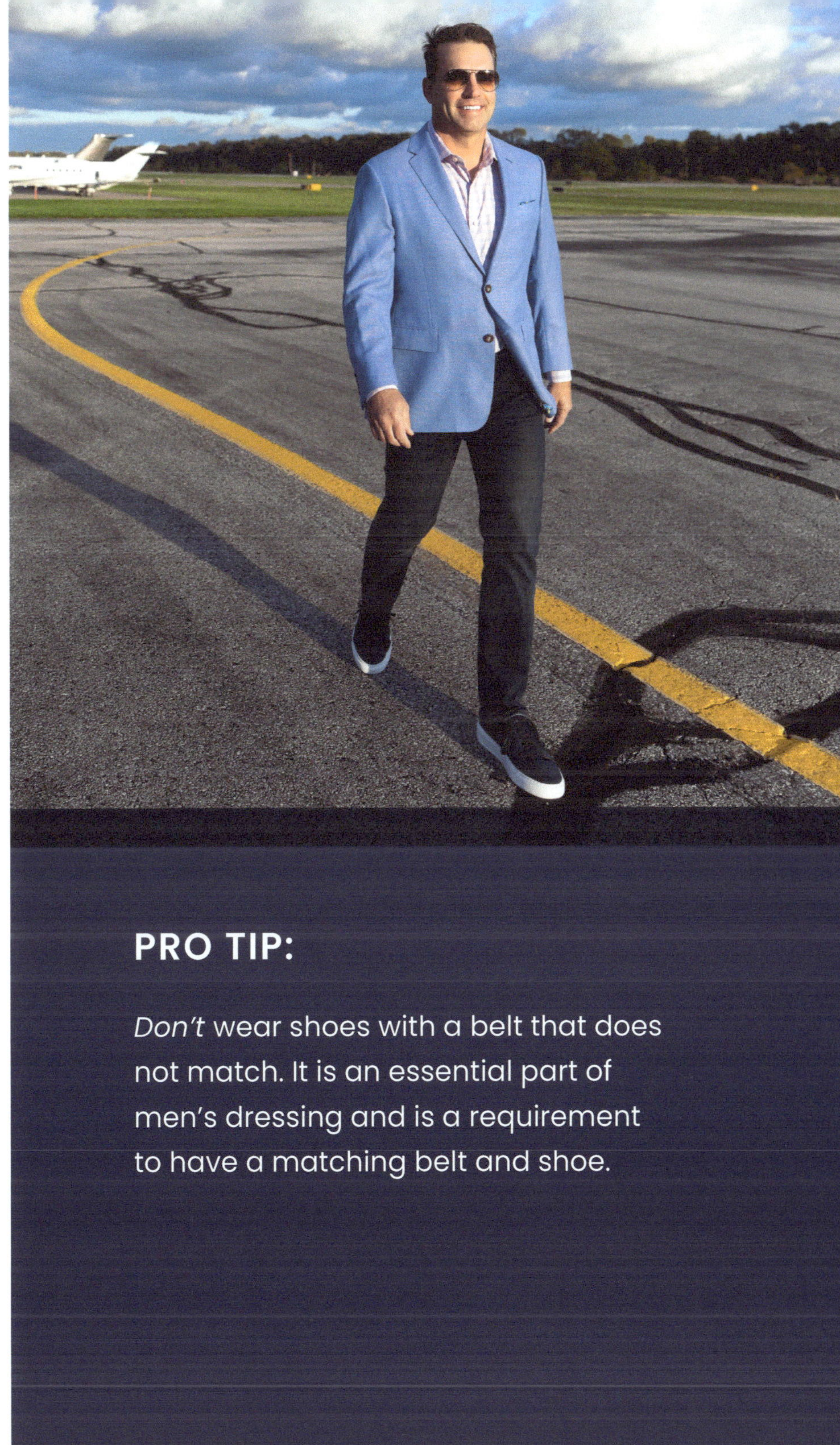

PRO TIP:

Don't wear shoes with a belt that does not match. It is an essential part of men's dressing and is a requirement to have a matching belt and shoe.

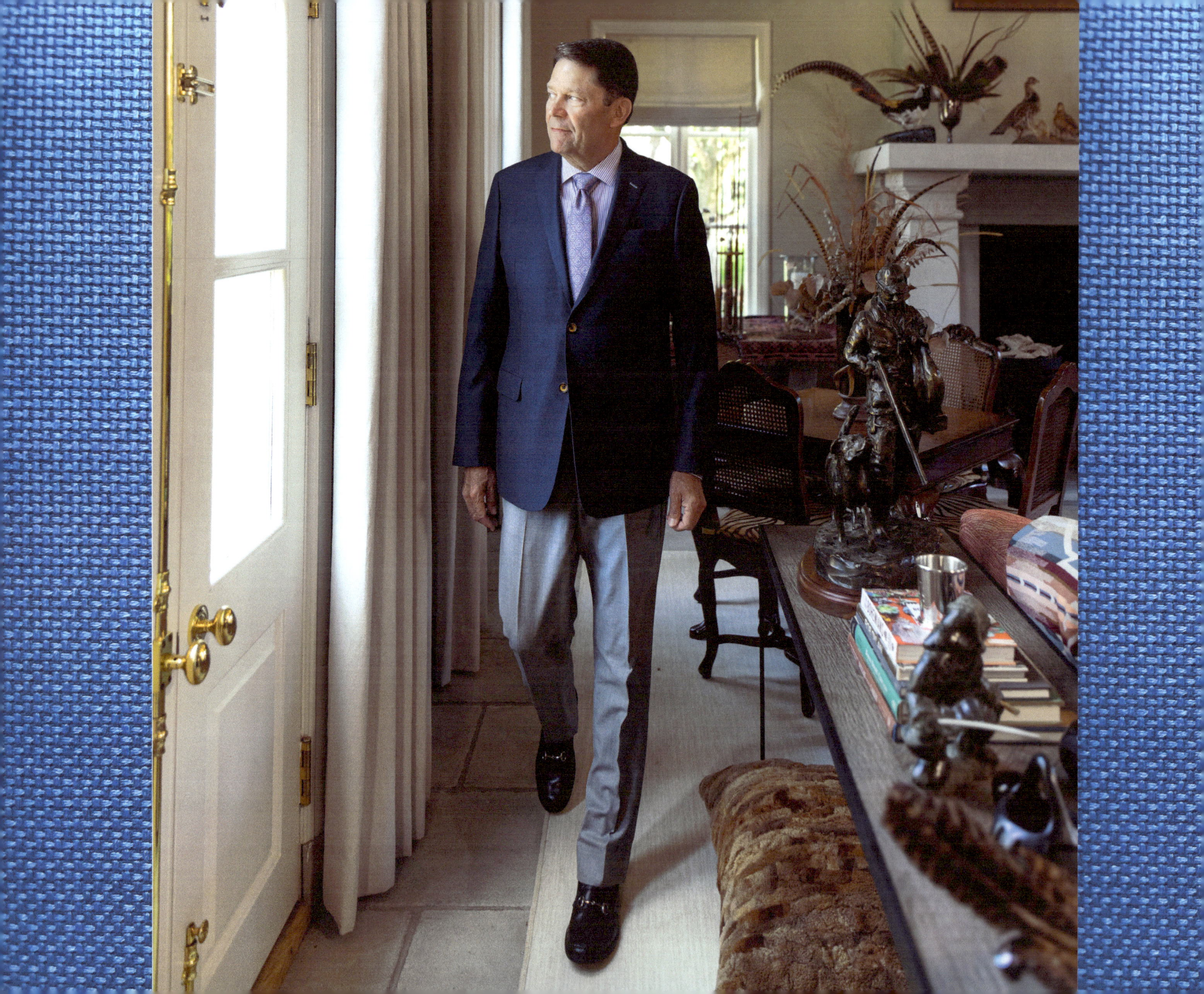

BLUE

TRADITIONAL • SIMPLE ELEGANCE • CLASSIC

Navy blazers have been a staple for many decades, and have an uncanny ability to adapt and survive even in modern times. Intentionally pair trousers with a blue blazer that have a contrasting shade to the jacket. It is inappropriate to wear navy, charcoal, or black pants with a traditional blue blazer. Instead, wear light grey, medium grey, light blue, or tan to achieve the required contrast.

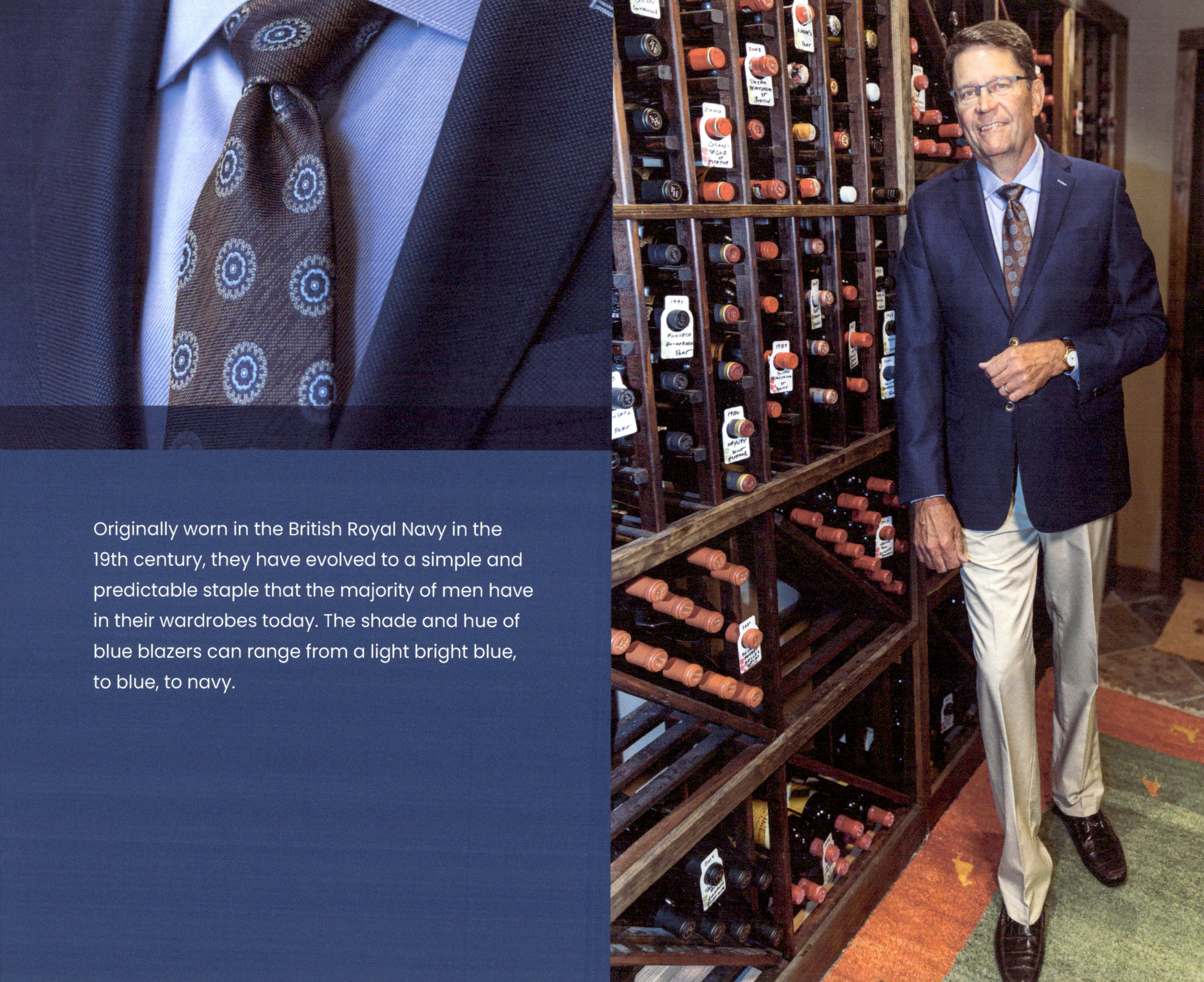
Originally worn in the British Royal Navy in the 19th century, they have evolved to a simple and predictable staple that the majority of men have in their wardrobes today. The shade and hue of blue blazers can range from a light bright blue, to blue, to navy.

WHAT TO WEAR WITH YOUR
BLUE BLAZER

SHIRTS TO MATCH

Solid Colors

White - Color Stripe or Pattern

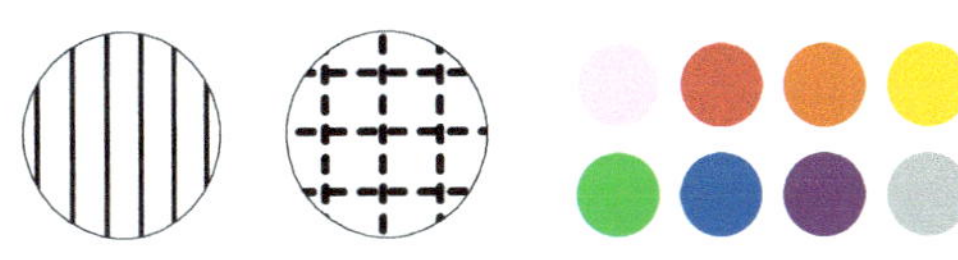

Blue - Color Stripe or Pattern

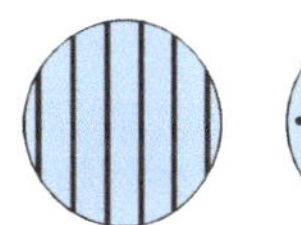
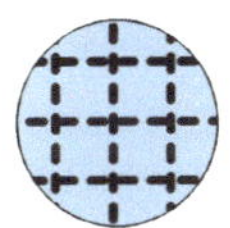
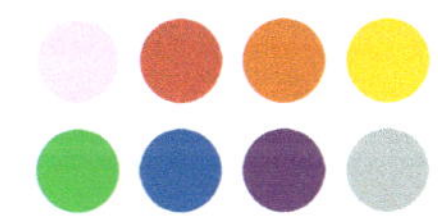

TROUSERS

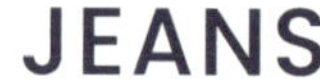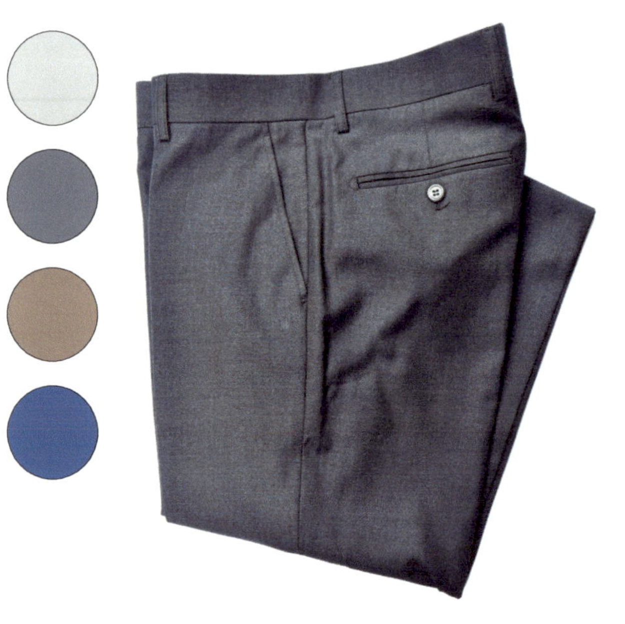

JEANS

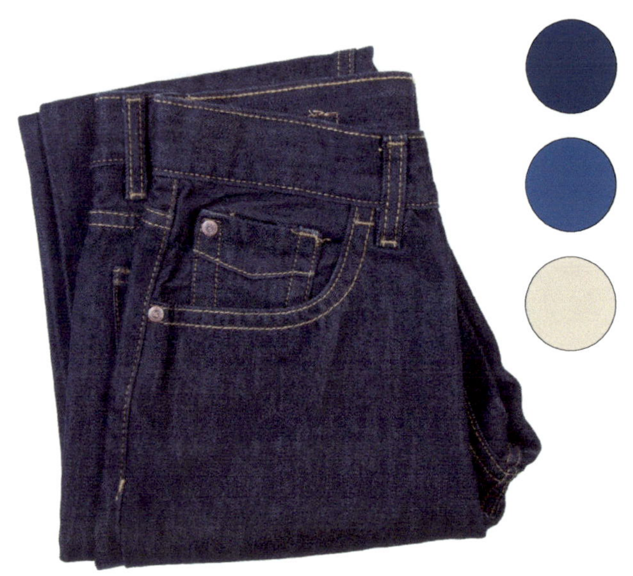

FOOTWEAR

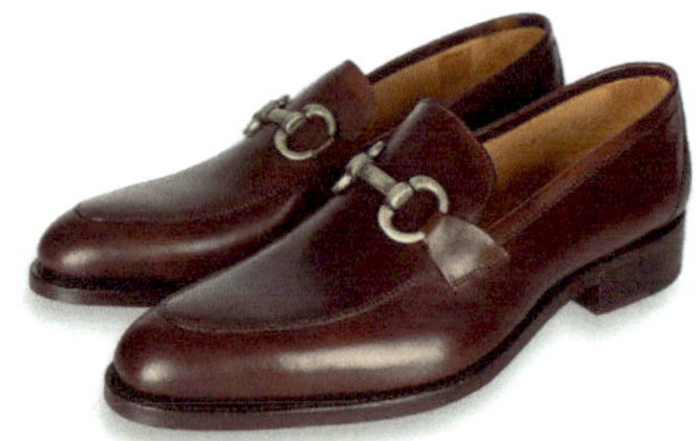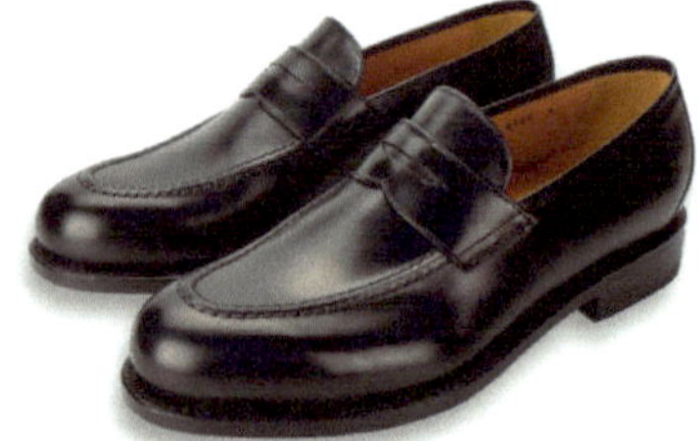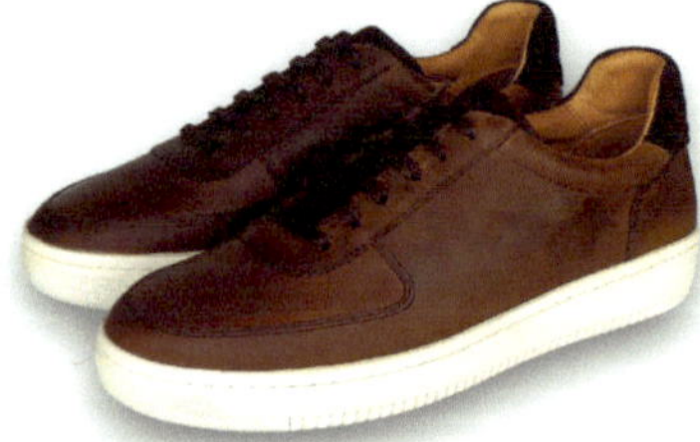

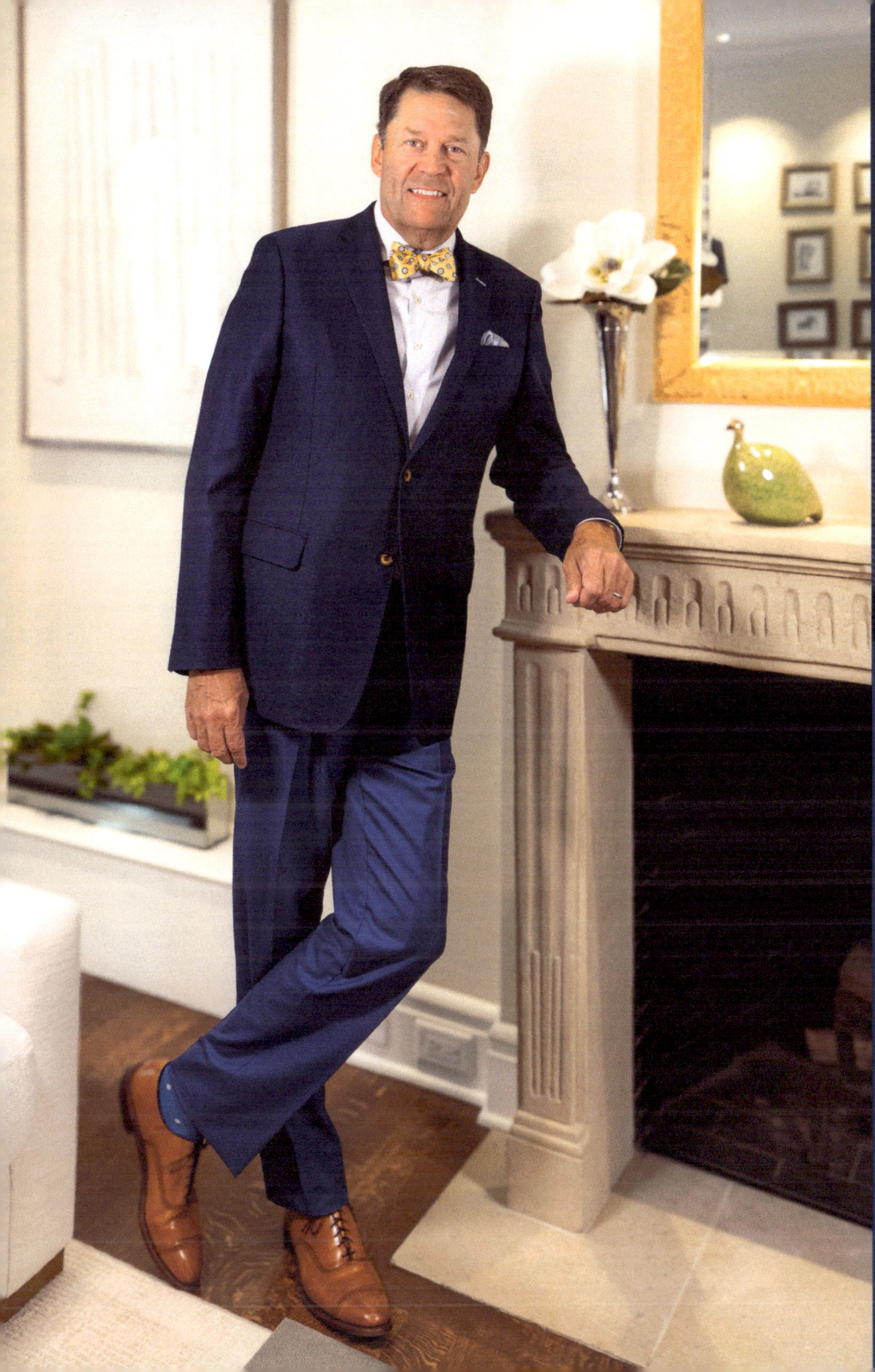

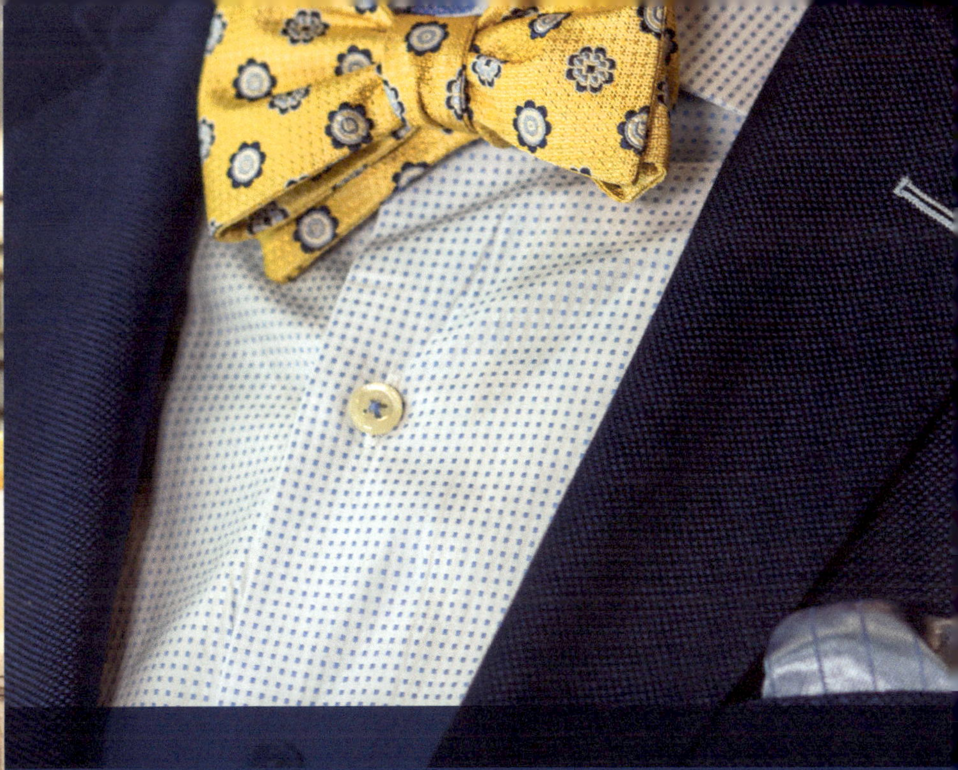

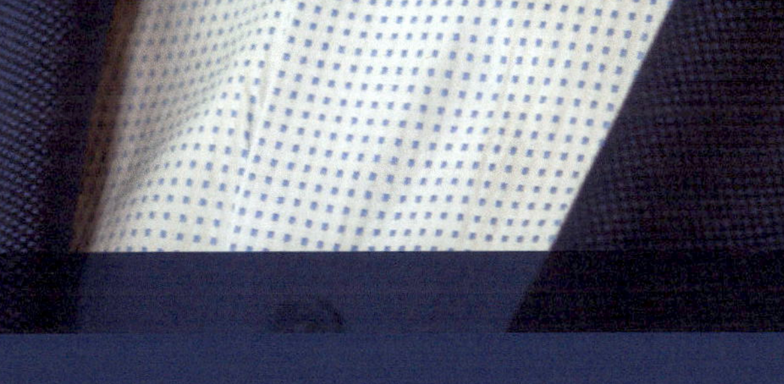

PRO TIP

Choose styles that complement your body shape. Not all trends are universally flattering. For example, tall and slender gentlemen can wear a 3 button jacket or a double breasted jacket because they have the torso length to accommodate the additional fabric, and it creates a balanced look. Those of low to medium height with a stout body shape should stick to a 2 button jacket.

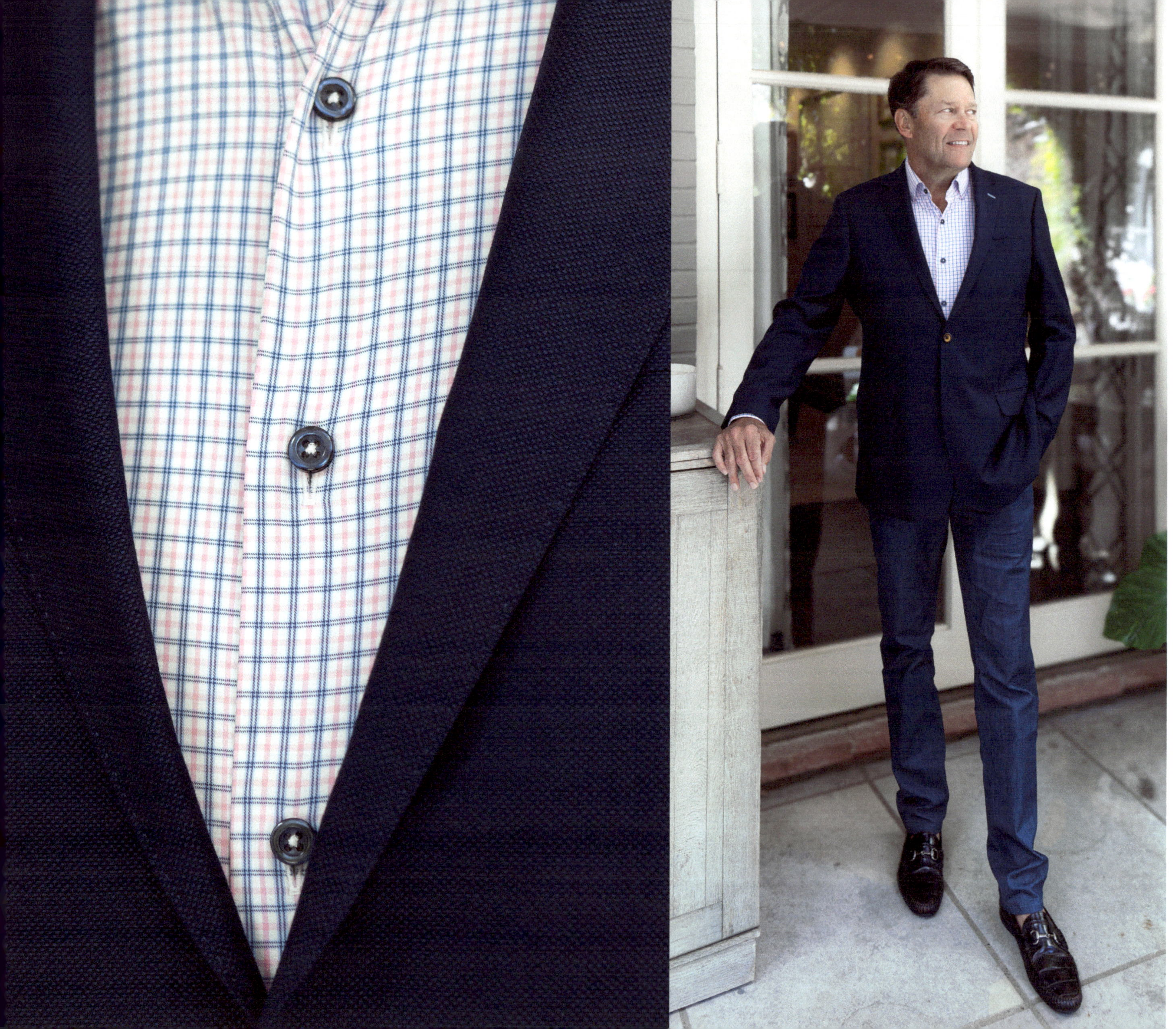

Russell Browning

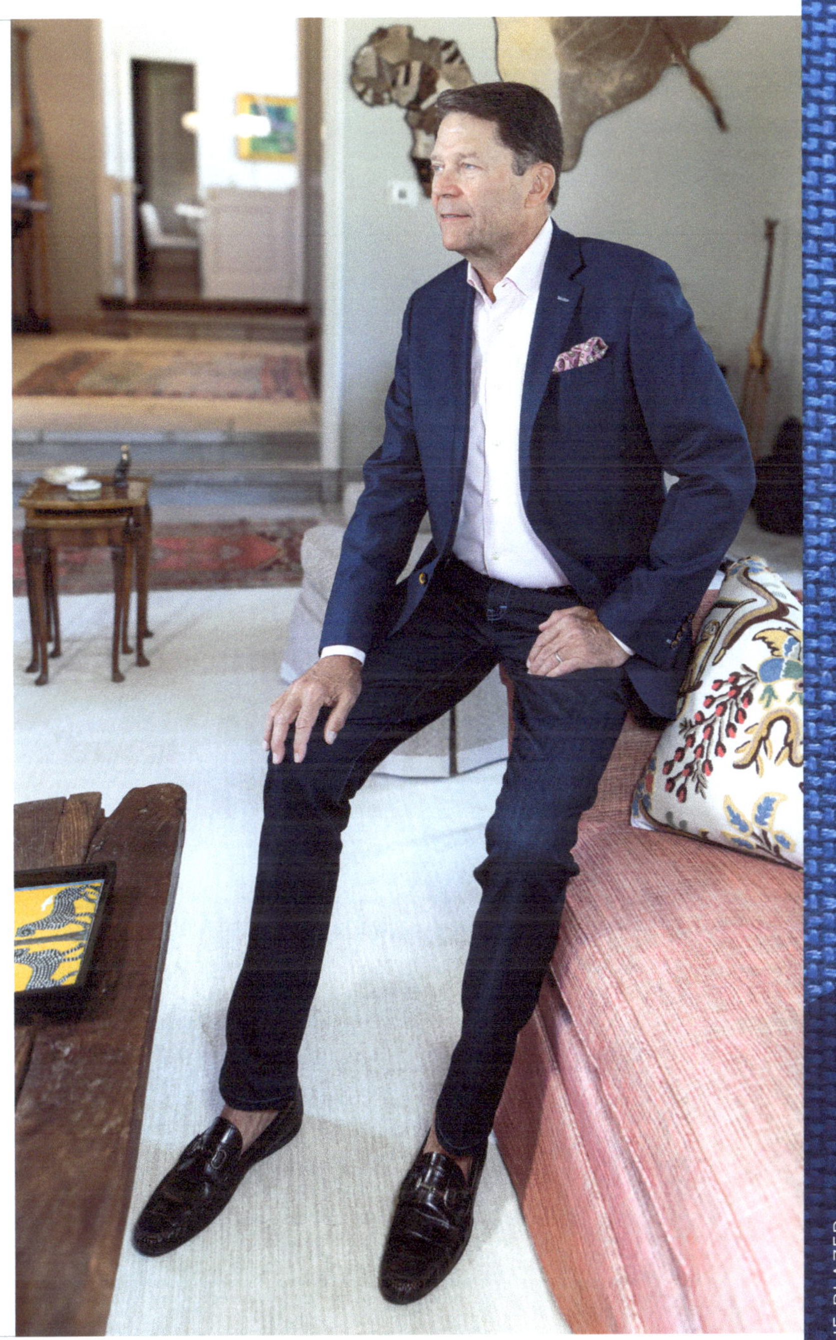

WHAT IS YOUR OCCUPATION?

Private investor for our Family Office

WHAT ARE YOUR HOBBIES AND INTERESTS?

Spending quality time with my wife and ever growing family! We like to travel, boat, golf, fly fish, and collect (and drink!) wine.

WHAT IS A FUN FACT ABOUT YOU?

Private pilot with an instrument rating (I can fly in the clouds). Proud owner of a 1963 port!

WHAT IMPACT HAS DRESSING WELL HAD ON YOUR CAREER?

When you dress well, you have a high degree of self confidence, and a higher professional impact.

WHAT IS IMPORTANT TO YOU IN THE QUALITY OF YOUR CLOTHING?

Individually tailored clothing is important and key to dressing well. Appreciation for quality is a consistent part of my life. I appreciate a well made, high quality, and a long lasting garment.

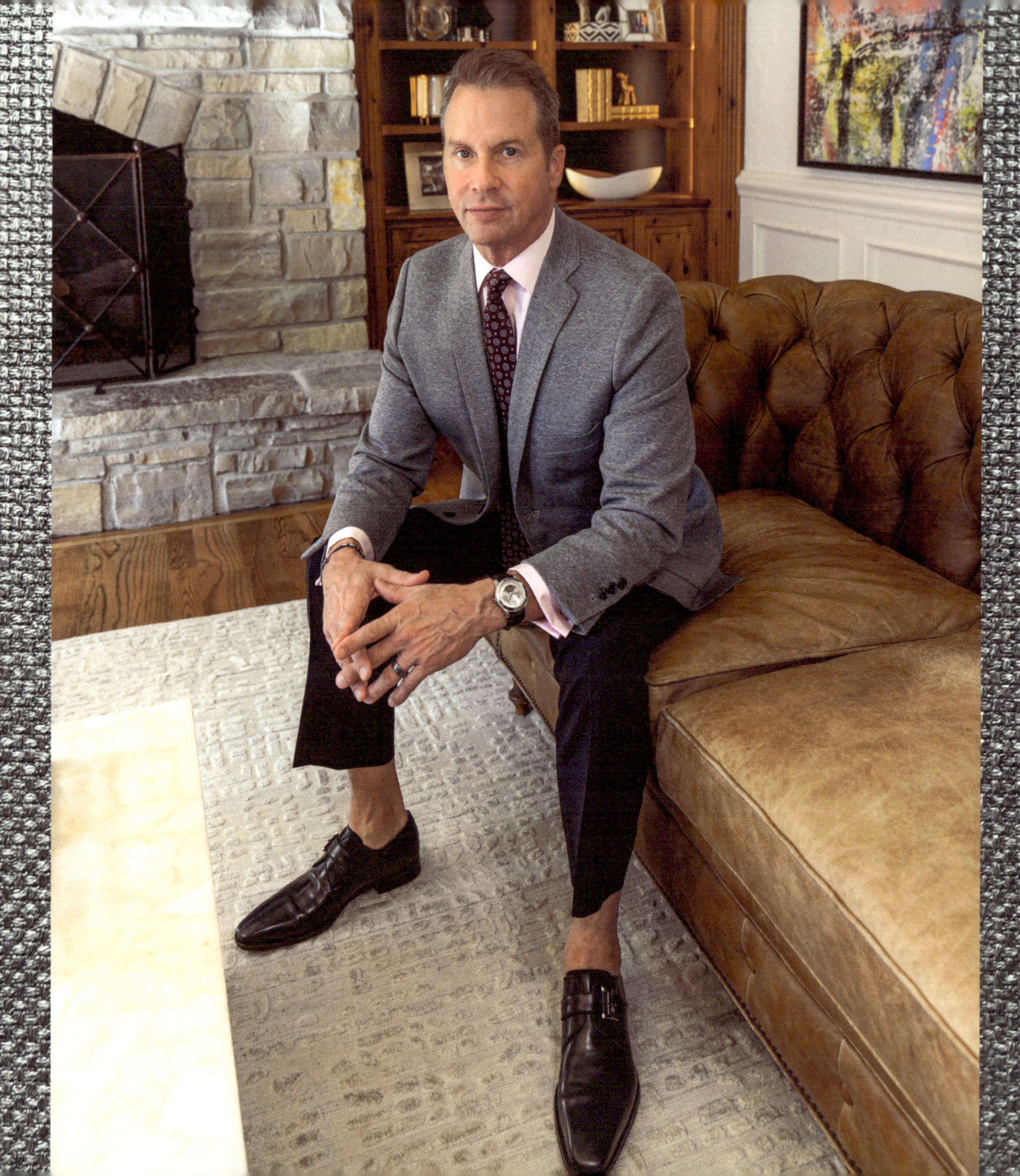

GREY

COOL • NEUTRAL • SLEEK • URBAN • MODERN

Cool, modern and steadfast, grey blazers of any shade present a refined and timeless image and can be worn in professional or casual settings.

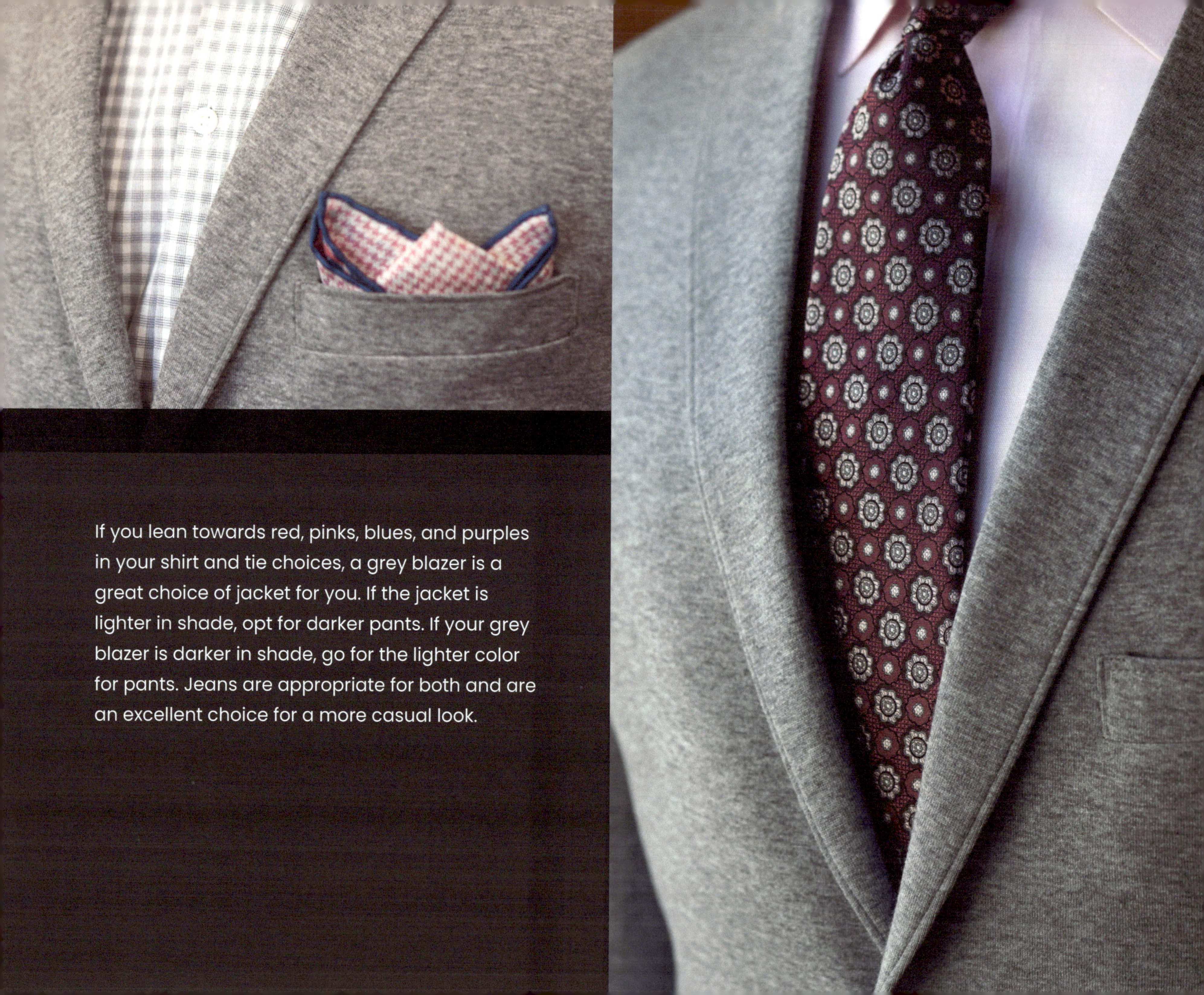

If you lean towards red, pinks, blues, and purples in your shirt and tie choices, a grey blazer is a great choice of jacket for you. If the jacket is lighter in shade, opt for darker pants. If your grey blazer is darker in shade, go for the lighter color for pants. Jeans are appropriate for both and are an excellent choice for a more casual look.

GREY BLAZER

SHIRTS TO MATCH

Solid Colors

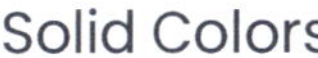

White - Color Stripe or Pattern

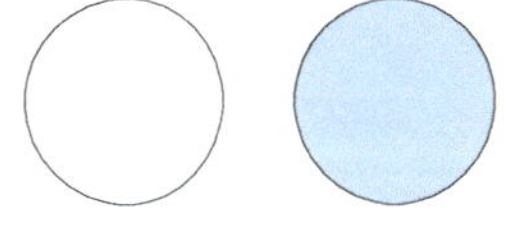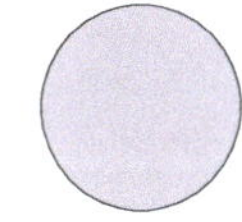

Blue - Color Stripe or Pattern

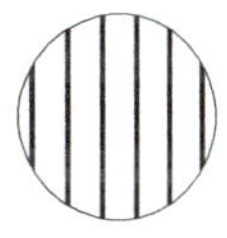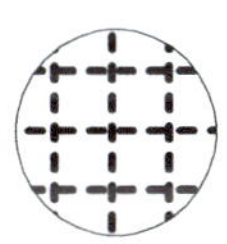

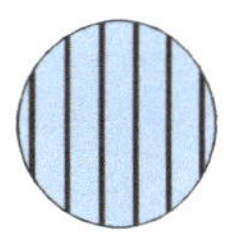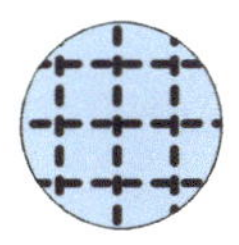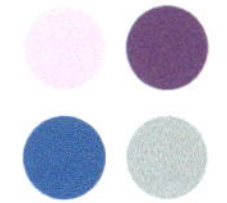

TROUSERS

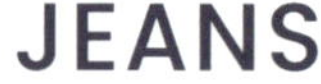

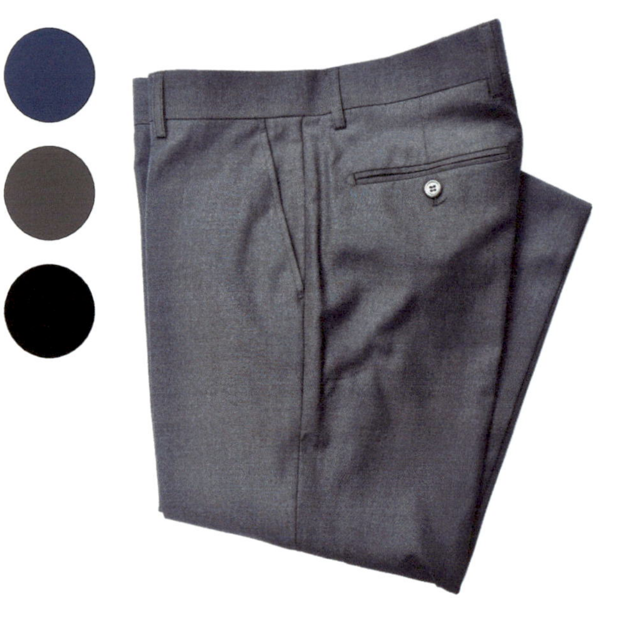

JEANS

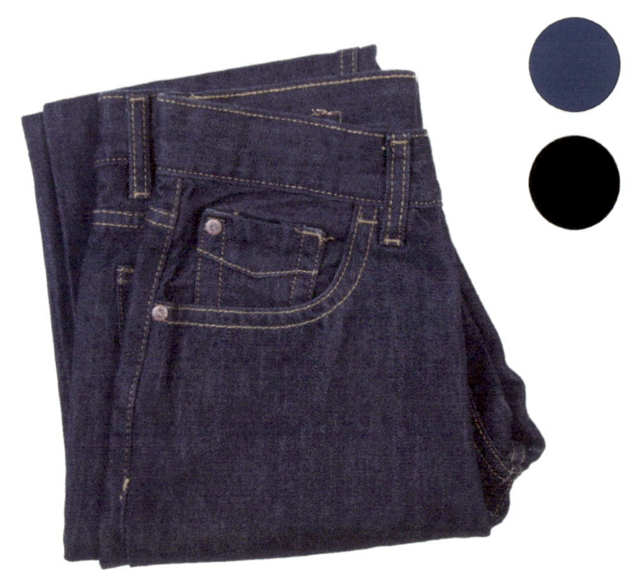

FOOTWEAR

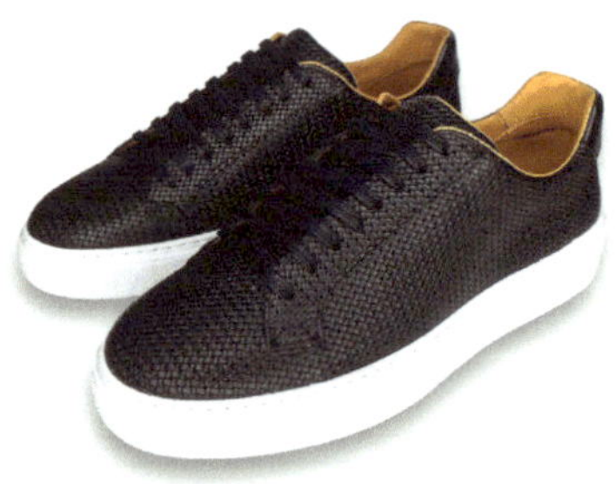

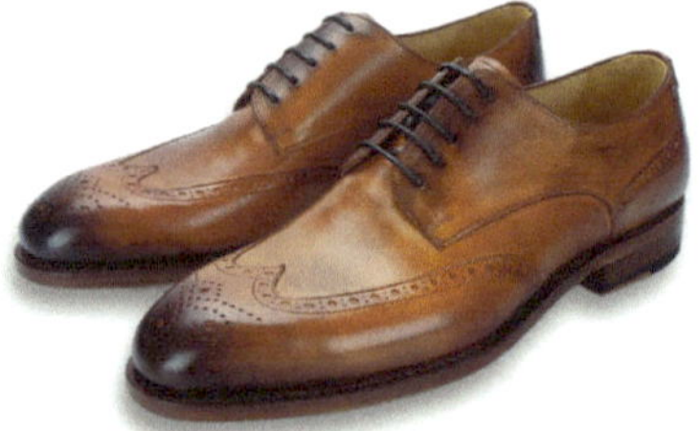

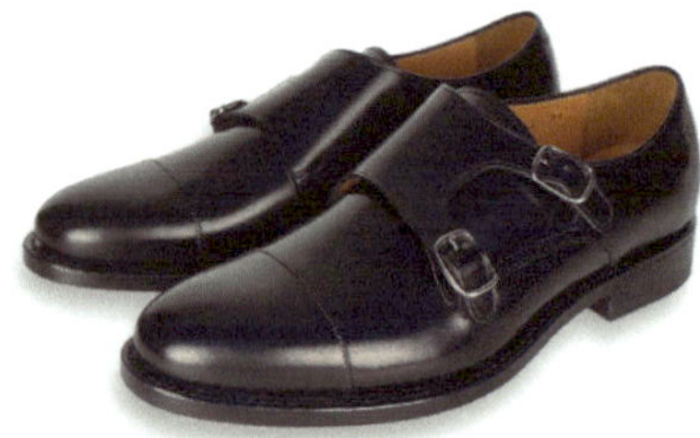

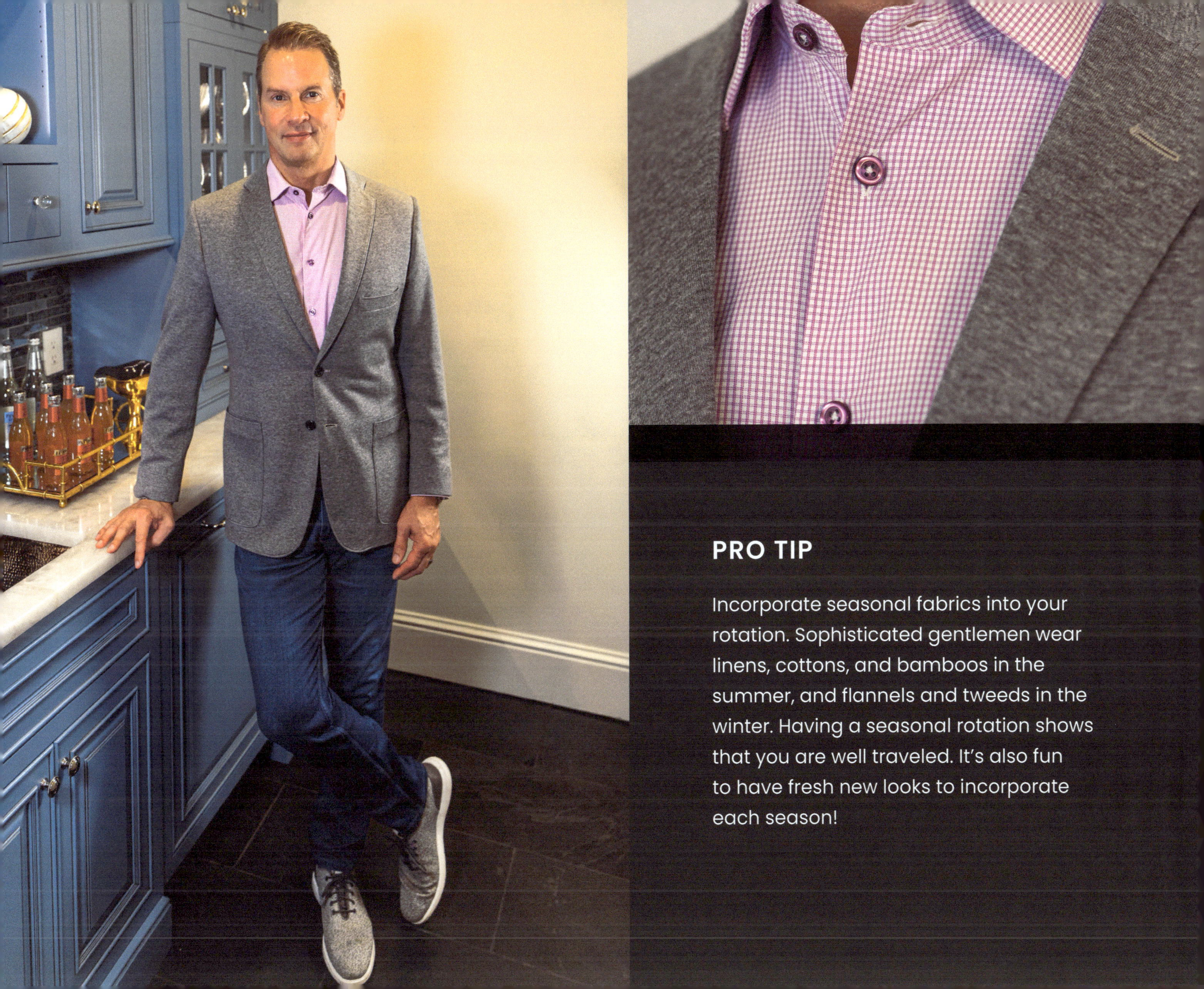

PRO TIP

Incorporate seasonal fabrics into your rotation. Sophisticated gentlemen wear linens, cottons, and bamboos in the summer, and flannels and tweeds in the winter. Having a seasonal rotation shows that you are well traveled. It's also fun to have fresh new looks to incorporate each season!

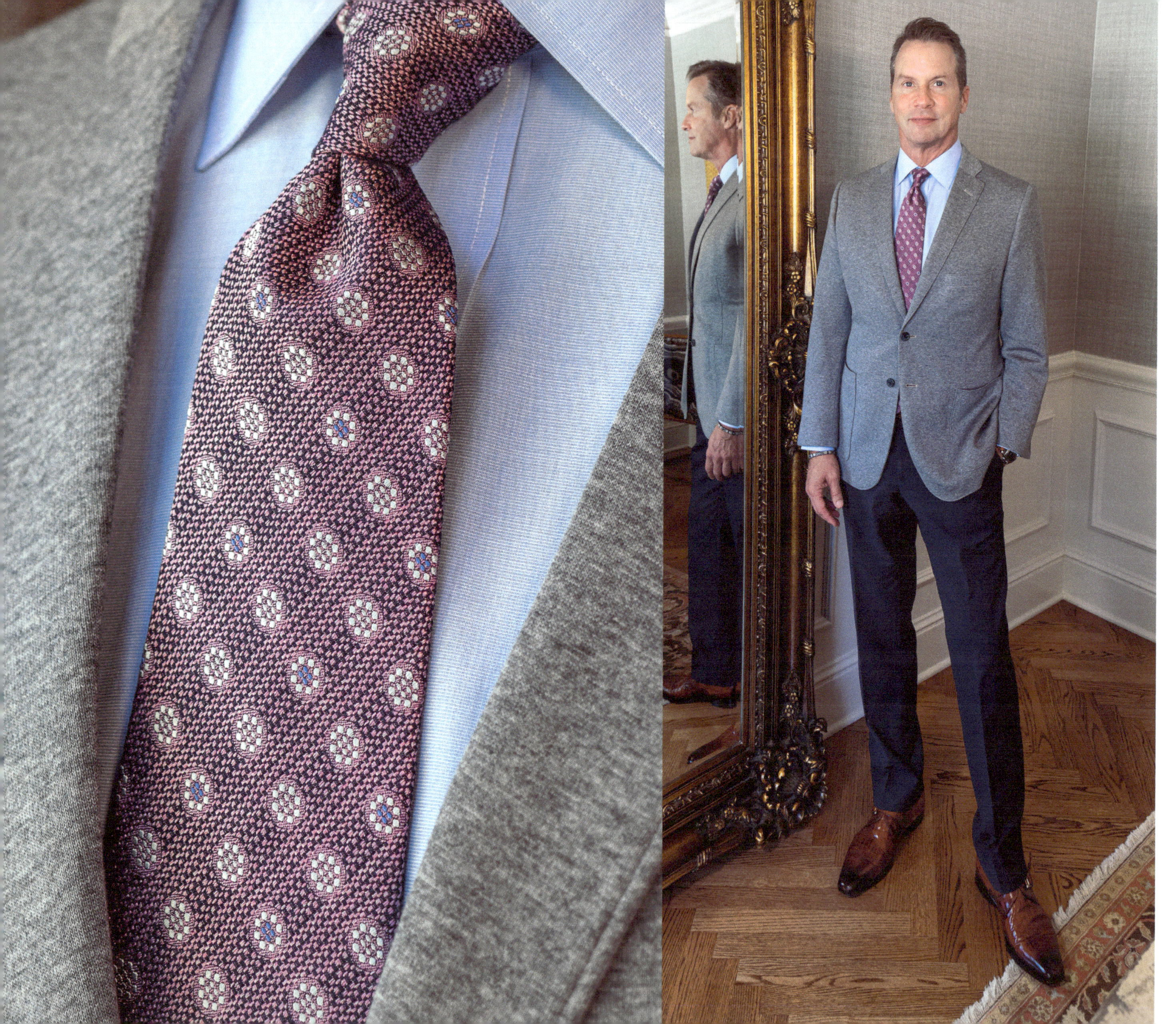

Bill Schmidt

WHAT IS YOUR OCCUPATION?

Managing Partner, Cultivation Capital

WHAT ARE YOUR HOBBIES AND INTERESTS?

I enjoy music and sports, skiing, collecting art, shooting hoops and traveling the world.

WHAT IS A FUN FACT ABOUT YOU?

I carried the Olympic Torch in 2008 Beijing Olympics.

IS THERE SOMEONE IN YOUR FAMILY WHO INFLUENCED YOU ON HOW TO DRESS?

Yes, my father. He never had the finest clothing, but his clothing was always impeccably tailored and he insisted on wearing well-fitting garments.

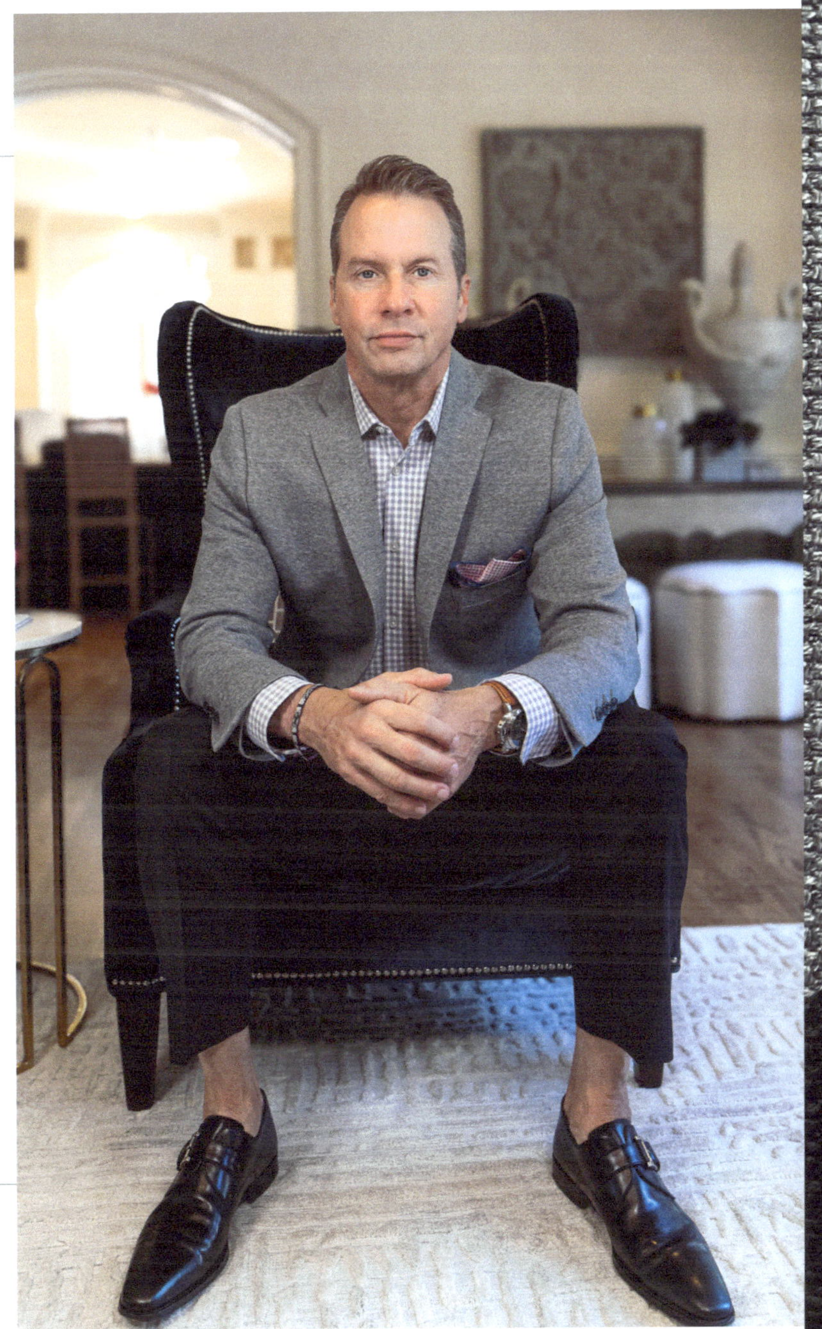

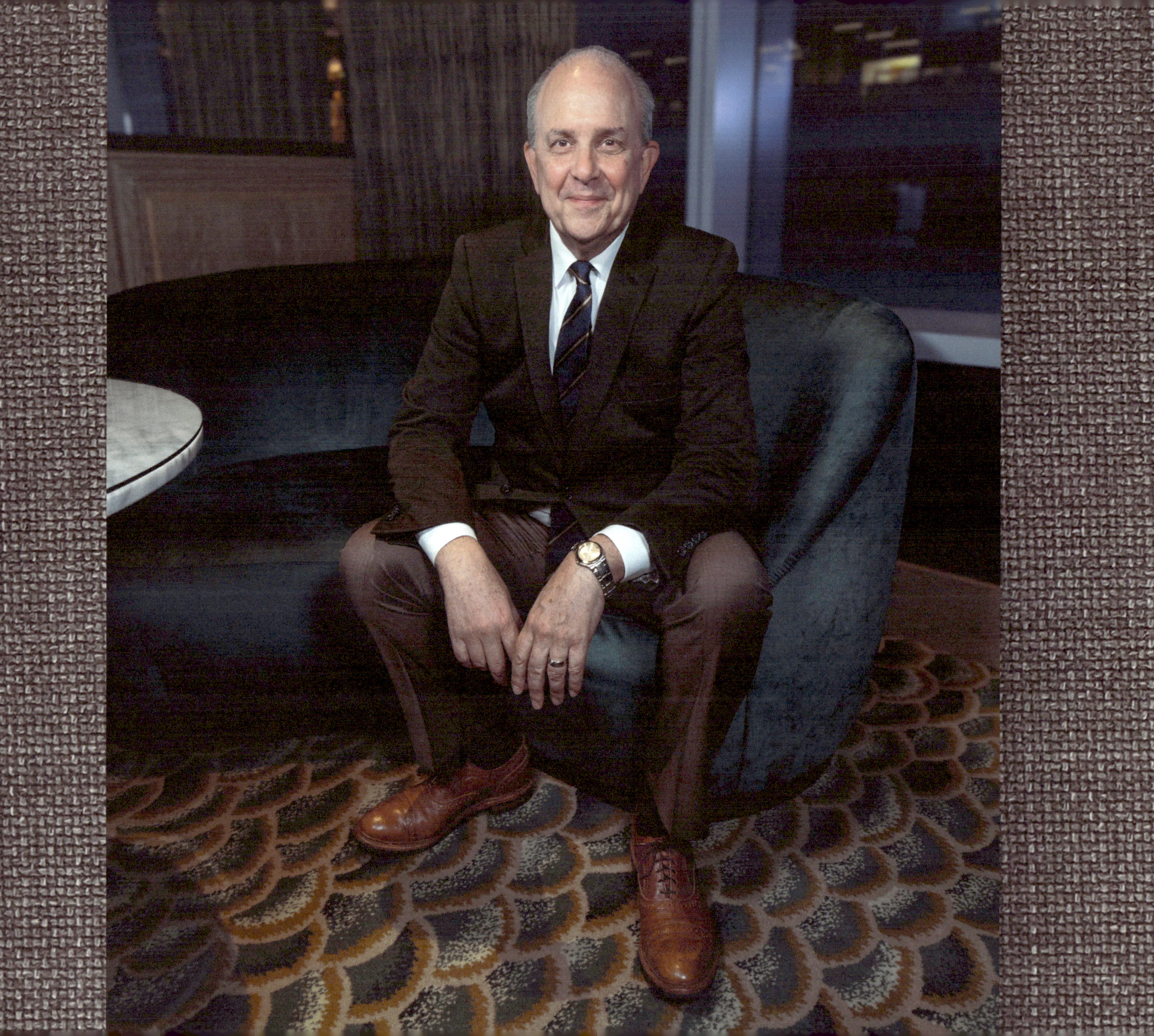

EARTH TONE

WARM • APPROACHABLE • COMFORTABLE • TRUSTWORTHY

Earth tones include colors like: brown, tan, khaki, olive green, rust, beige, caramel, moss green, taupe or camel. They all project a sense of calmness and create an immediate feeling that you can be trusted and approached with the issue at hand.

If you need to deliver bad news, earth tones are a great color to wear. If you are looking to appeal to an empathetic audience or create a trusting and not intimidating environment, earth tone jackets (and suits) are the right choice. Earth tones also tend to be more casual, especially as jackets, and are great to wear to the office when you do not have any client meetings, but still want to have a jacket on. You could also wear them out to dinner at a more casual restaurant. For those who have a pale skin tone and have no hair or light color hair, avoid the lighter colored earth tones as they will make you look washed out.

When pairing trousers with earth tone blazers, do not wear a trouser of a similar color to the jacket. For example, wear a brown blazer with a tan pant. Wear a tan jacket with a chocolate brown trouser. Jeans are always a great choice for a more casual look, and complement any earth tone blazer well. Avoid shirt colors that have red, pinks or purples and stick with blues, rust, tan, cream, terracotta, and gold.

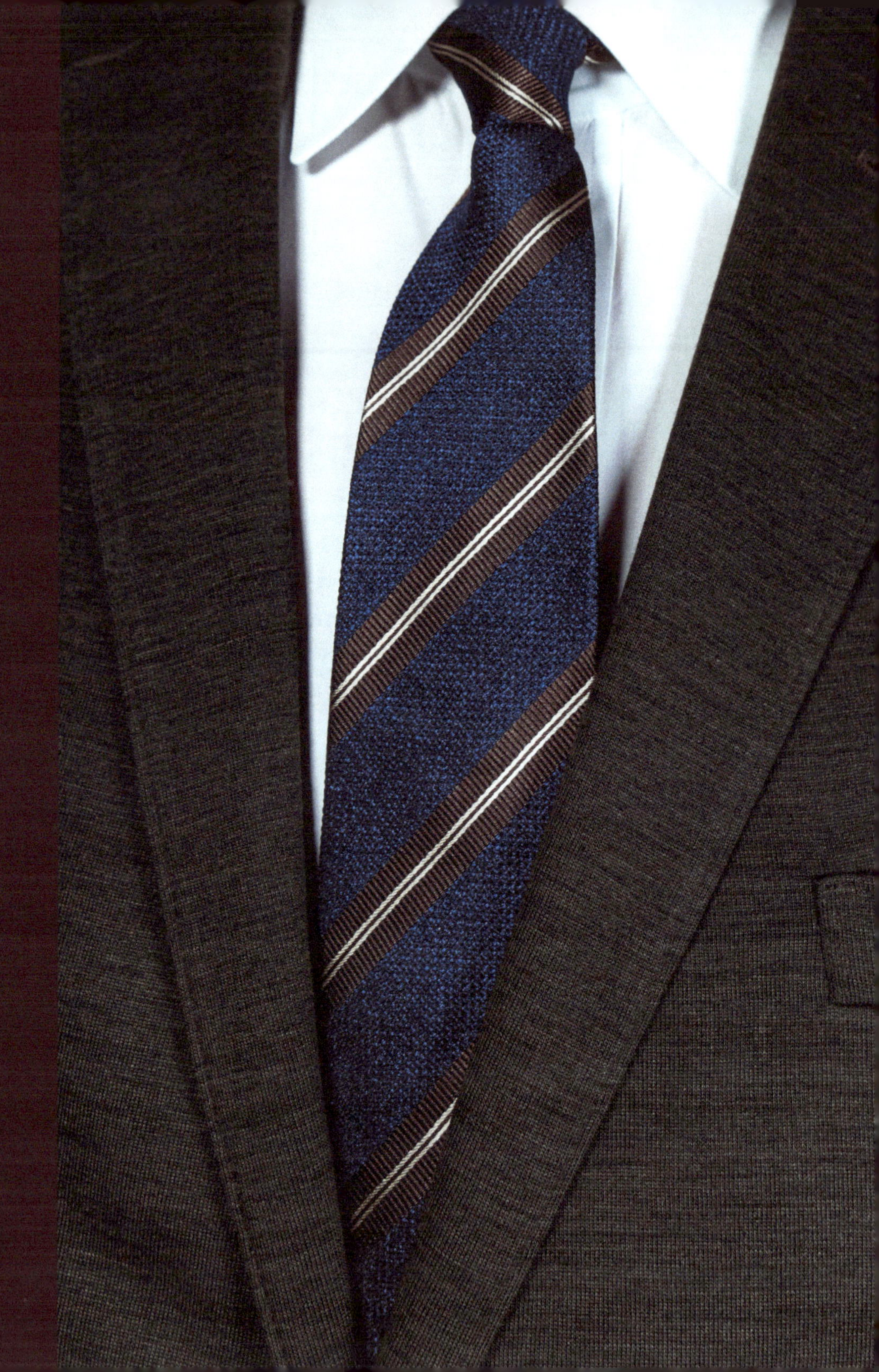

EARTH TONE BLAZER

SHIRTS TO MATCH

Solid Colors

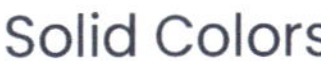

White - Color Stripe or Pattern

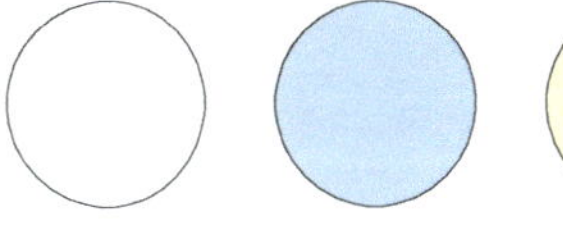

Blue - Color Stripe or Pattern

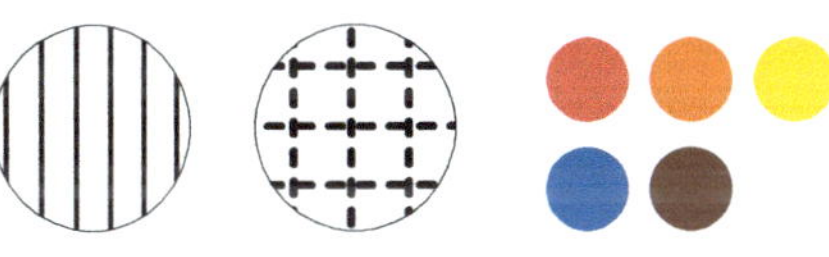

TROUSERS

JEANS

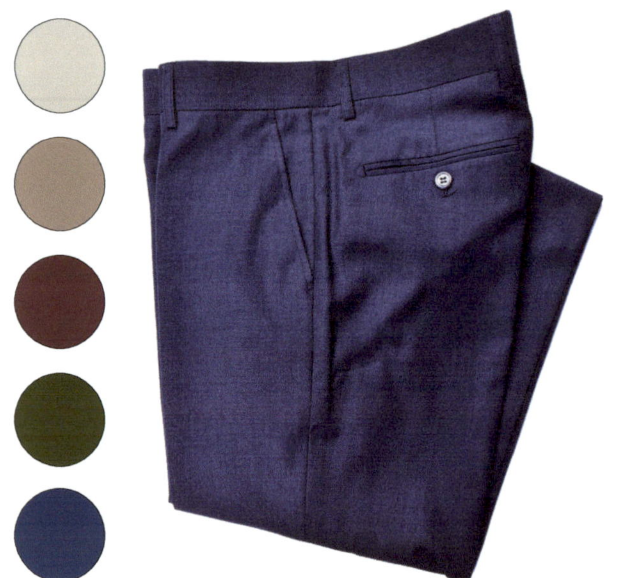

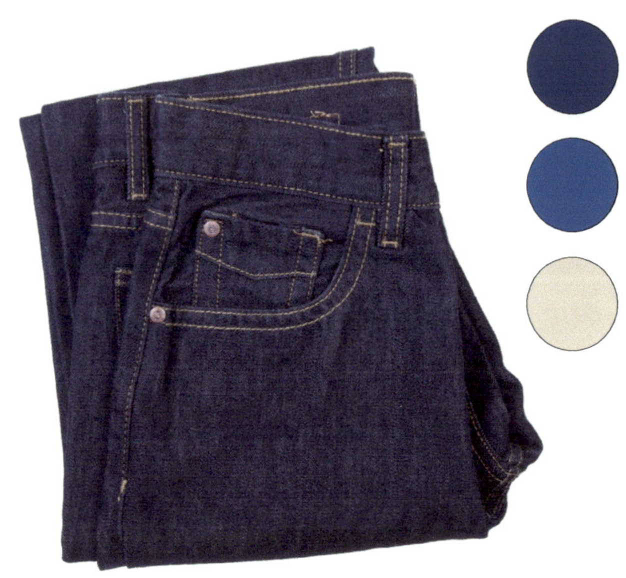

FOOTWEAR

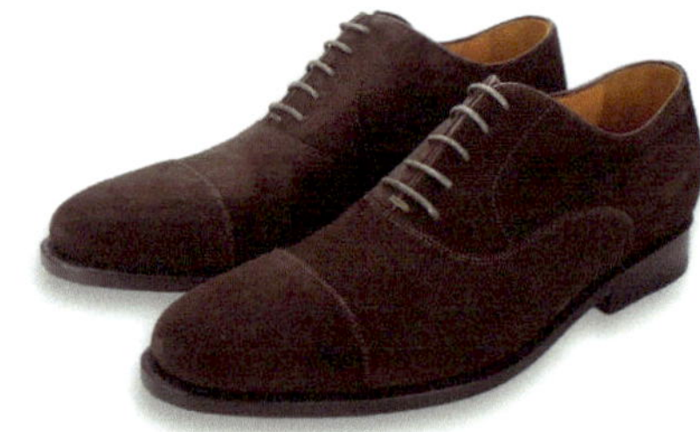

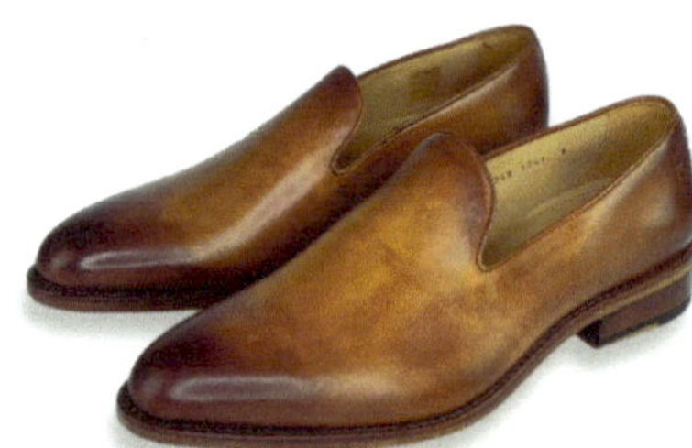

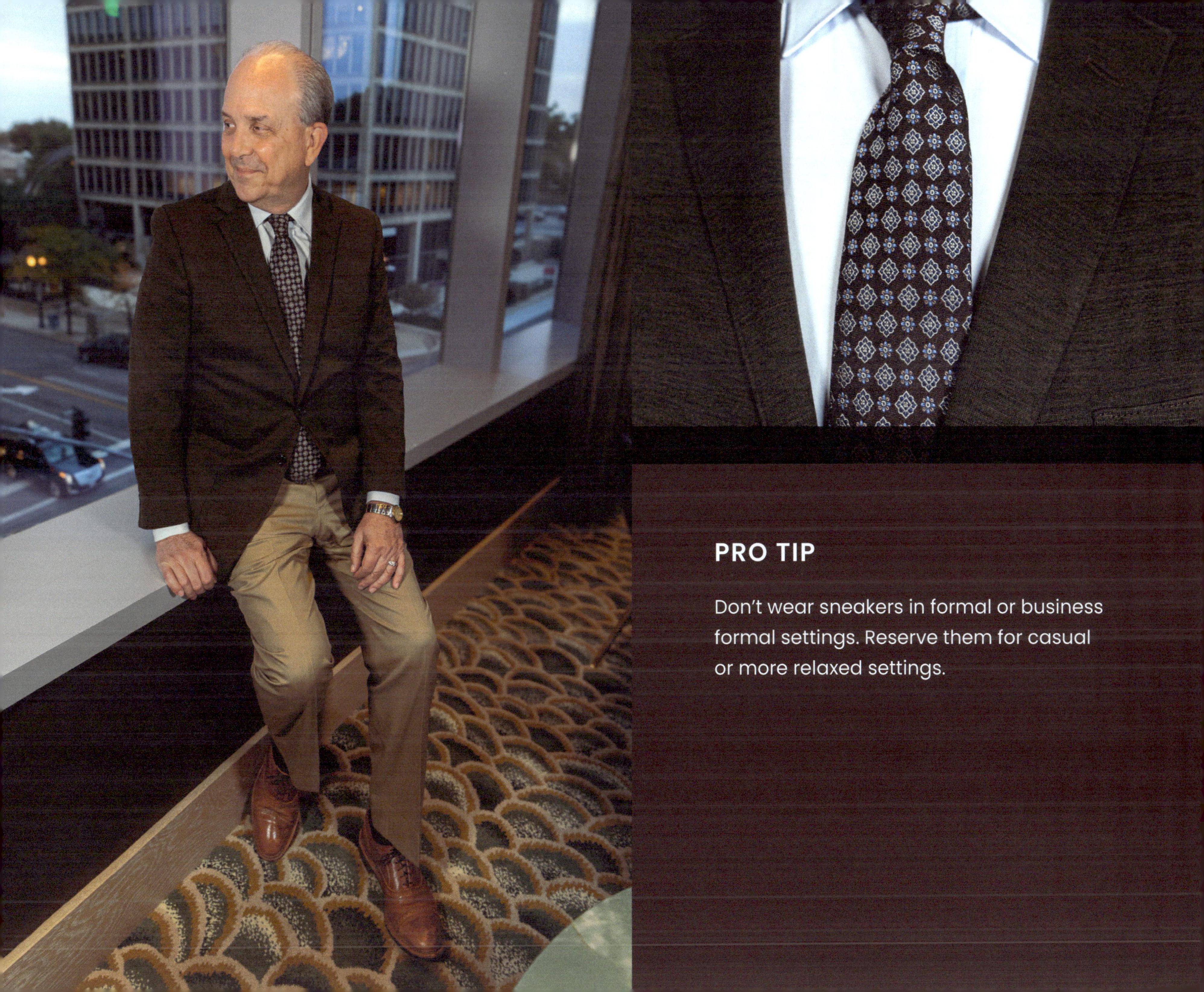
PRO TIP

Don't wear sneakers in formal or business formal settings. Reserve them for casual or more relaxed settings.

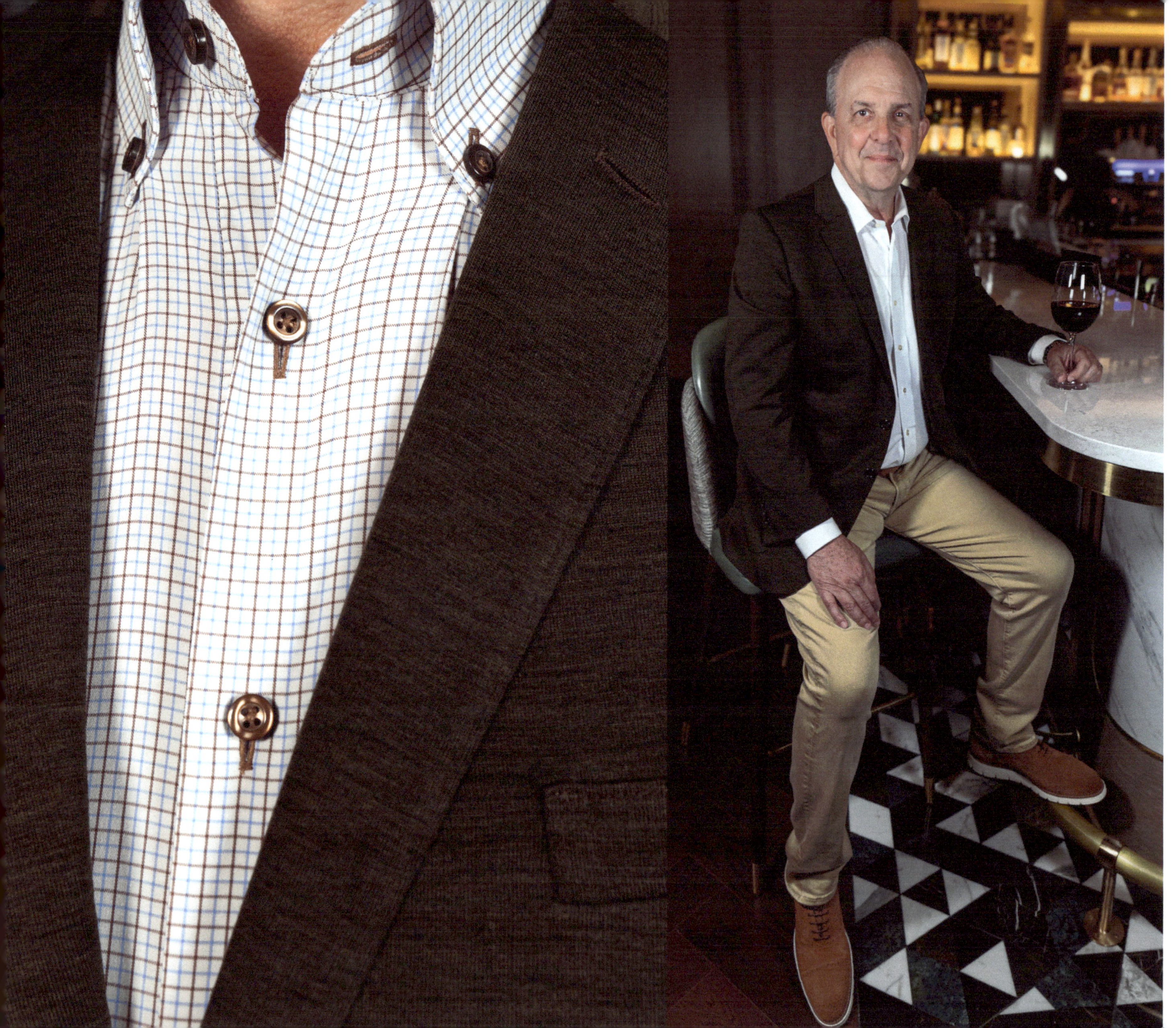

John Weber

WHAT IS YOUR OCCUPATION?

Financial Advisor

WHAT ARE YOUR HOBBIES AND INTERESTS?

I like to spend my time cooking, traveling, fly fishing, collecting wine, bourbon, and skiing.

WHAT IS A FUN FACT ABOUT YOU?

I have visited 35 countries. I'm also an Eagle Scout and have earned the national merit award as Scoutmaster.

WHAT IS MOST IMPORTANT TO YOU, FIT, QUALITY, OR SELECTION?

Quality. I want something to look great, but more importantly, I want it to last.

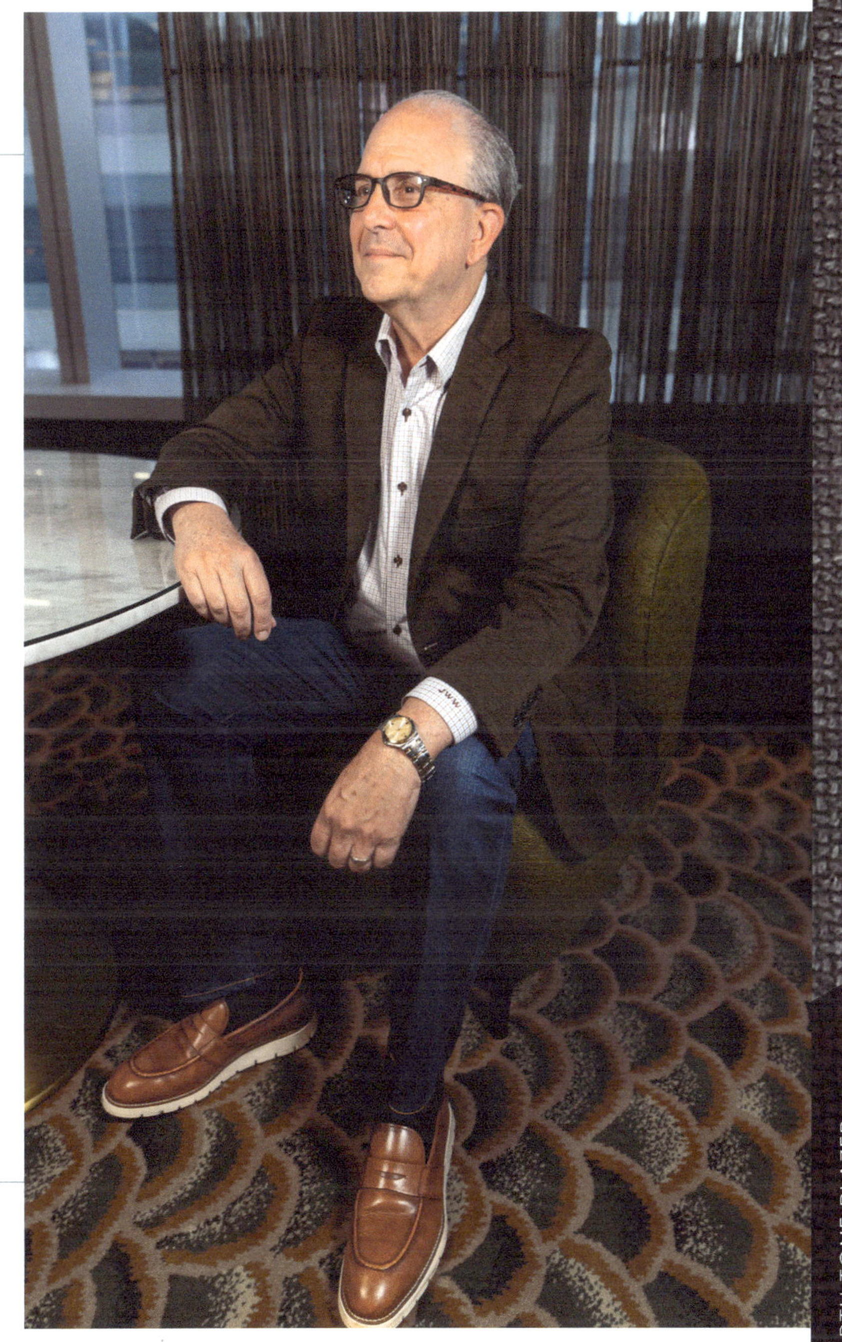

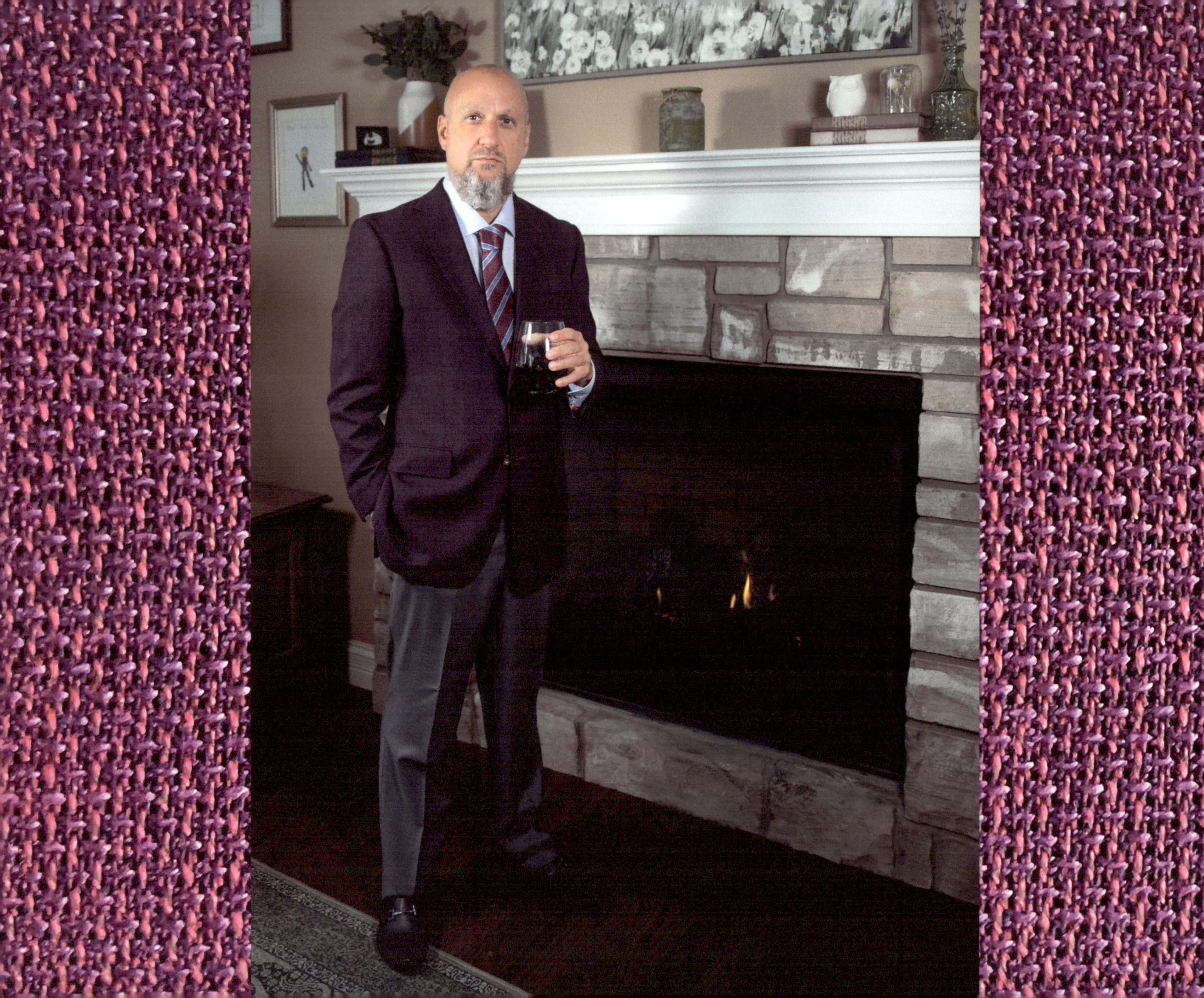

WINE

RICH • DEEP • REFRESHING • ROYAL

Majestic and sophisticated, wine blazers have come in with a bang to diversify the solid-jacket rotation. Wine, merlot, or burgundy blazers are surprisingly versatile and effortlessly transition from business to social occasions.

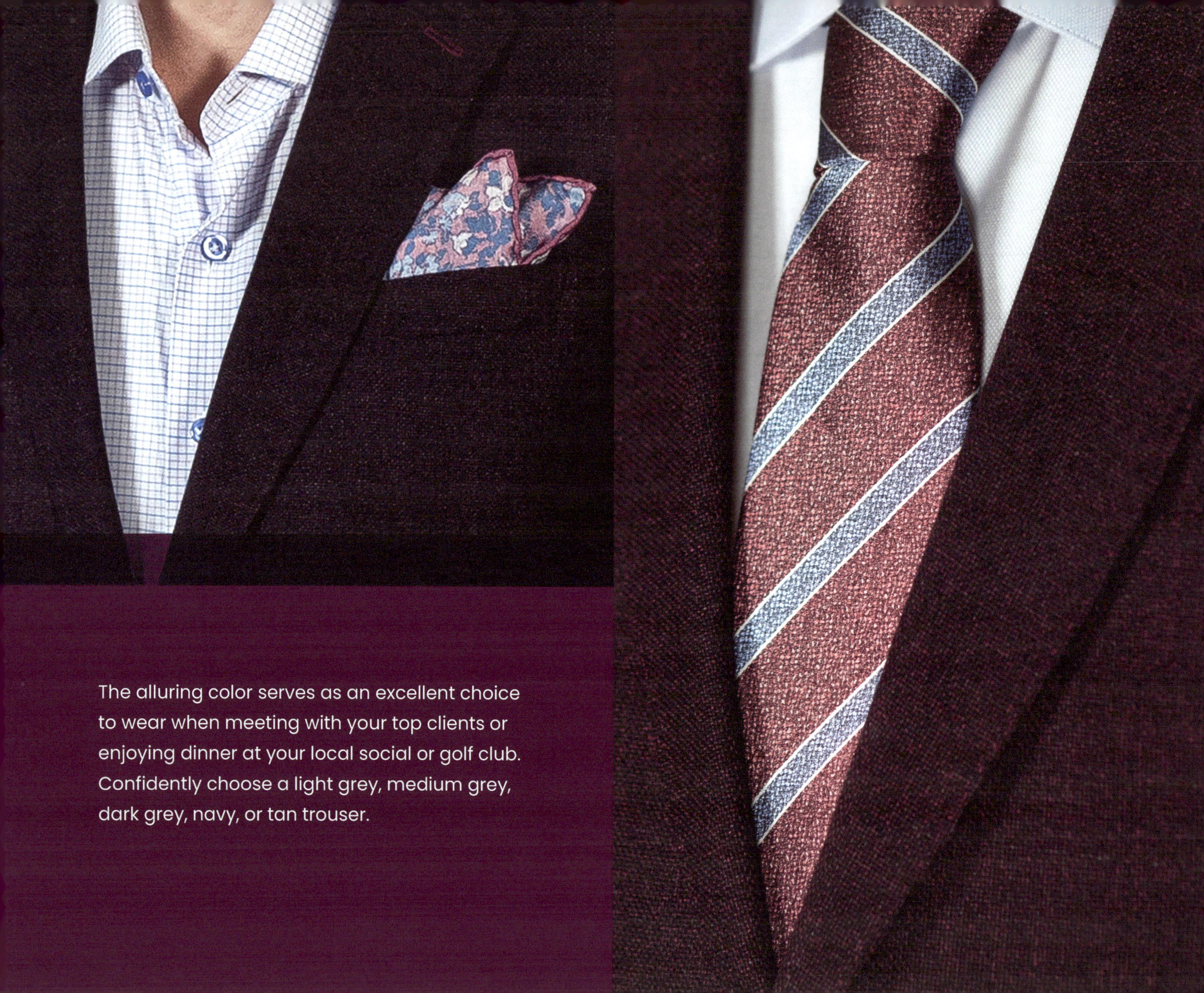

The alluring color serves as an excellent choice to wear when meeting with your top clients or enjoying dinner at your local social or golf club. Confidently choose a light grey, medium grey, dark grey, navy, or tan trouser.

WINE BLAZER

SHIRTS TO MATCH

Solid Colors

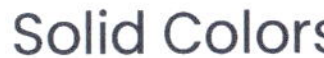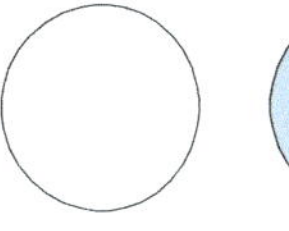

White - Color Stripe or Pattern

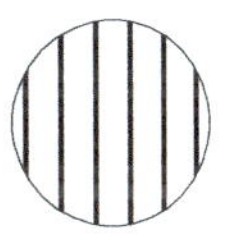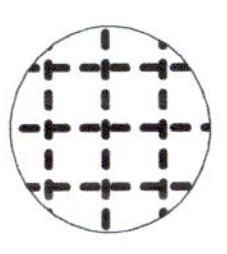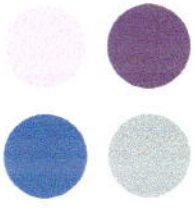

Blue - Color Stripe or Pattern

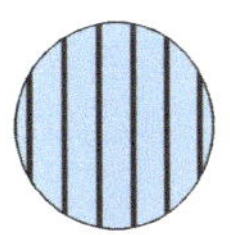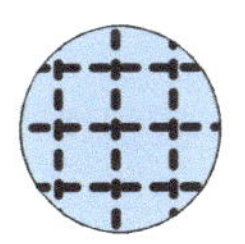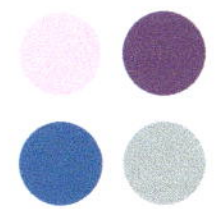

TROUSERS

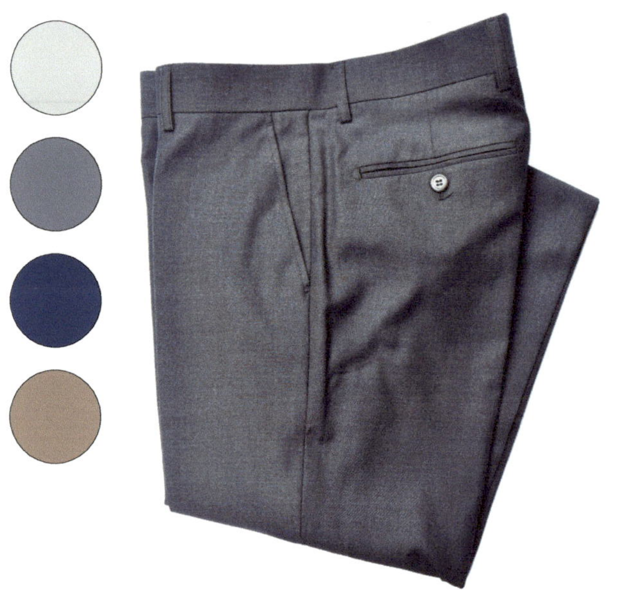

JEANS

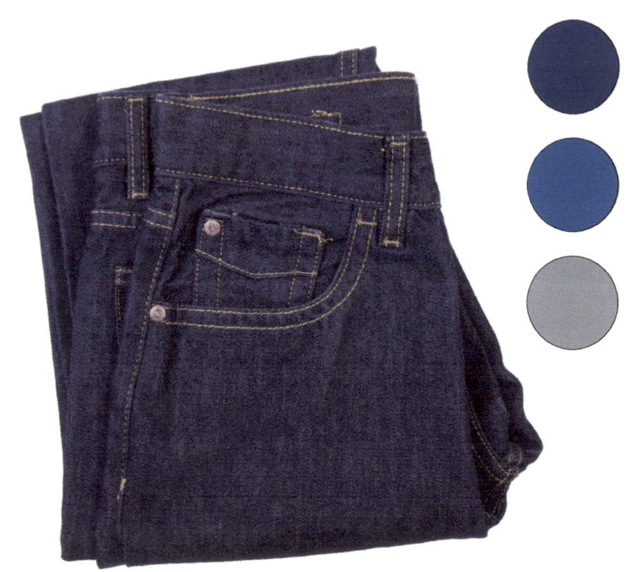

FOOTWEAR

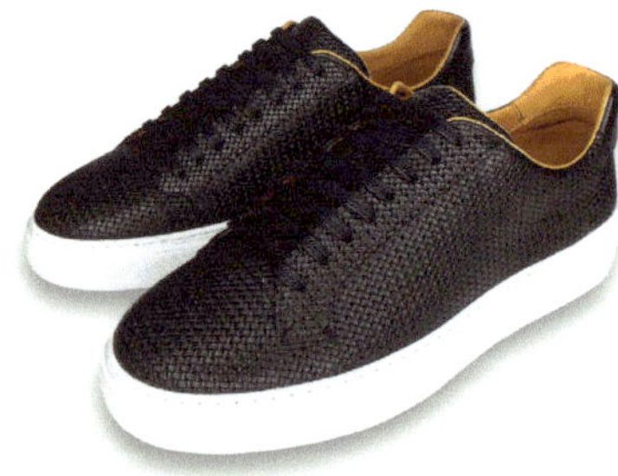

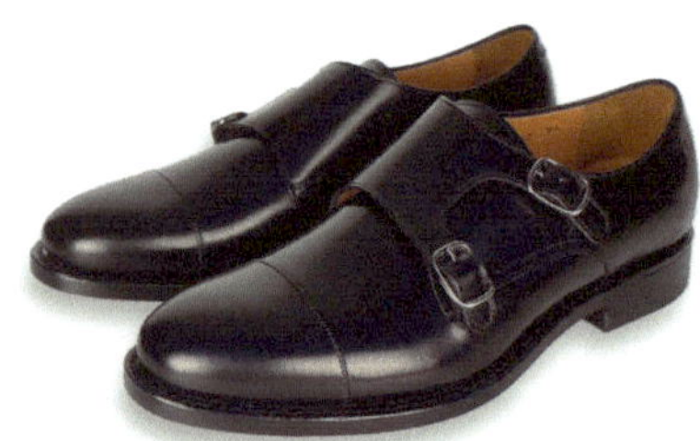

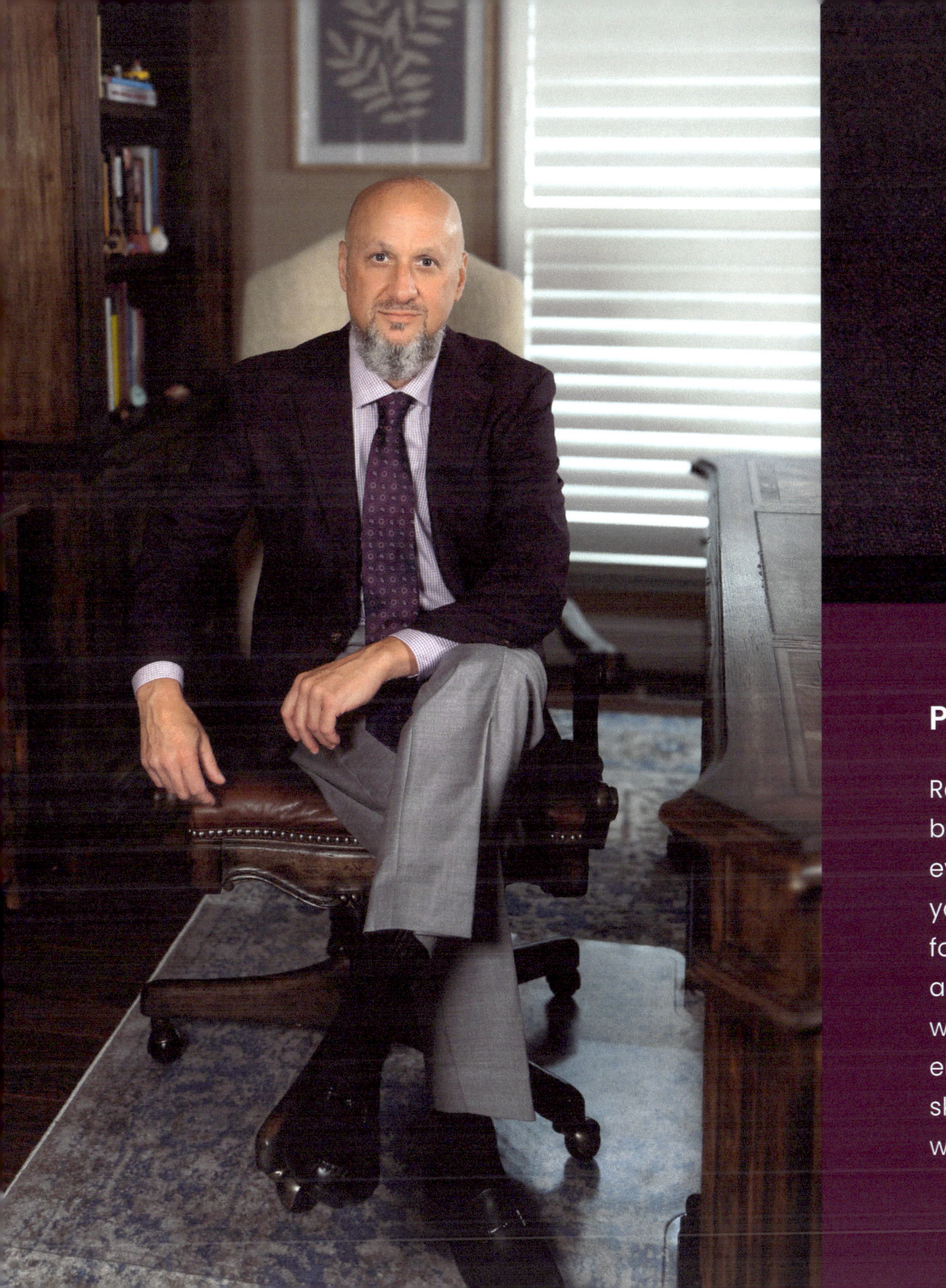

PRO TIP

Research what colors look best on you based on your skin tone, hair color, and eye color. Most men wear a lot of blue, but you may enjoy finding additional options for shirts, ties, jackets and suits that flatter and enhance your coloring to add to your wardrobe. Wearing colors that do not emphasize your hair color, eye color, and skin tone can make you appear drained, washed out, or unhealthy.

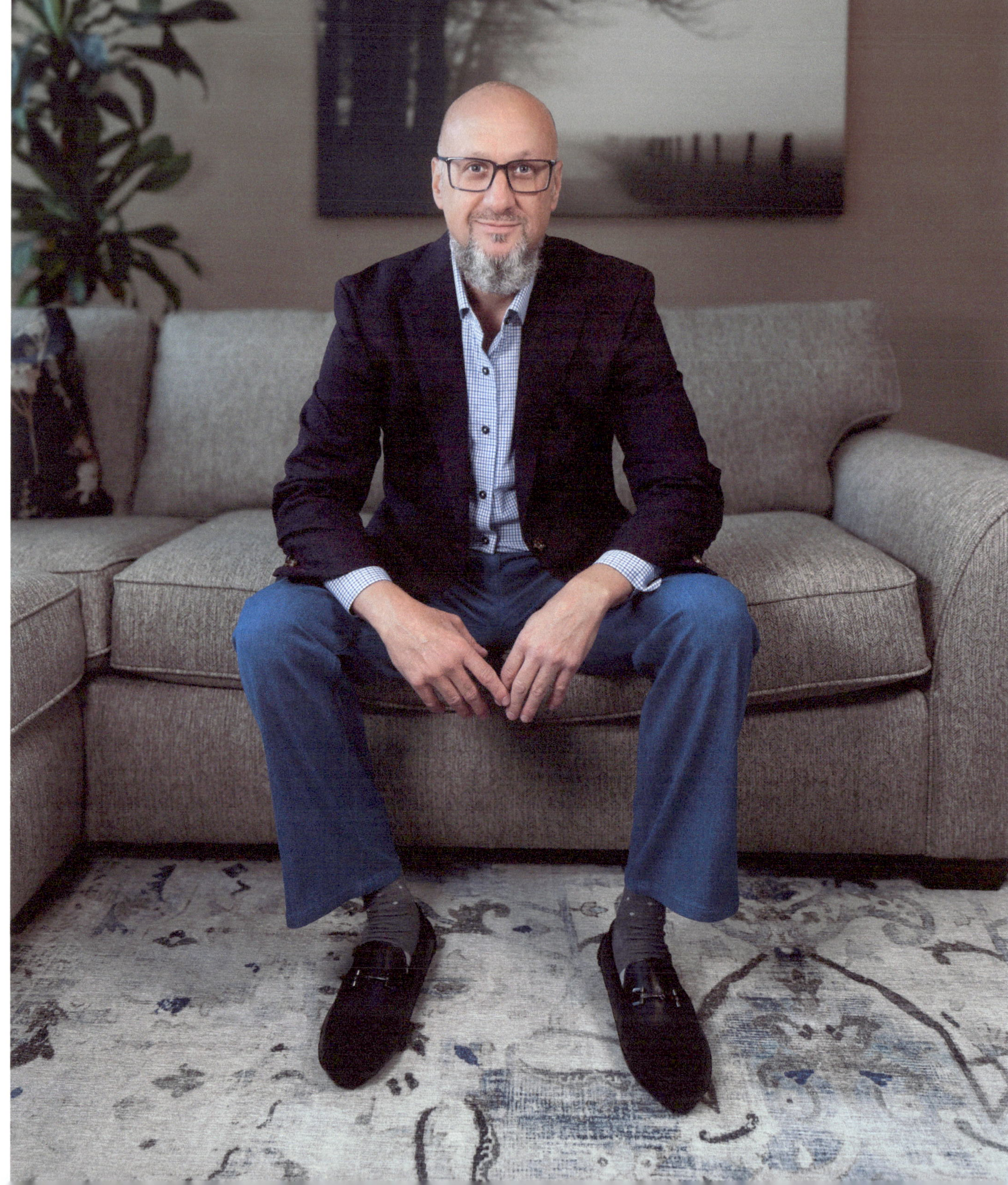

Kevin Lathrop

WHAT IS YOUR OCCUPATION?

Healthcare Consultant

WHAT ARE YOUR HOBBIES AND INTERESTS?

I spend my free time cooking, gardening, reading, practicing yoga, and traveling.

DO YOU PREFER WEARING BOLD, COLORFUL AND EXCITING COLORS OR DO YOU LIKE MORE MUTED TRADITIONAL COLORS?

Calm and traditional colors. I look and feel better in them.

WHAT IS A FUN FACT ABOUT YOU?

I'm a Master Black Belt in Six Sigma.

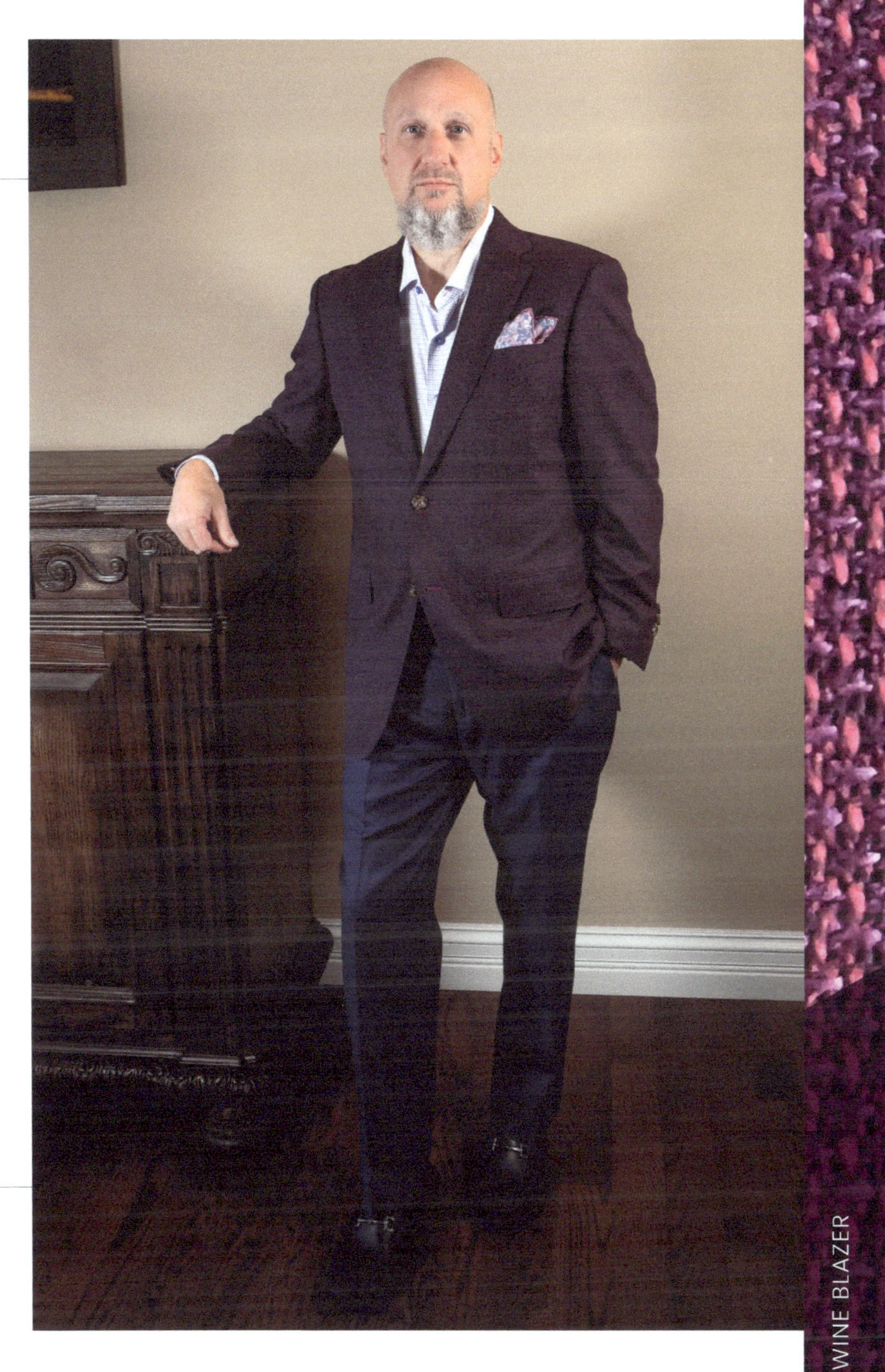

FORMAL WEAR

Elegance is not about being noticed,
it's about being remembered.

GIORGIO ARMANI

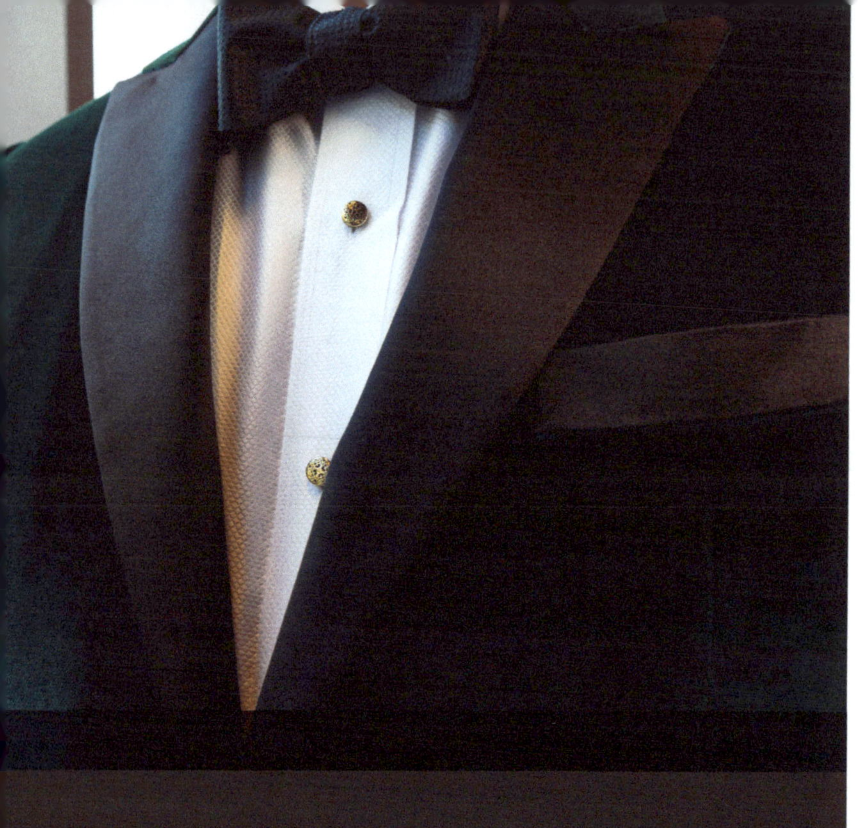

When it comes to formal wear, the solid black tuxedo stands as the most common and traditional option. However, fashion forward gentlemen are often seen wearing navy, creme, burgundy, gold, green, patterned, or striped tuxedos at formal events. A tuxedo resembles a suit featuring satin lapels, satin breast pocket welt, satin pocket cording, fabric covered buttons, and a satin braid down the leg of the trouser. This classic look should be paired with a crisp white shirt, stud fronts, and cufflinks with a bow tie, or a tie with cufflinks. Wearing a black suit and calling it a tuxedo is a faux pas!

Diversifying your formal wear rotation is essential, so you can stand out without appearing ostentatious in a setting where everyone is dressed their best. That is why dinner jackets are such a popular choice for formal wear. Unlike traditional tuxedos, dinner jackets have a contrasting fabric to the trouser, much like a sport coat or blazer. They often include satin trimmings and should be worn with a trouser with a satin braid down the peg. Dinner jackets offer room for creativity and expression through color, pattern and texture making formal wear interesting and enjoyable.

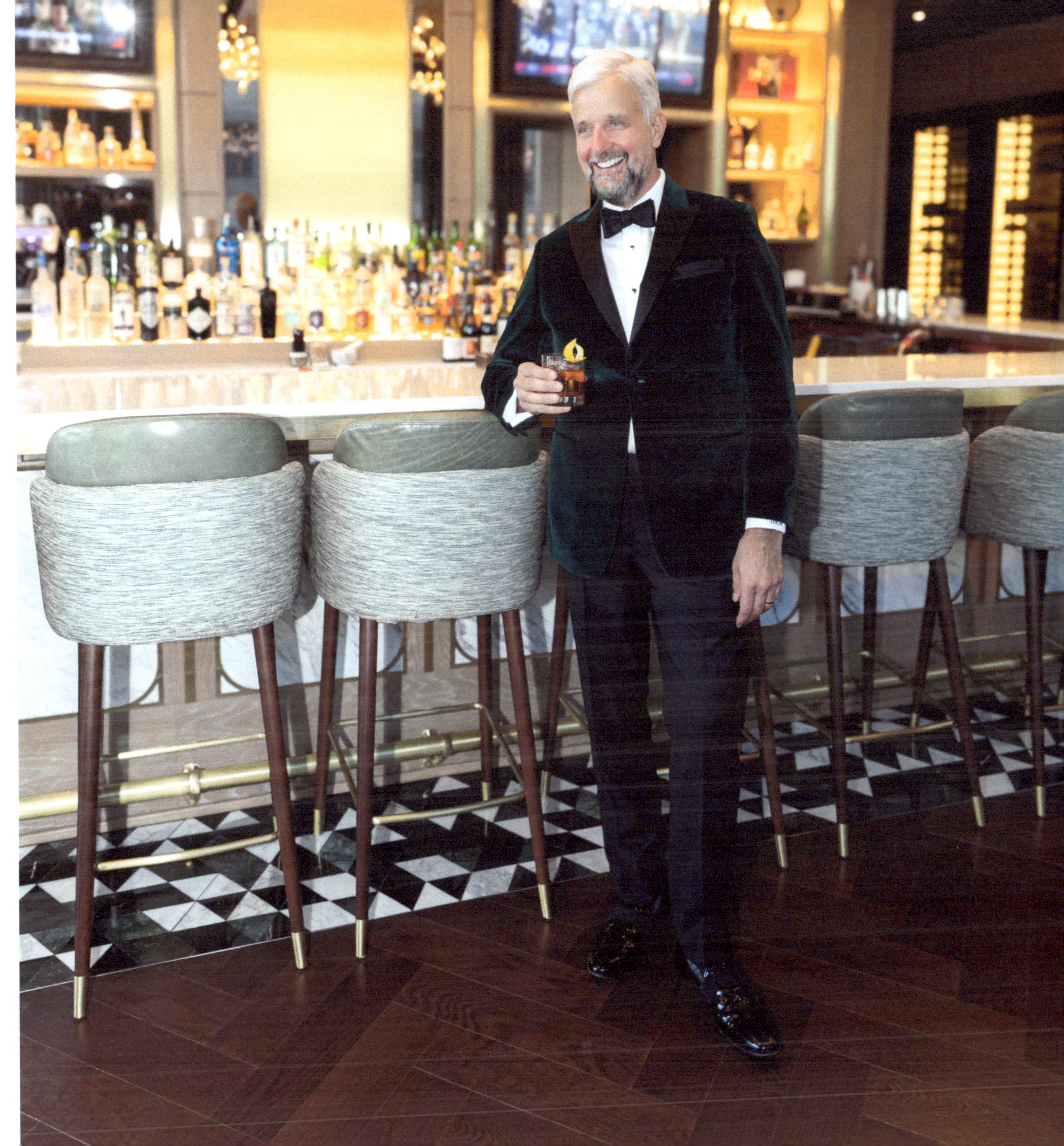

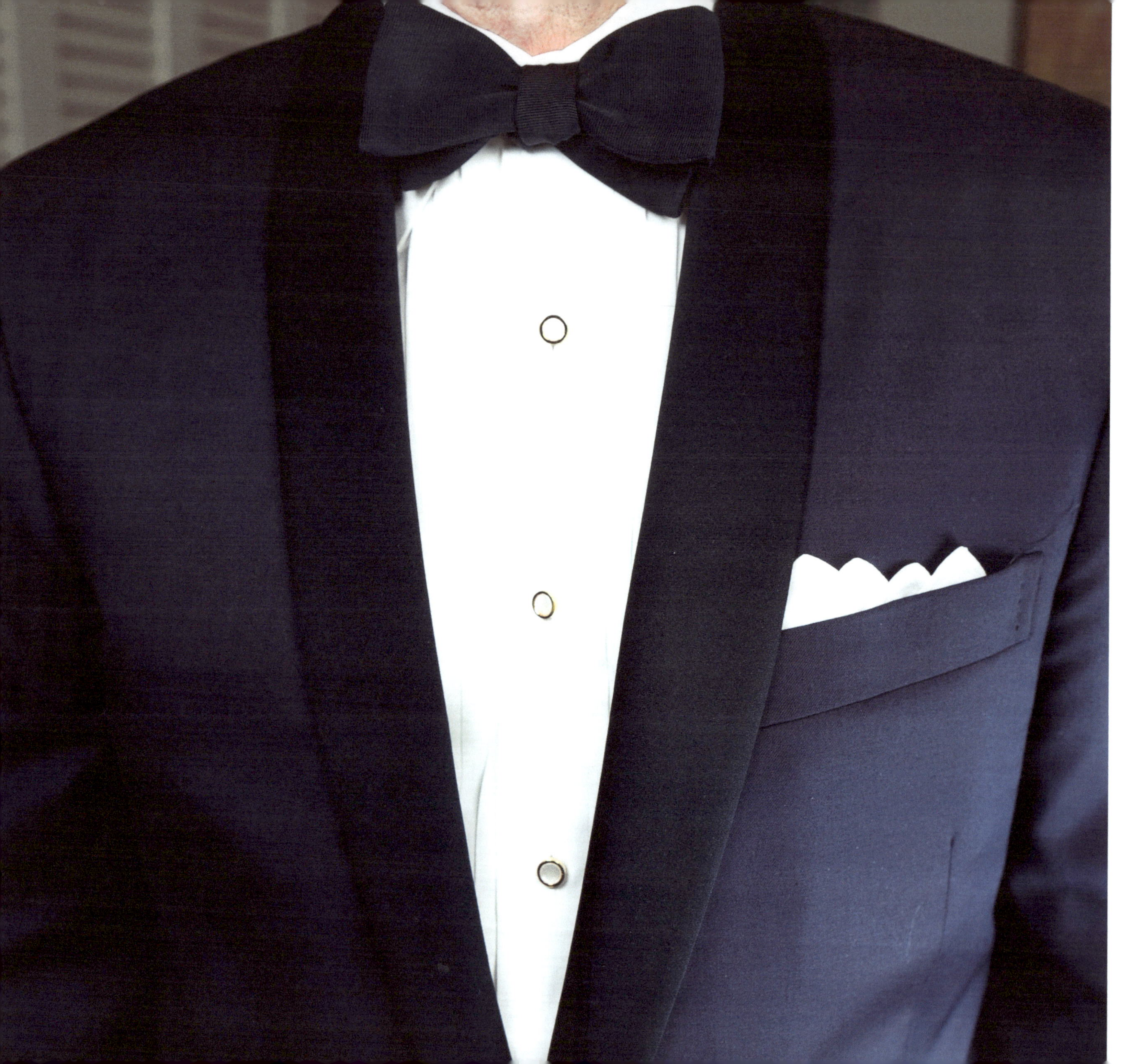

Allan Ivie

WHAT IS YOUR OCCUPATION?

Banker

WHAT ARE YOUR HOBBIES AND INTERESTS?

I am committed to giving back to the community and thus enjoy volunteering for a number of St. Louis area non-profits. I also enjoy gardening, working out, traveling, and hunting.

WHAT IS A FUN FACT ABOUT YOU?

I enjoyed working at menswear stores in high school and college where I first learned all about fabrics and men's fashion. Today, I am the proud owner of over 200 bow ties.

HOW DO YOU ORGANIZE YOUR CLOSET?

Shirts by color, white, blue stripe, solid blue, pink, miscellaneous. The majority of my shirts are white and blue variations. Bow ties are organized by color.

WHAT'S YOUR FAVORITE PART OF YOUR WARDROBE?

I'm a big believer in seasonal wear because of the variety. I love switching out spring and winter wear and I look forward to the selection of fabrics I have to choose from.

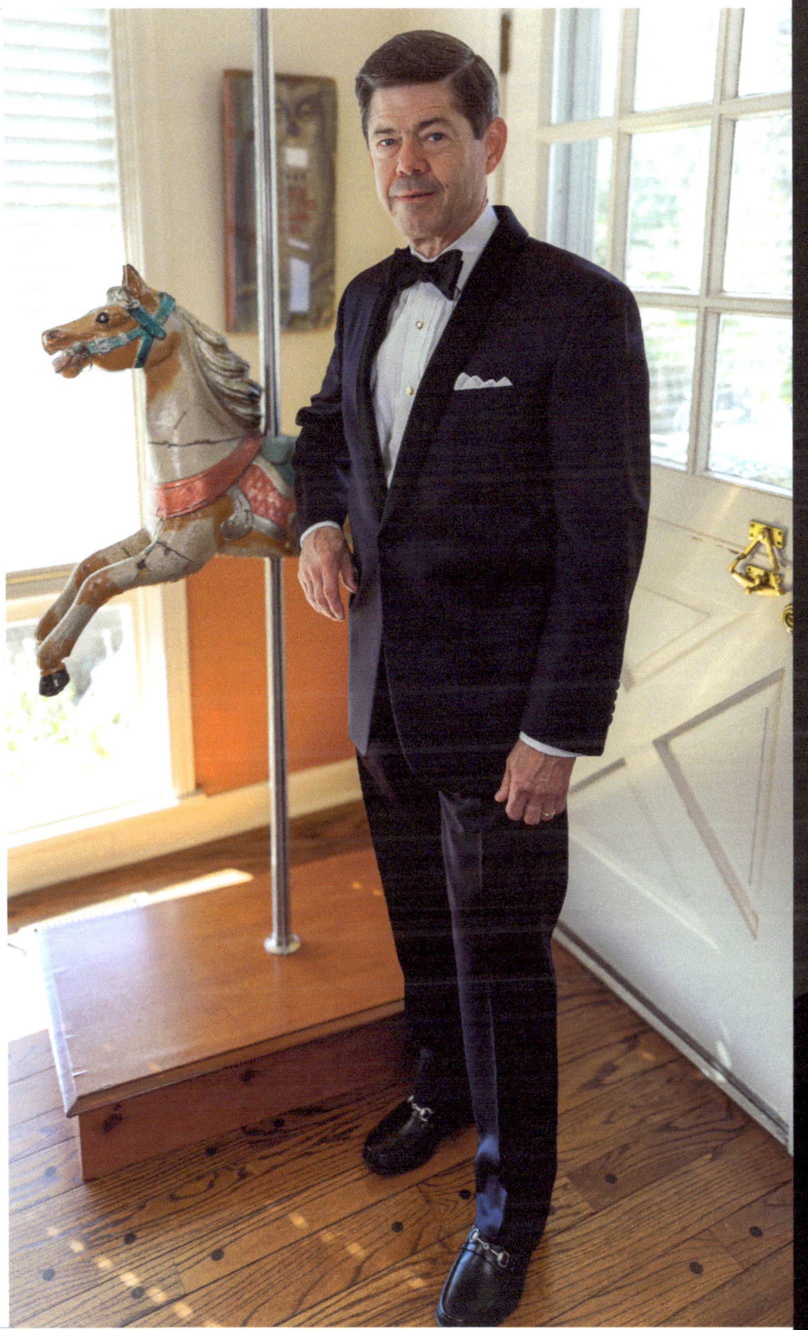

BOLD
MOVES

People will stare. Make it worth their while.

HARRY WINSTON

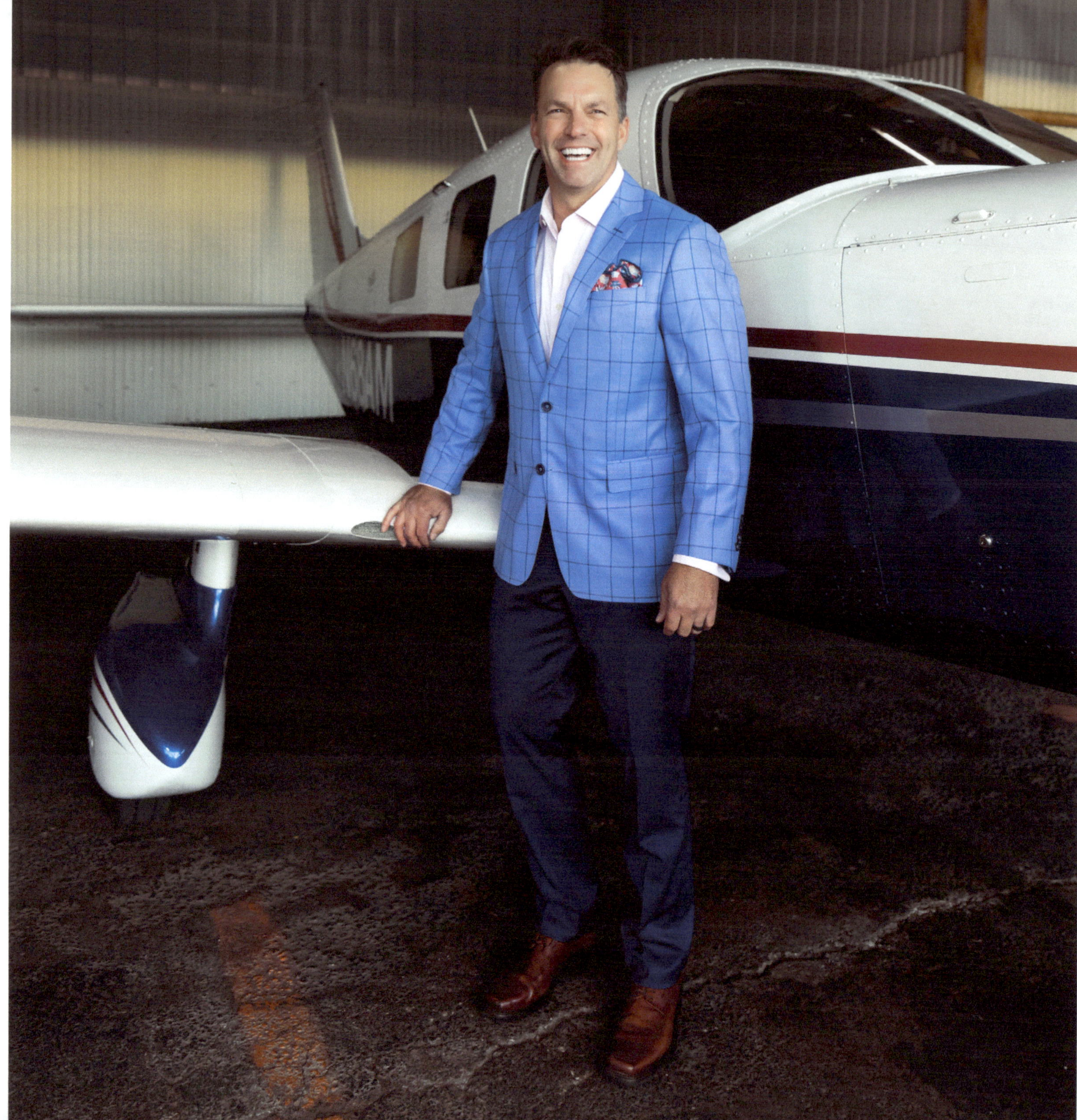

Ryan Barr

Owner of a National General Contractor,
Echelon Constructors

WHAT ARE YOUR HOBBIES AND INTERESTS?

I enjoy flying airplanes, mountain climbing,
scuba diving, CrossFit, skydiving, skiing, cycling,
hunting, and photography.

WHAT IS A FUN FACT ABOUT YOU?

Competed in 13 Ironman competitions, has over 600
skydives, is a CrossFit and scuba diving instructor and
has summited Mount Denali, Kilimanjaro and Rainier.

**CAN YOU SHARE A STORY OF
HOW DRESSING WELL PLAYS
A ROLE IN YOUR CAREER?**

A while back, a friend told me that my dress was out of style.
I realized I needed to update my wardrobe so I found Margo.
She helped me add suits, sport coats, shirts, and trousers to
my wardrobe. Not only that, she also helped me pick great
fabrics and coordinate my outfits! Now everything fits and
is back in style. I regularly get compliments on what I wear
and I feel confident wearing sport coats and suits on a
much more regular basis to my business meetings and
professional events.

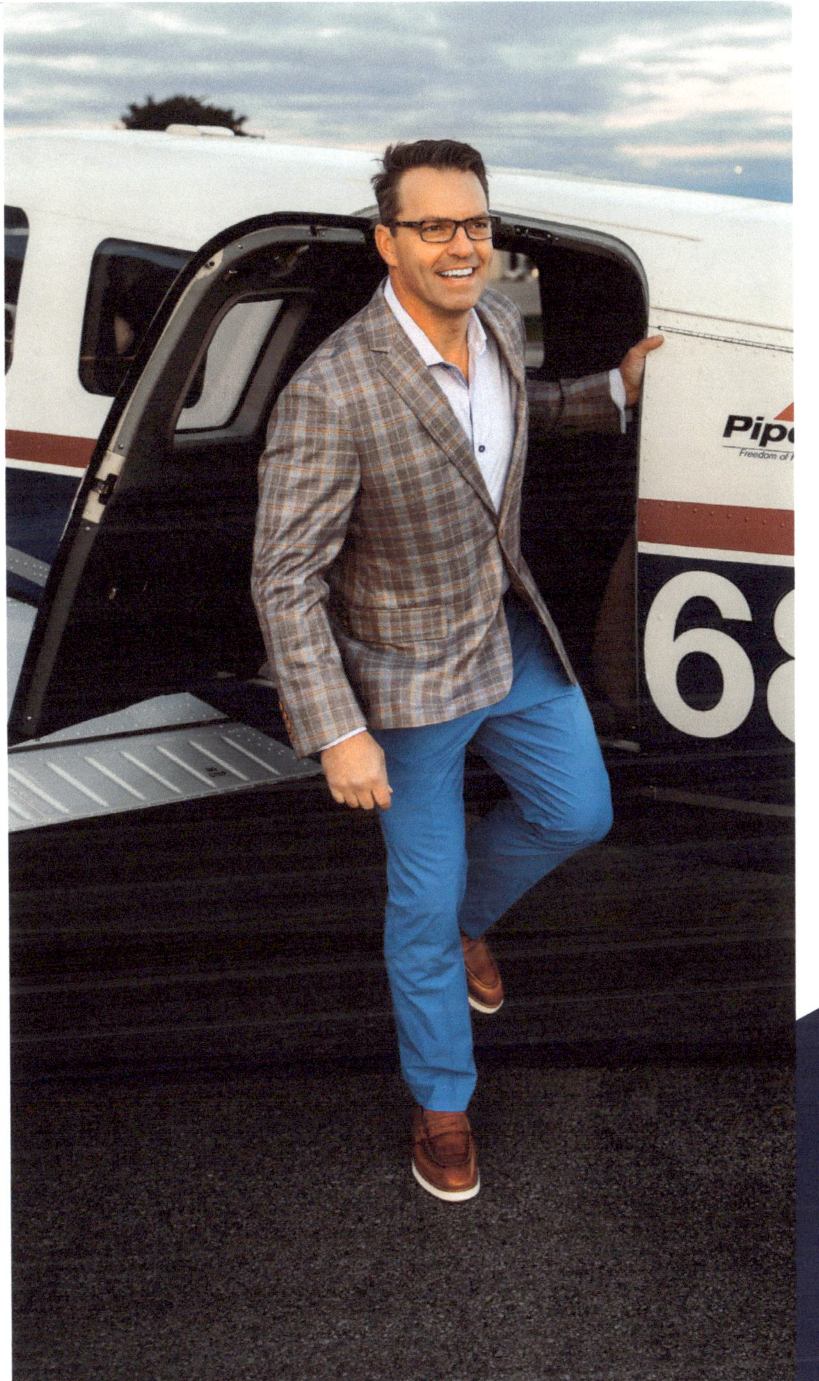

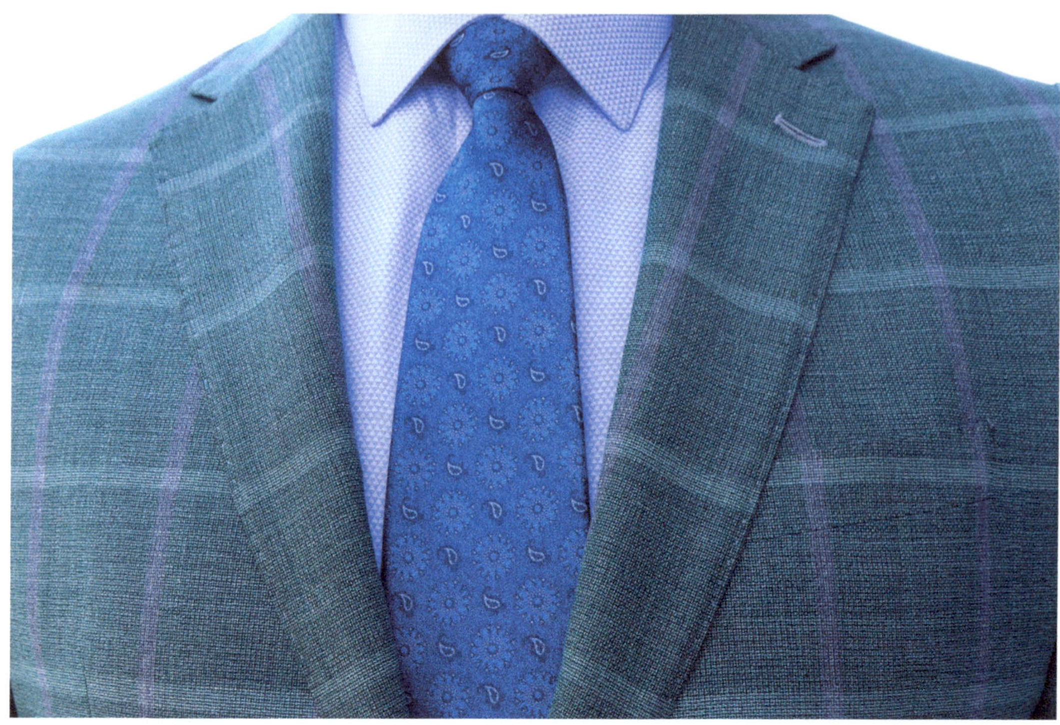

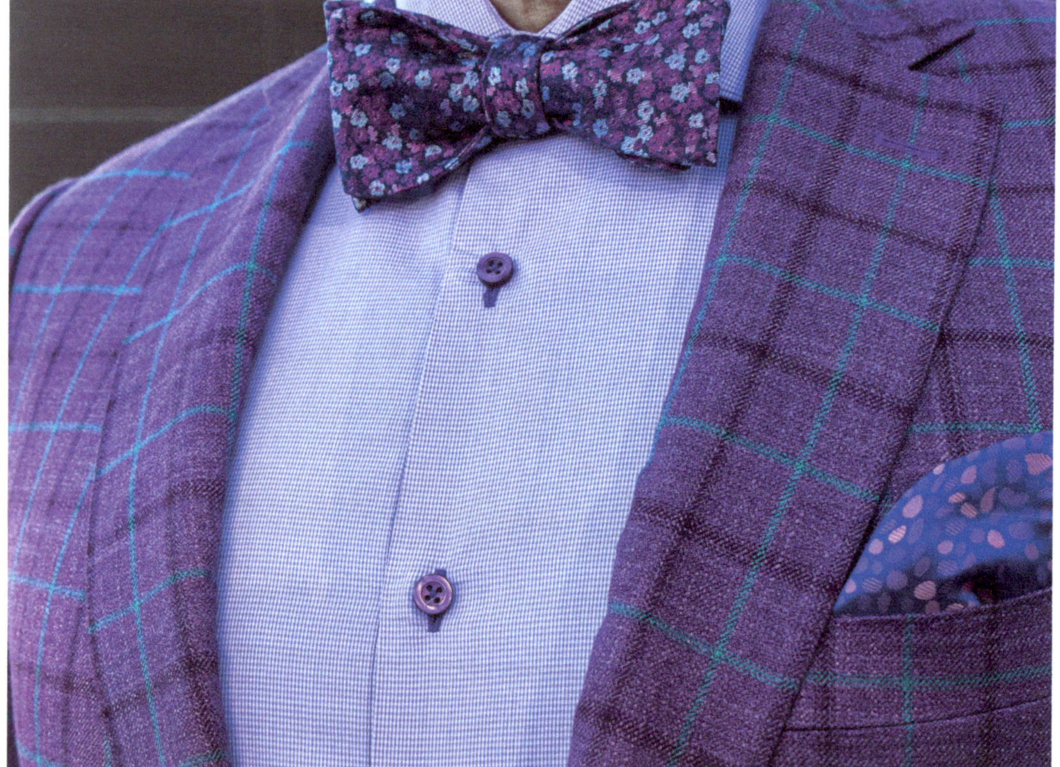

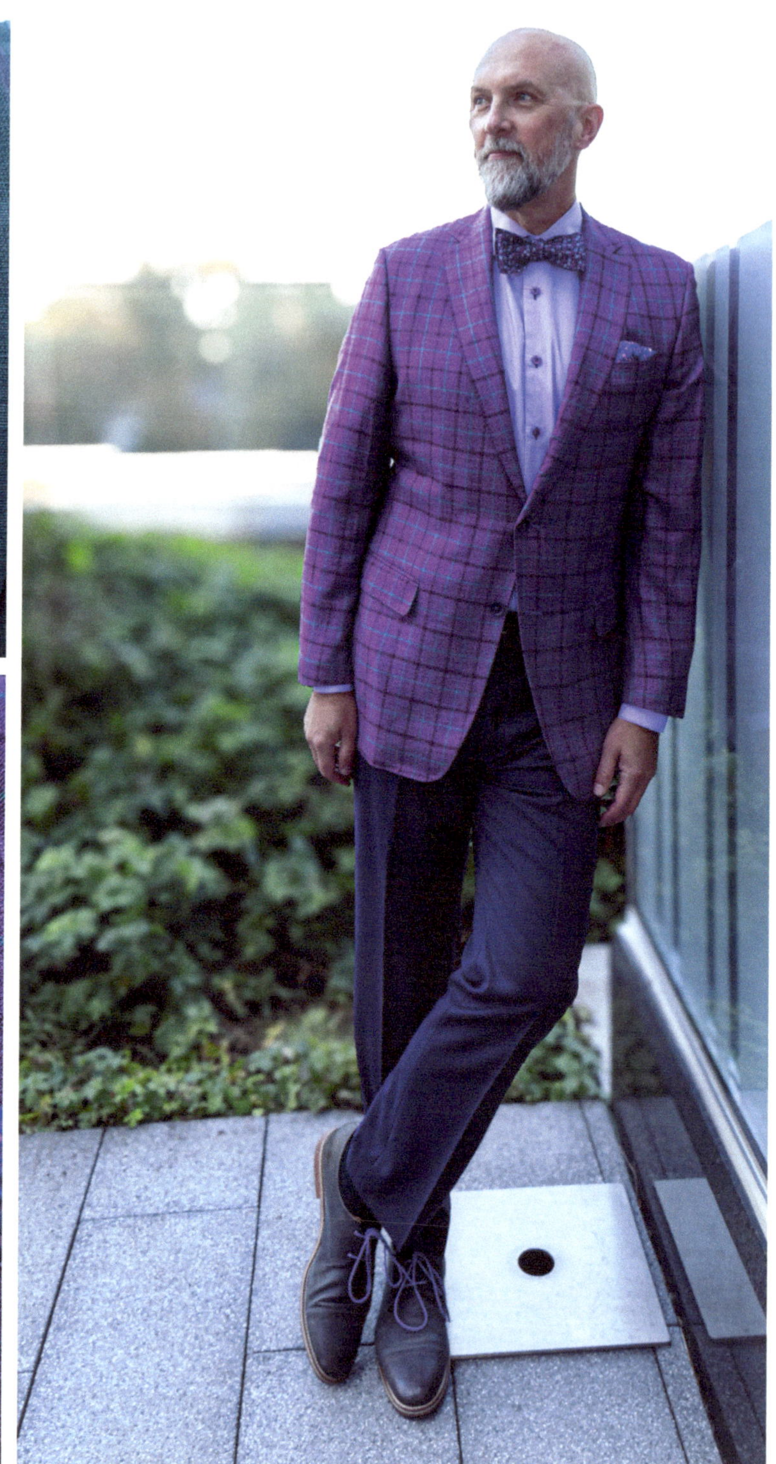

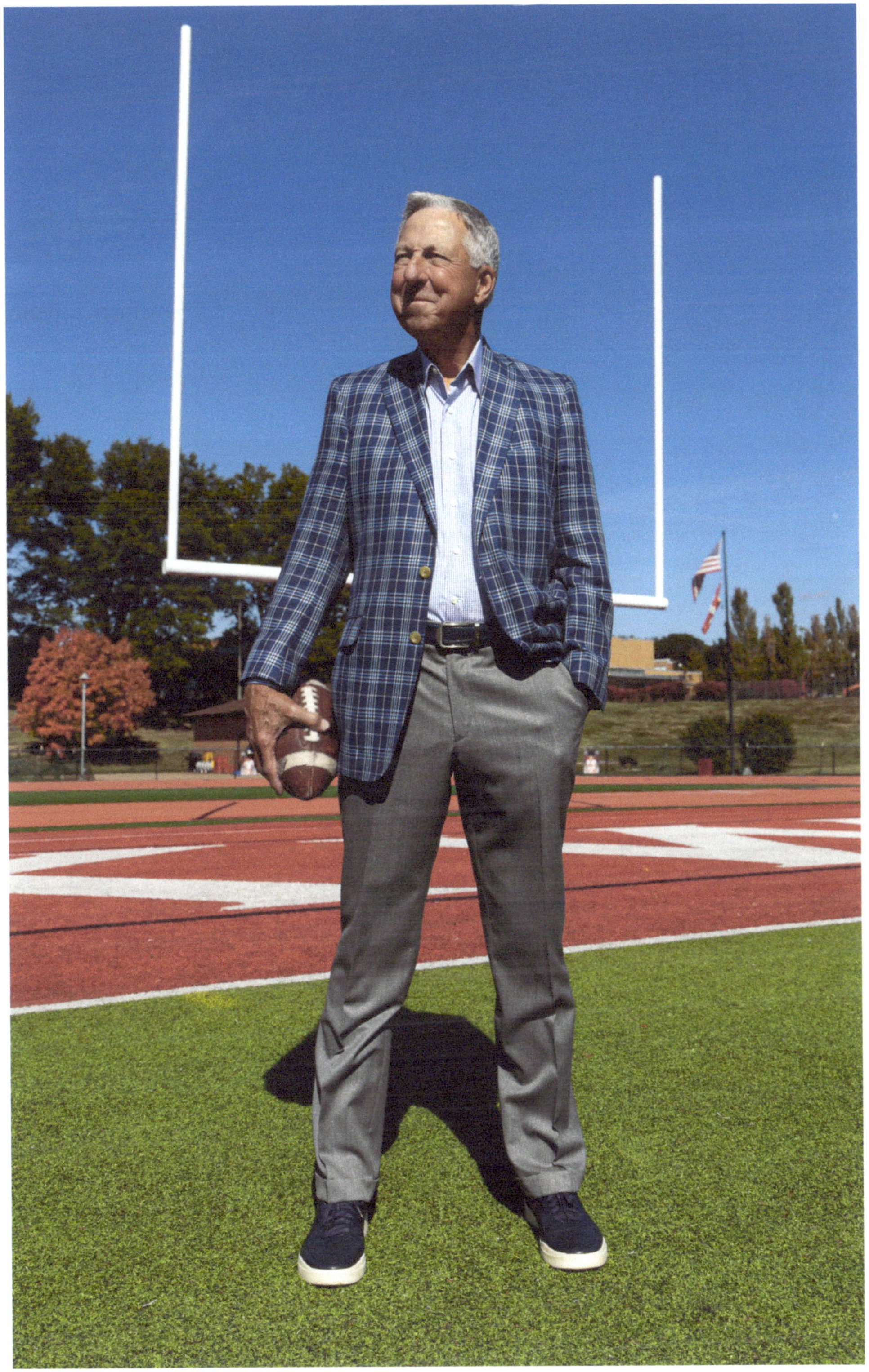

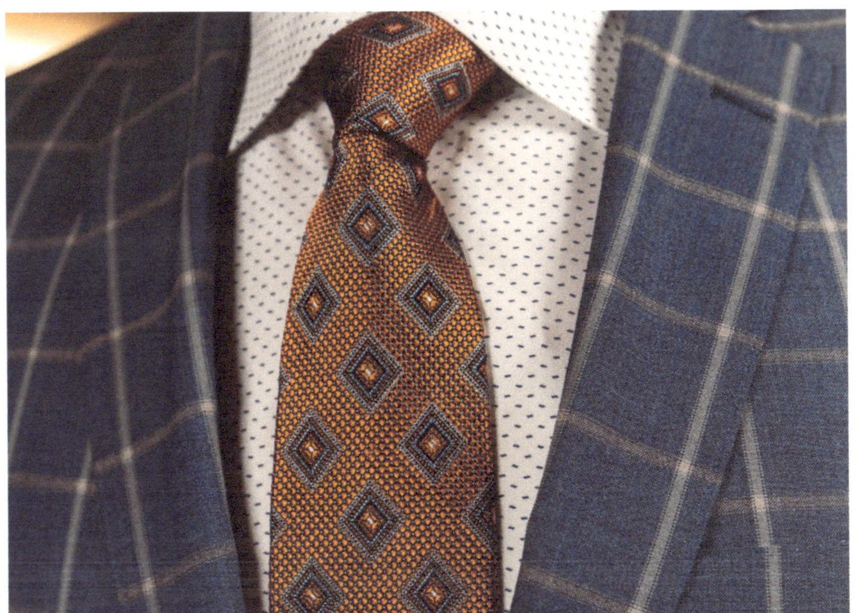

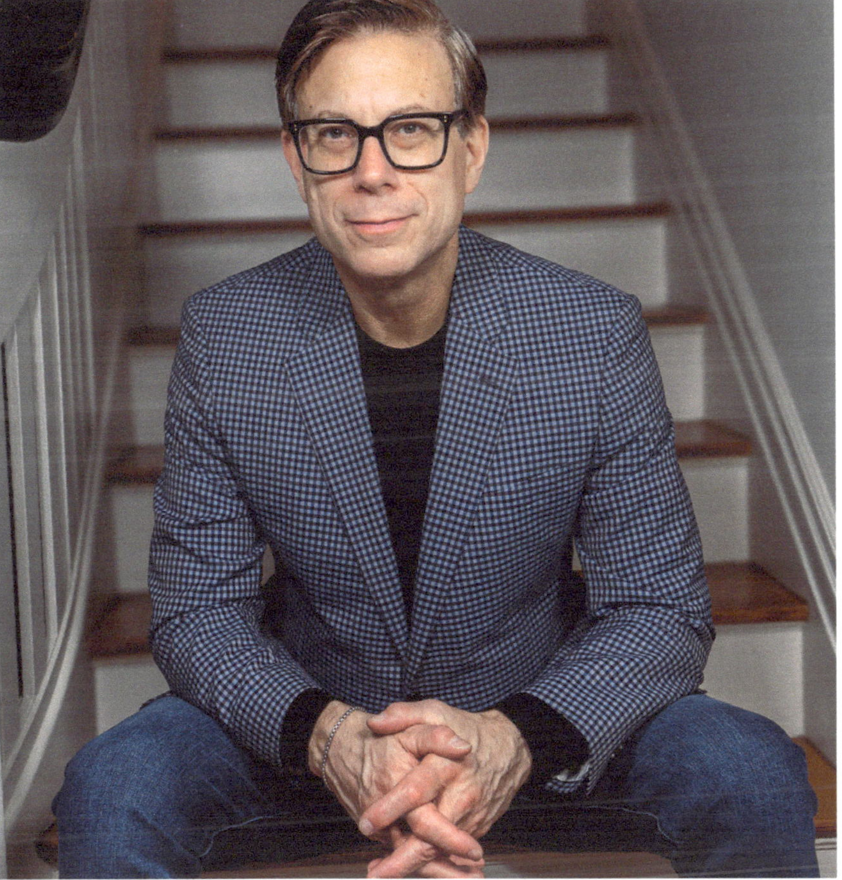

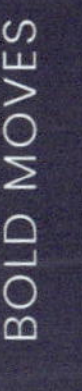
BOLD MOVES

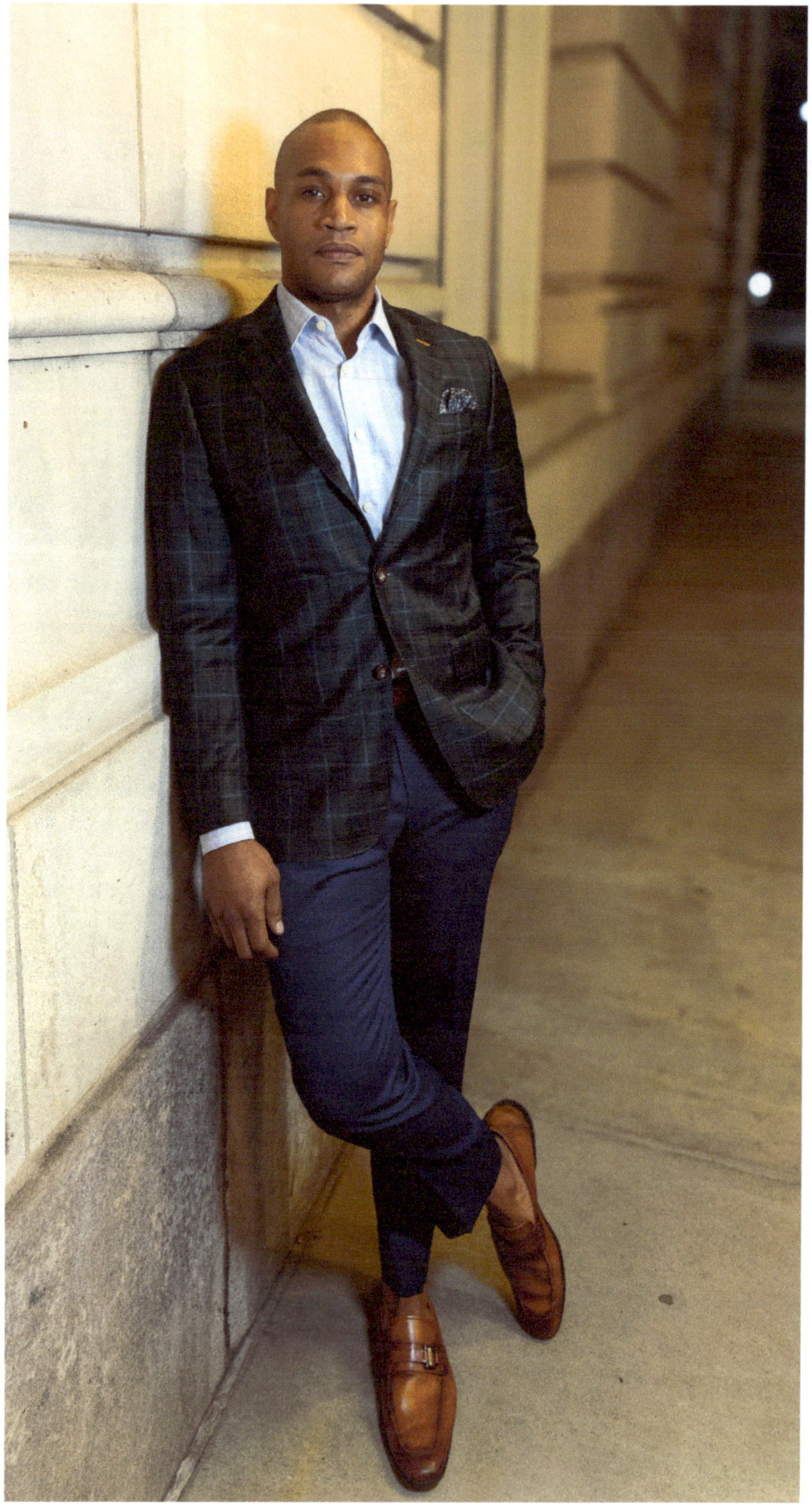

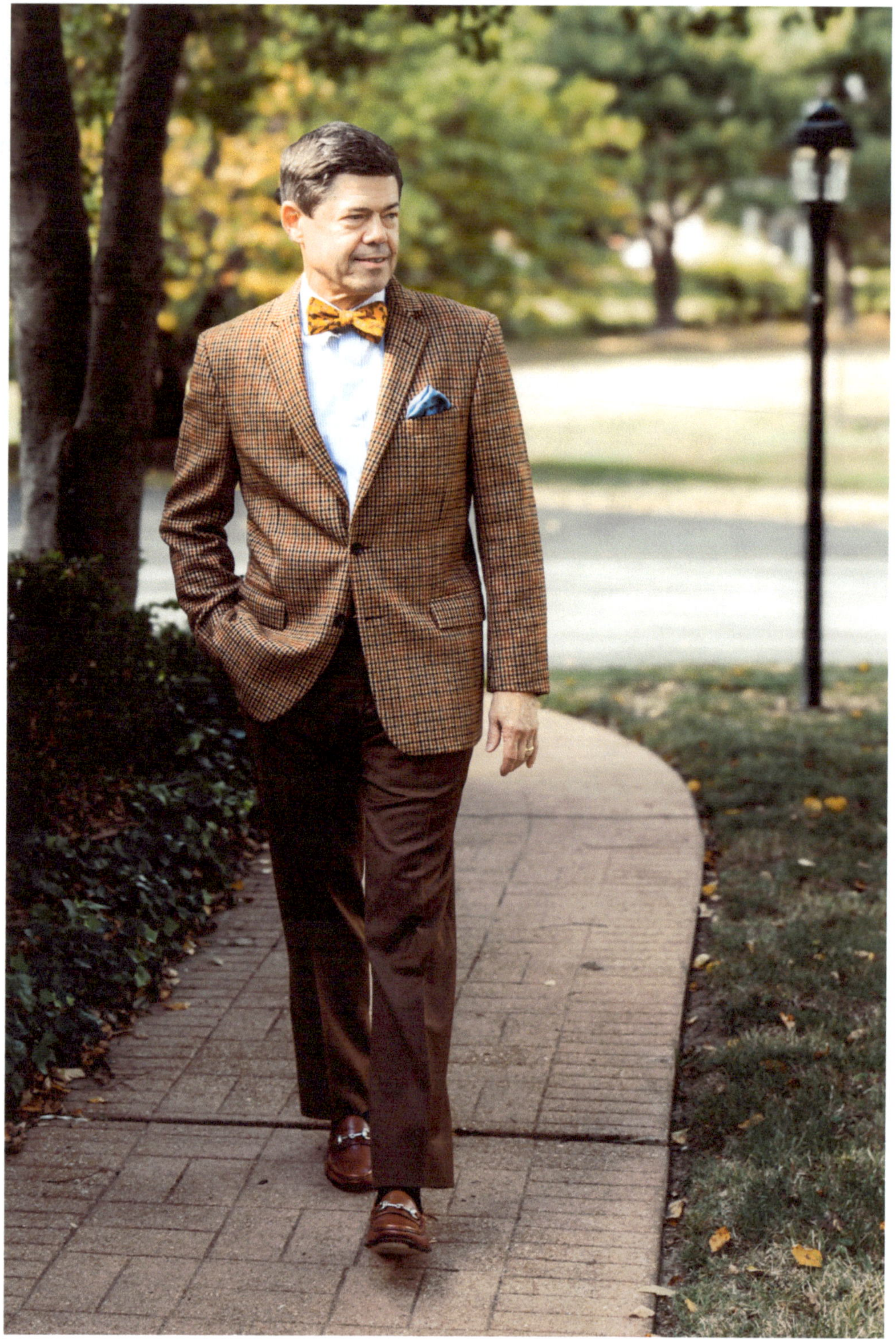

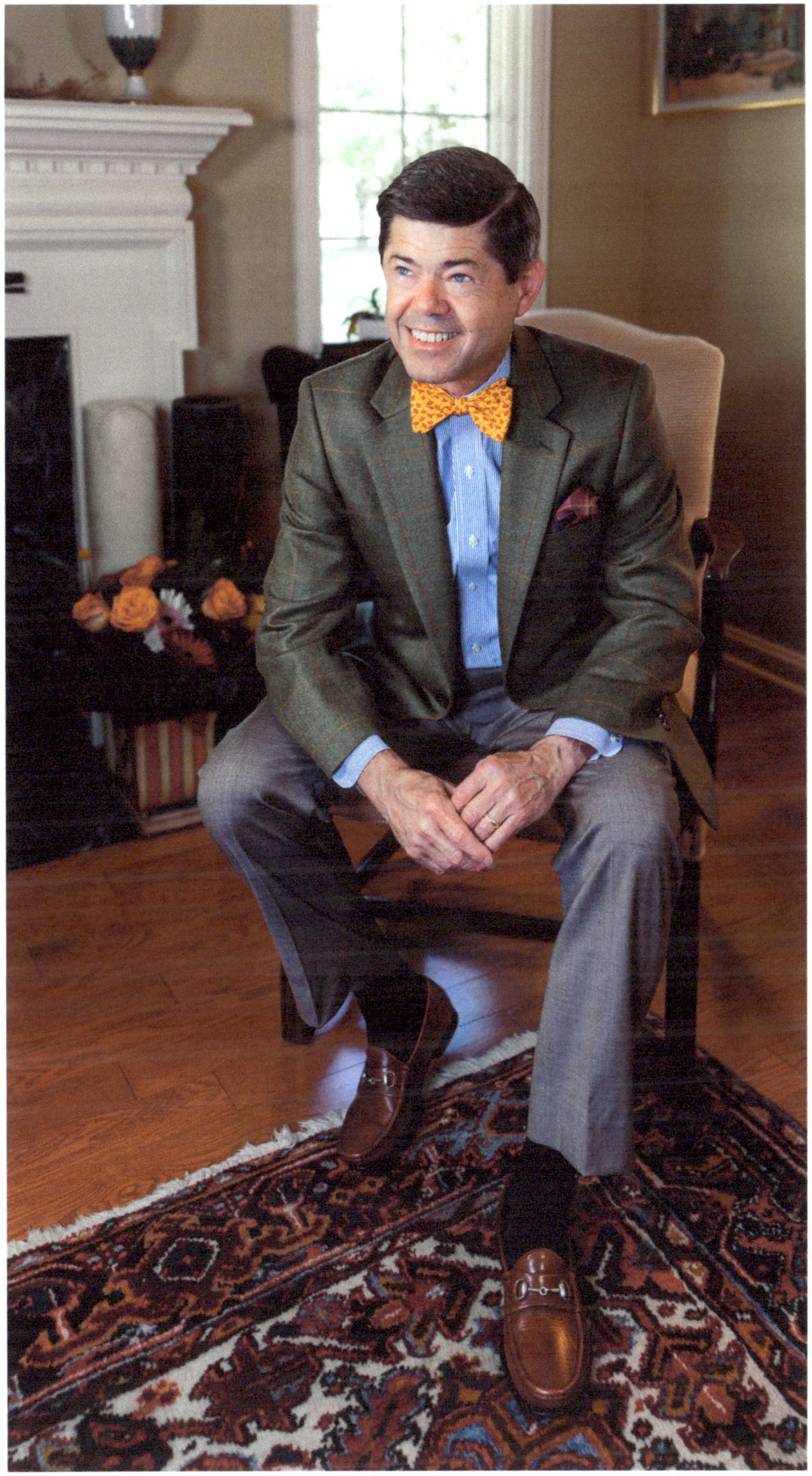

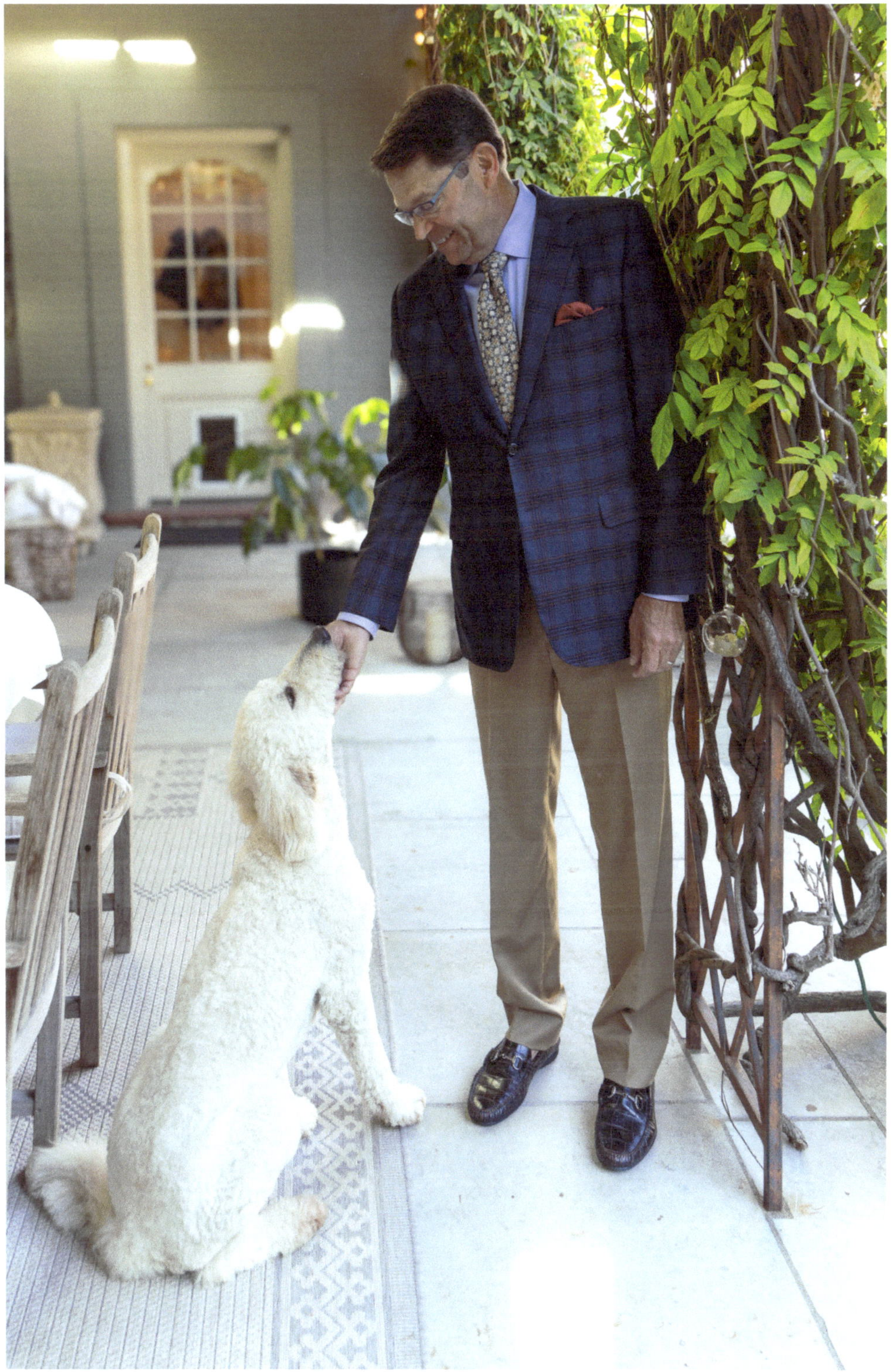

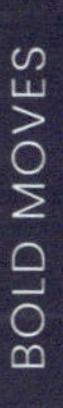

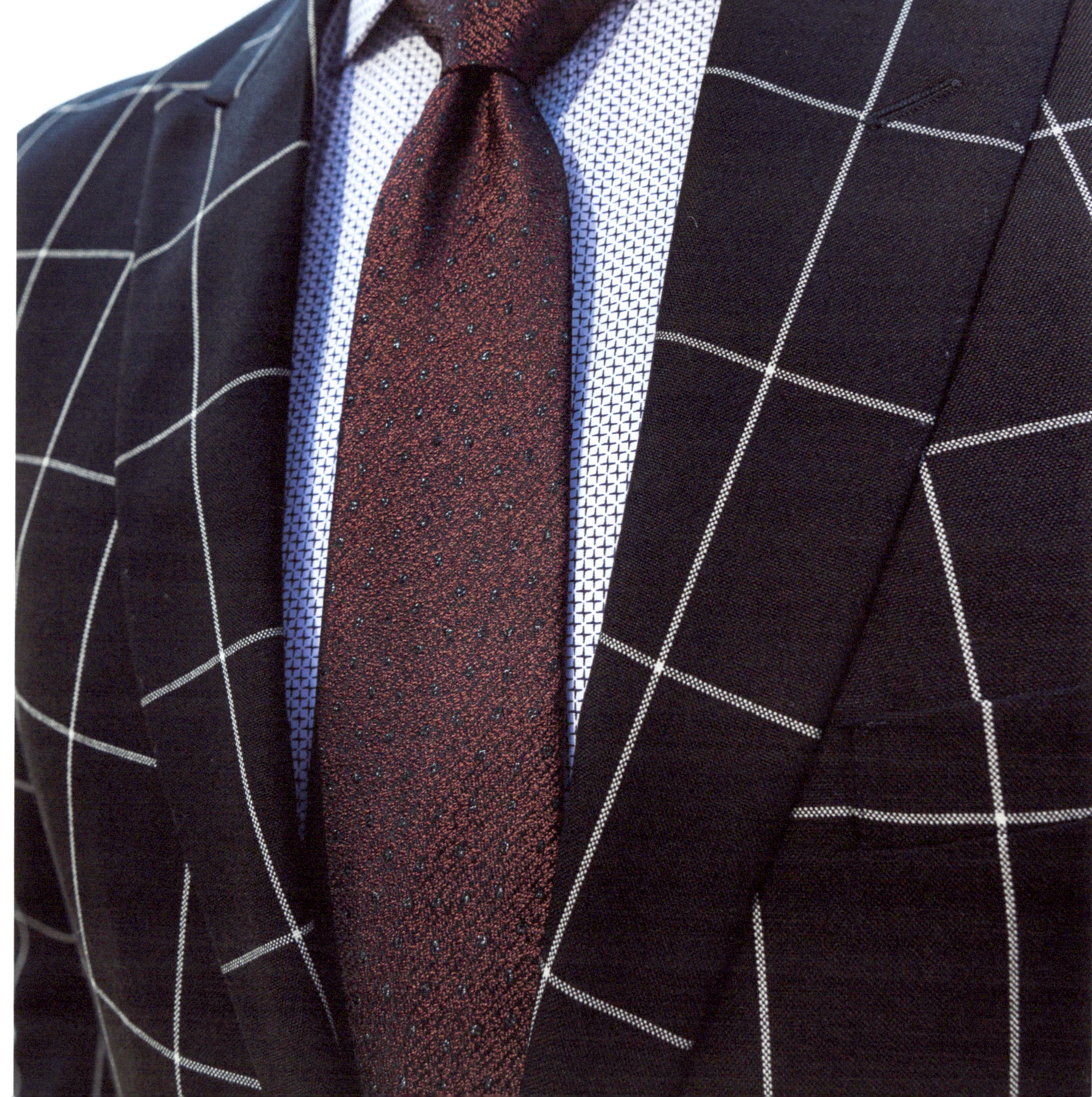

Paul Yarns

WHAT IS YOUR OCCUPATION?

Lawyer

WHAT ARE YOUR HOBBIES/INTERESTS?

I enjoy concerts, festivals, cigars, records,
University of Missouri Tigers, animals, and tattoos.

WHAT ADVICE WOULD YOU GIVE TO A YOUNG PROFESSIONAL IN REGARDS TO DRESSING?

Don't be afraid to be yourself and incorporate color
and pattern into your outfits.

WHAT IS YOUR FAVORITE ACCESSORY TO WEAR?

Vintage cufflinks and glasses

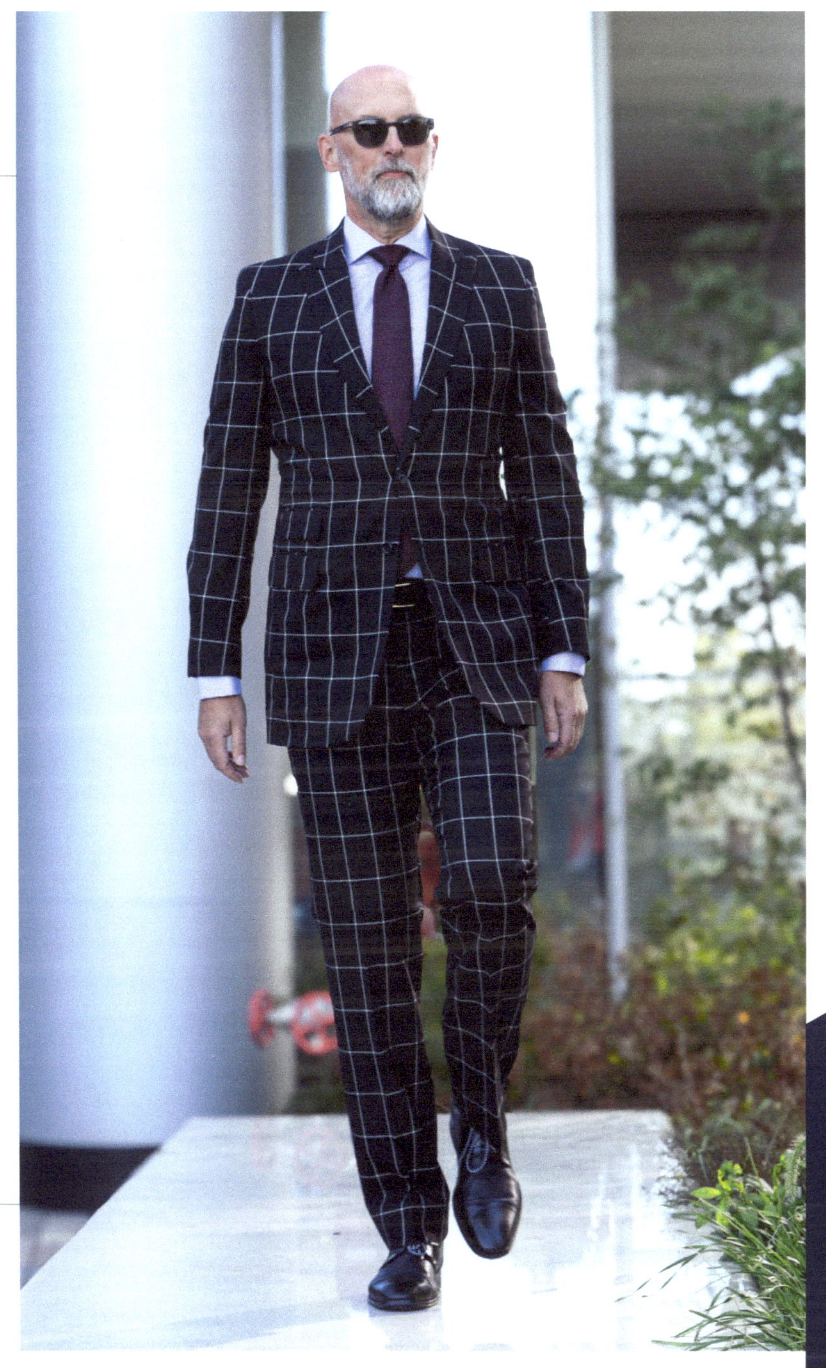

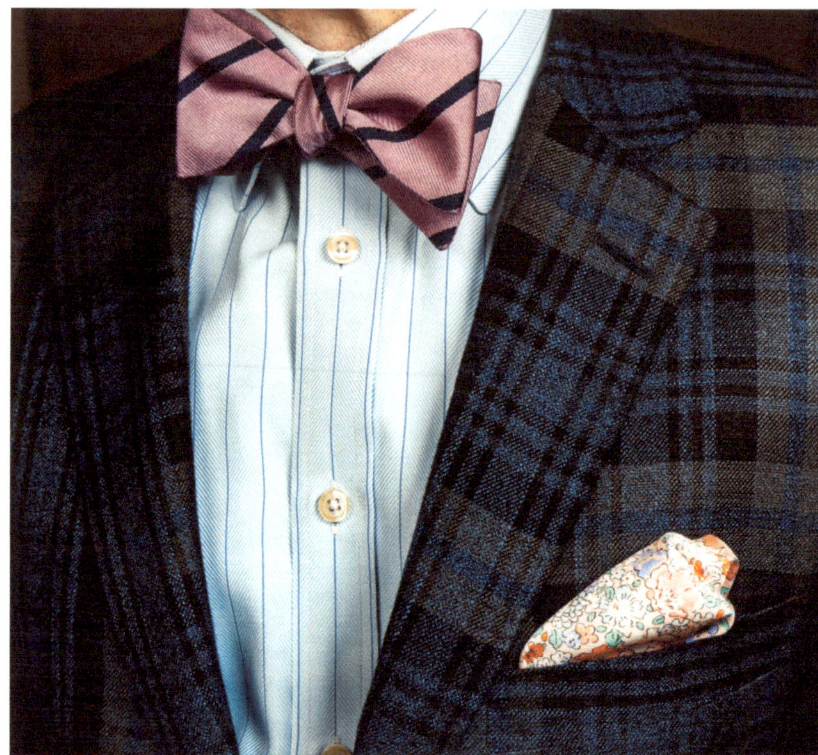
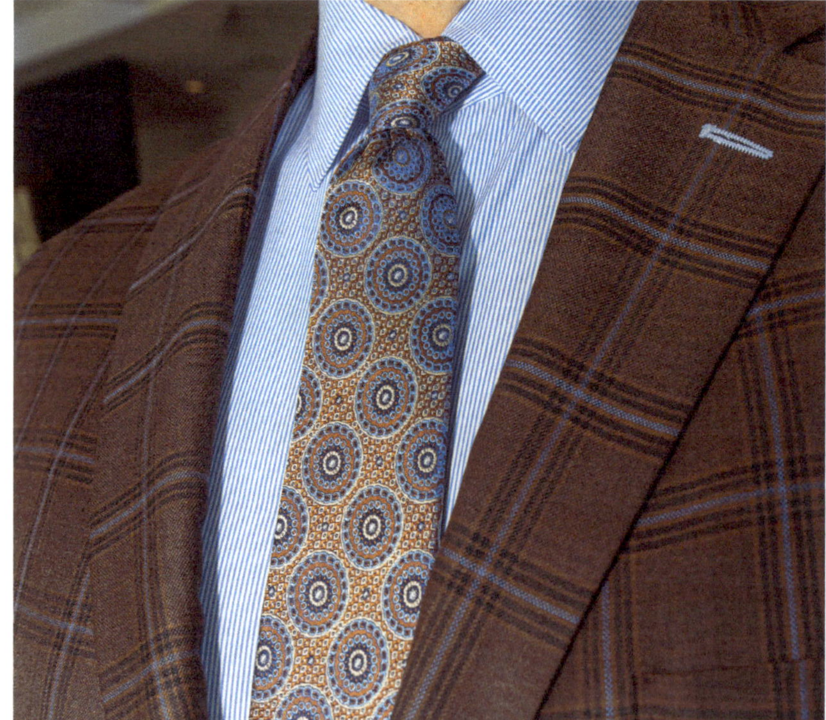

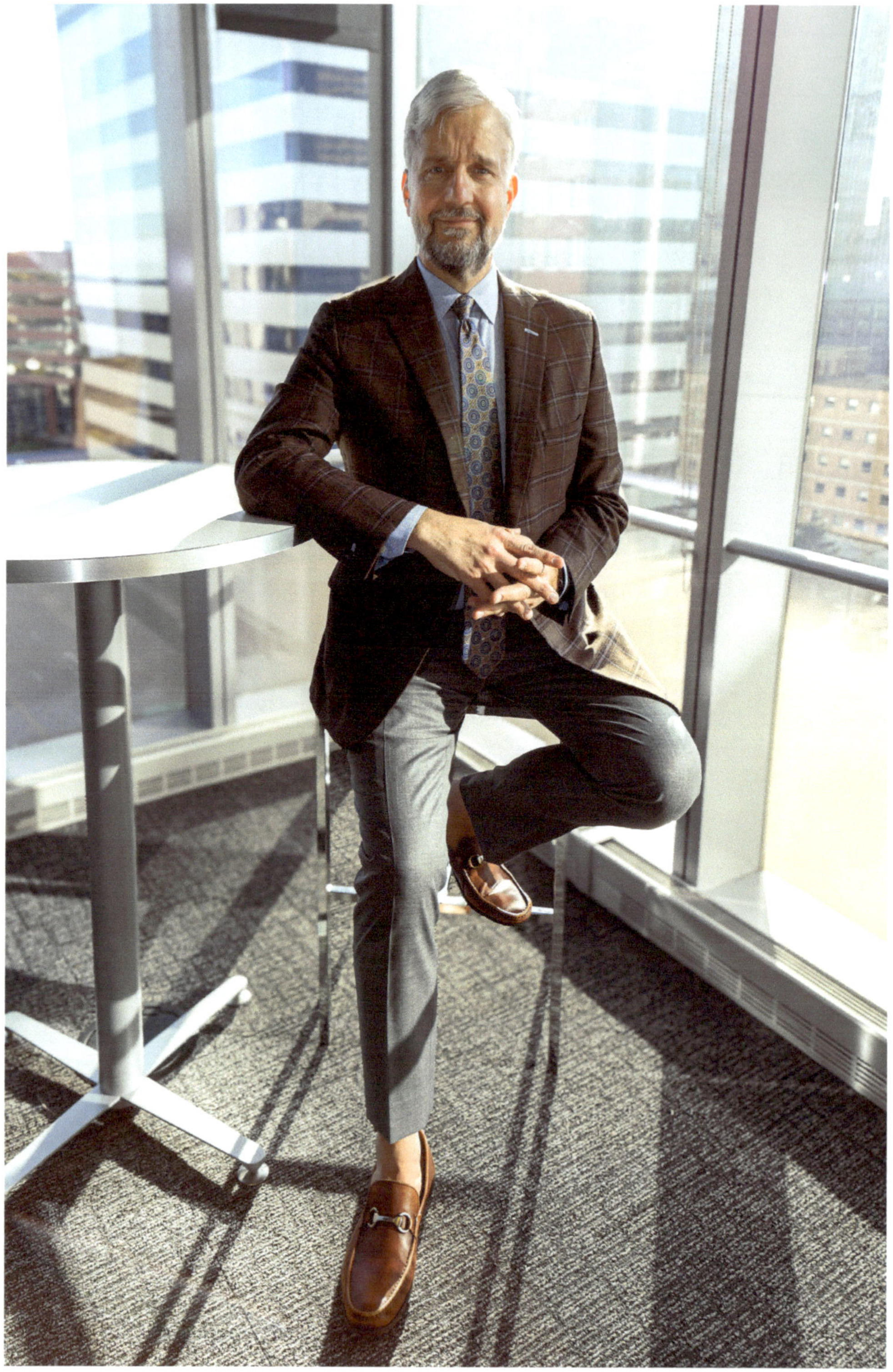

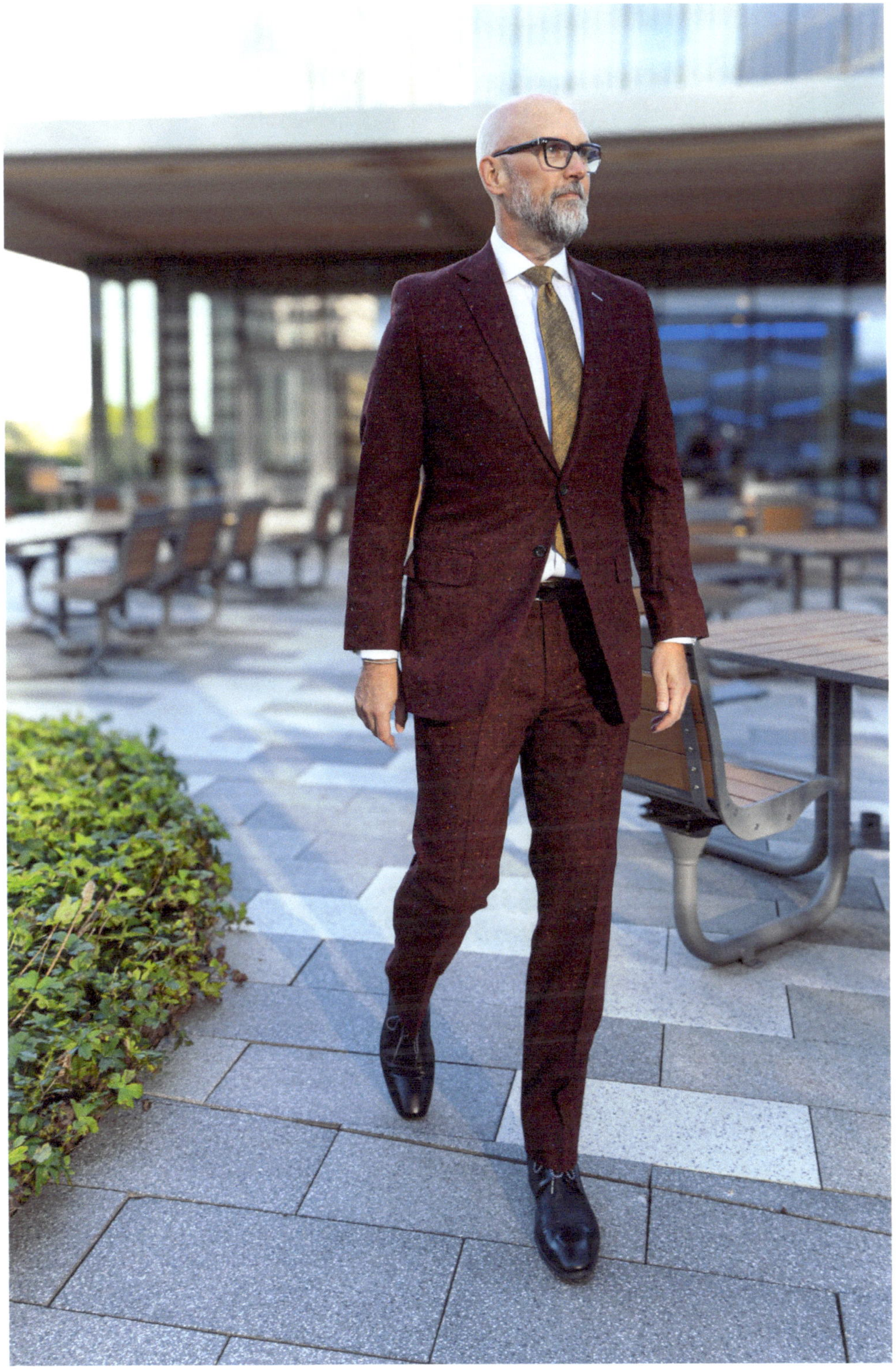

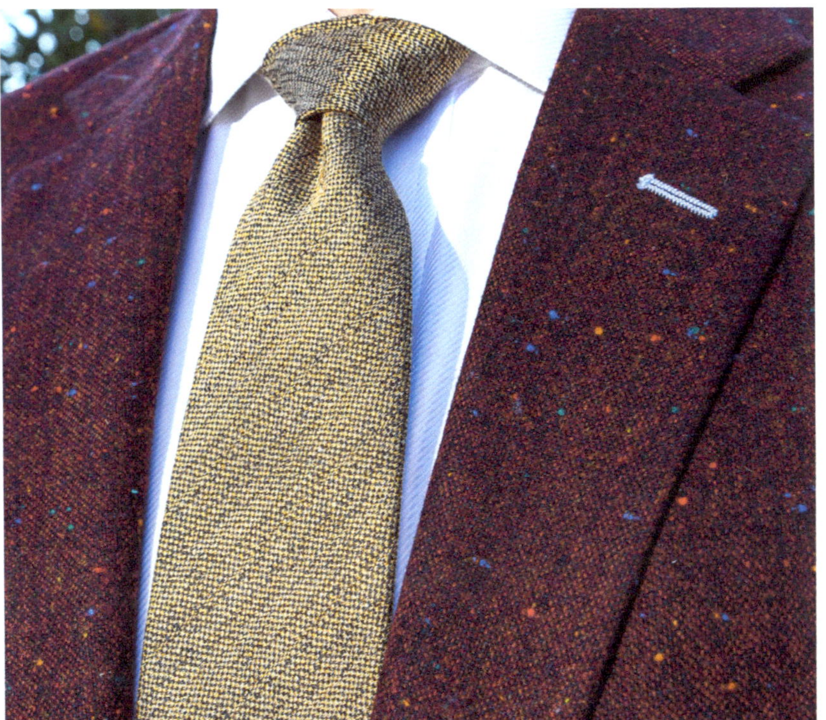

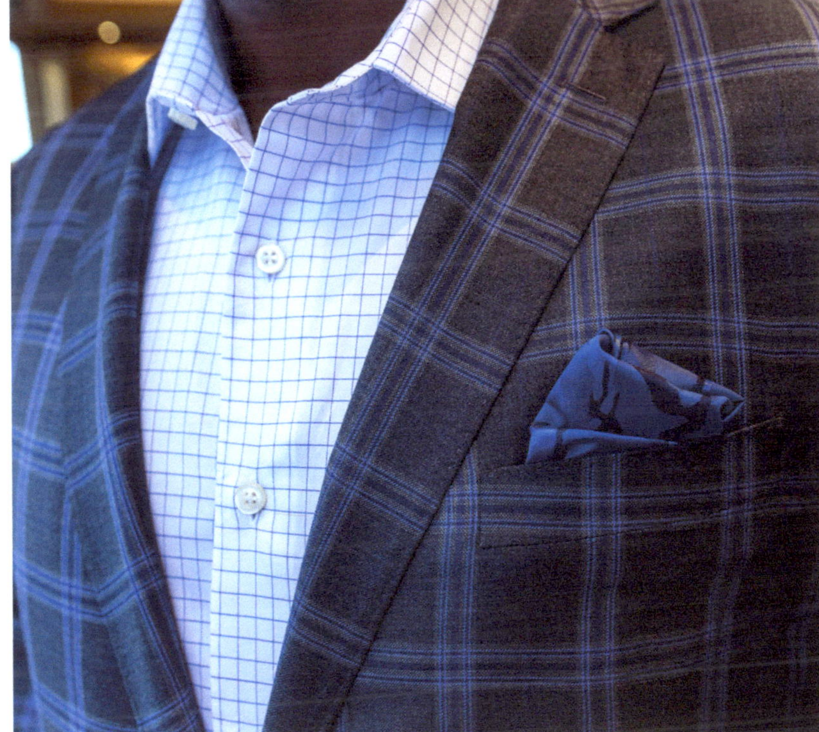

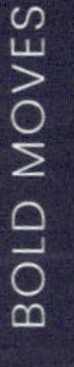
BOLD MOVES

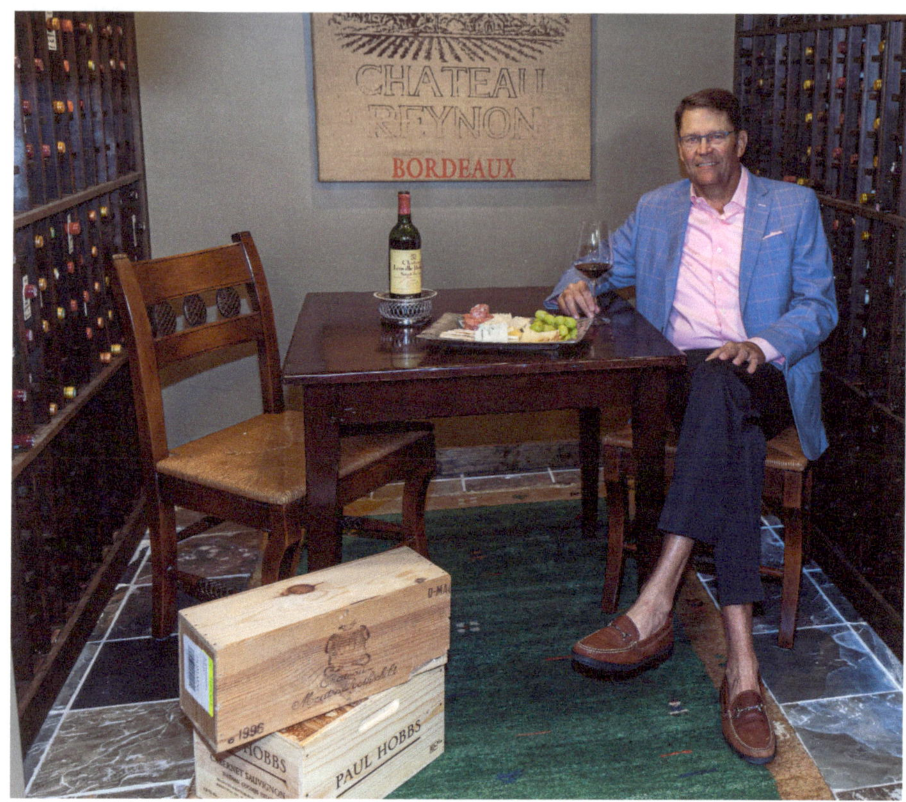

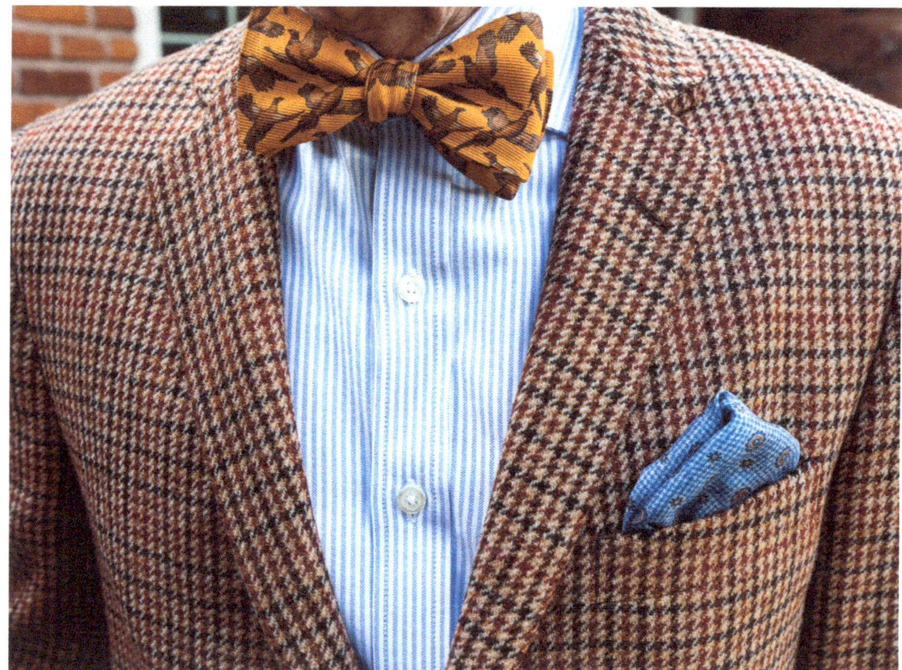

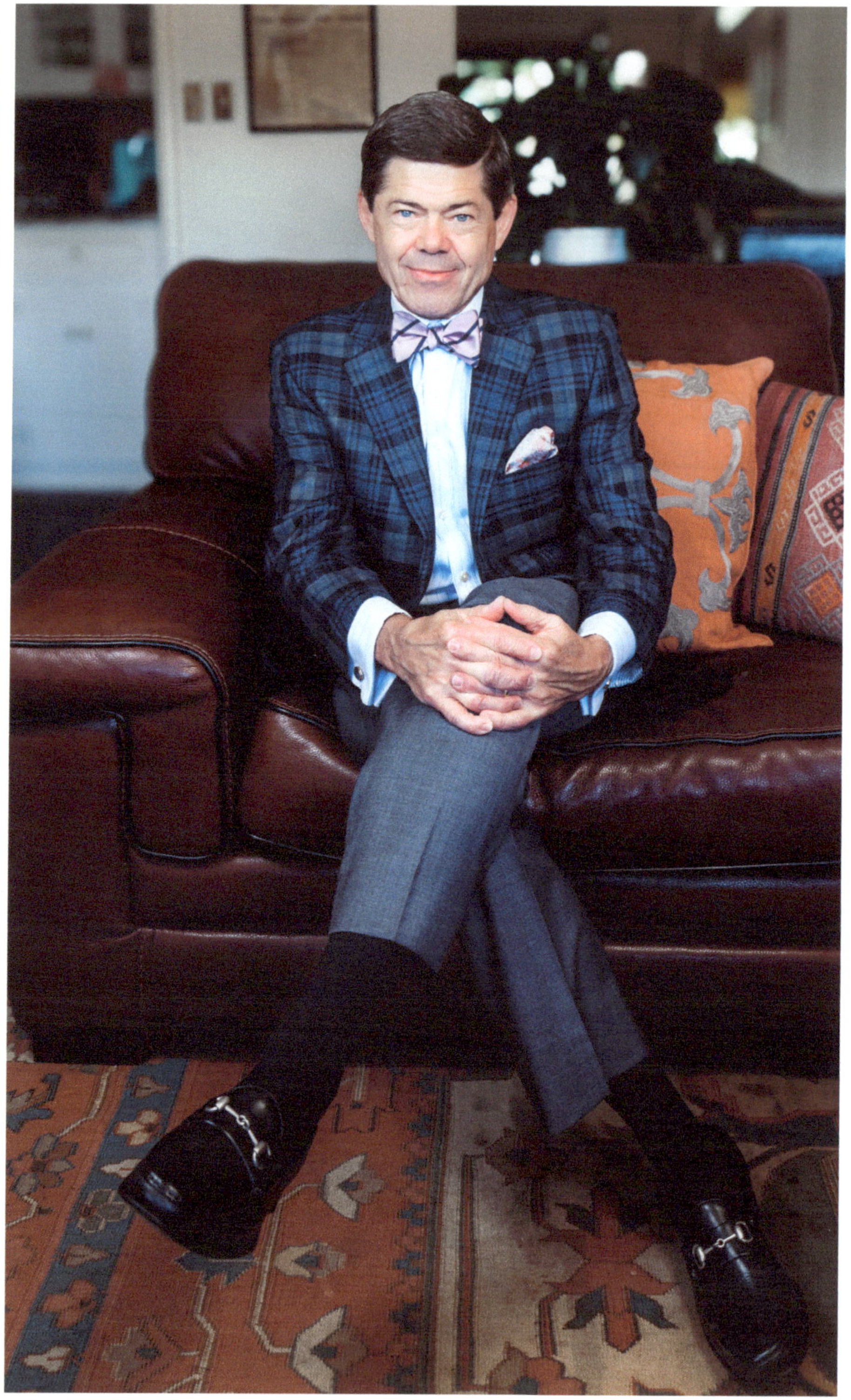

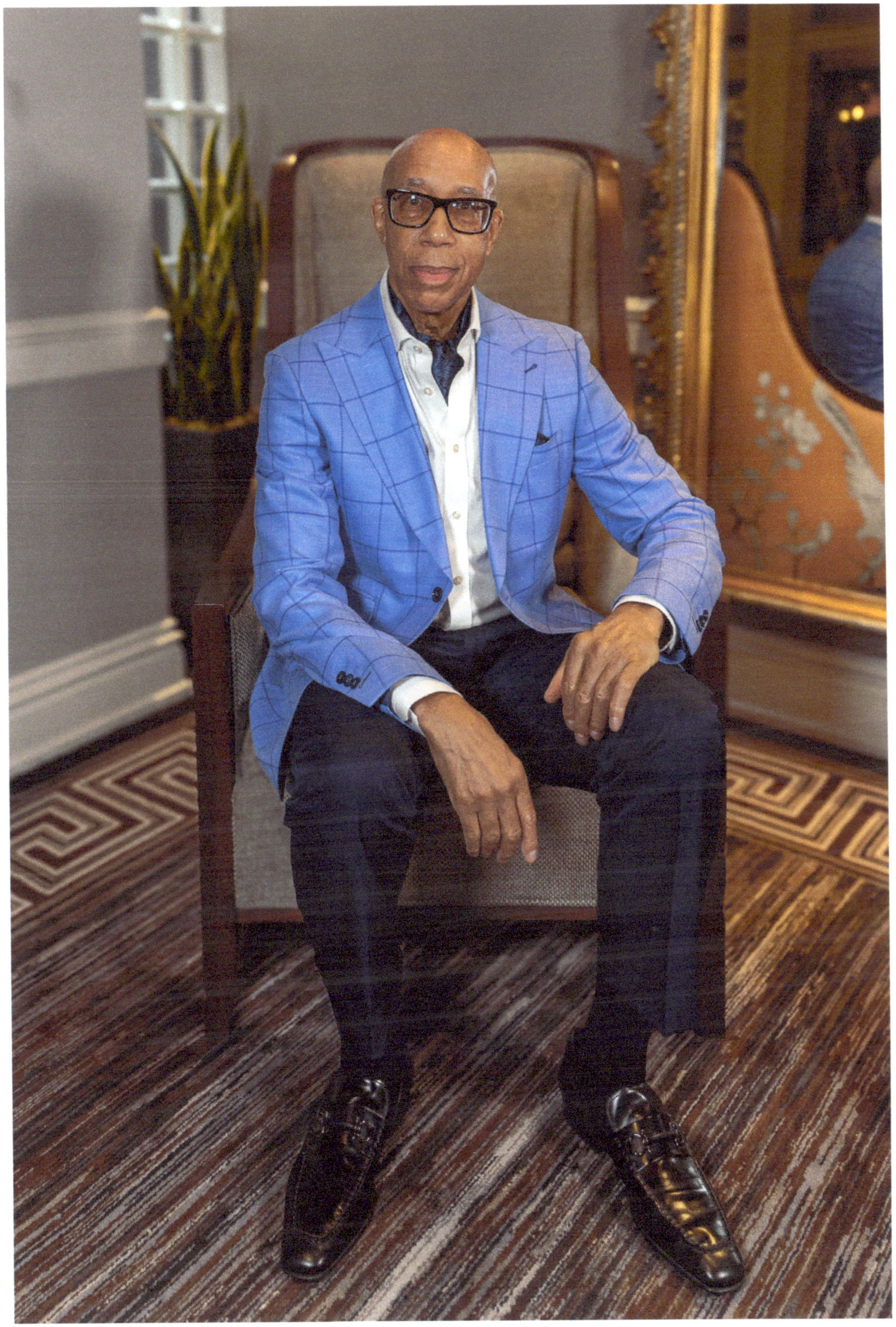

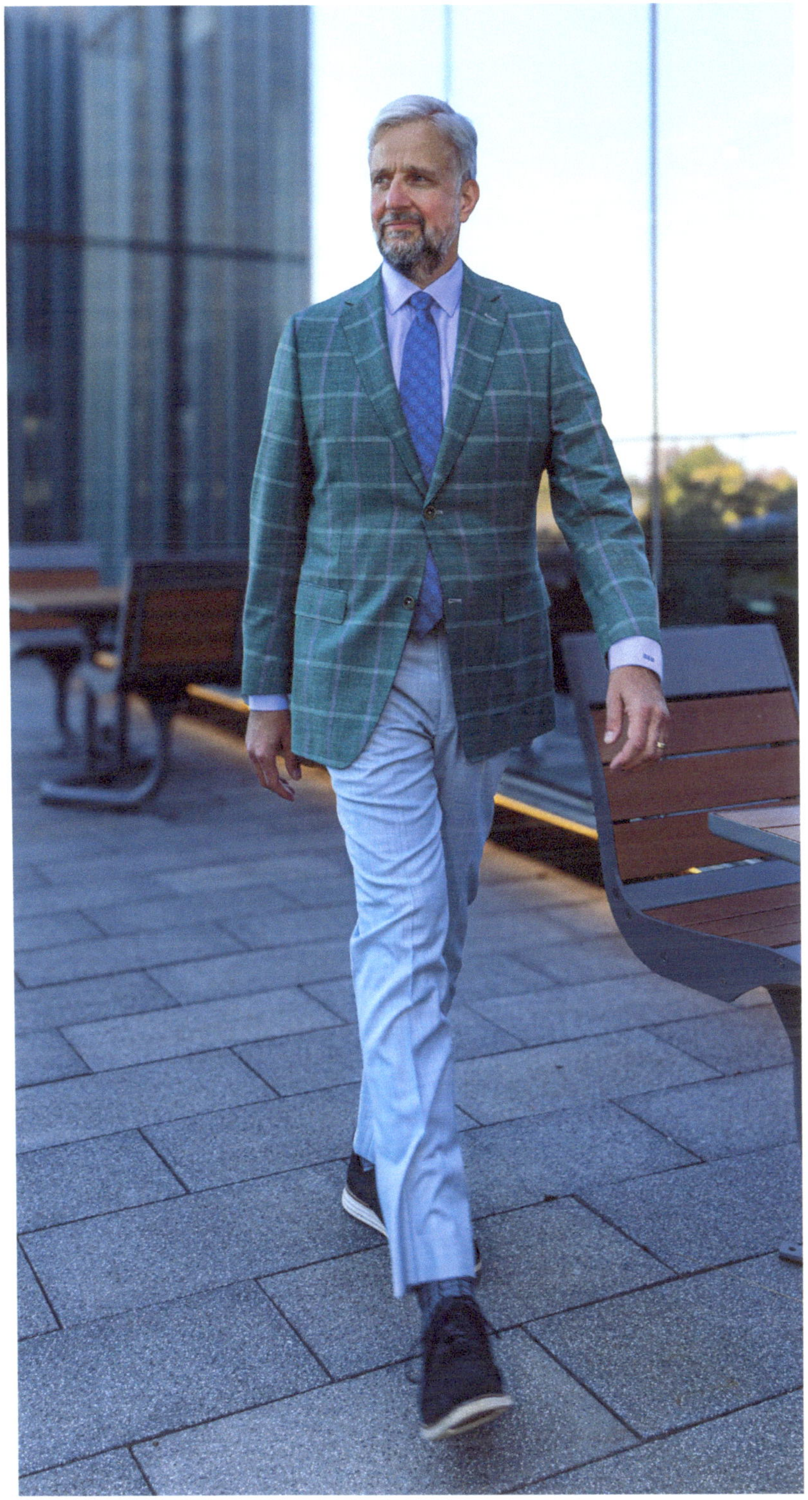

BOLD MOVES

About the Author

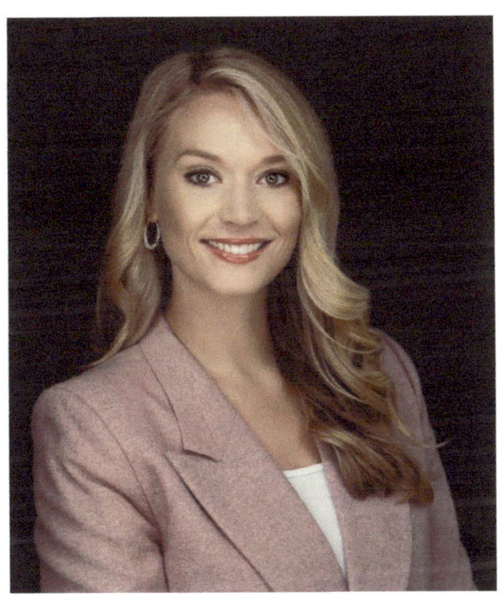

Margo Martinez is Owner and Founder of *Be the Man*, a Men's Image and Lifestyle Consulting firm focused on custom clothing for quality-seeking, hard-to-fit, busy, and successful gentlemen. Margo's purpose is to bring them confidence and happiness through their clothing and image. Many of her clients become dear friends, which is a true joy for her.

She was born and raised in Oklahoma on a cattle farm in a small town with one blinking stop light. She has fond childhood memories of building fence, hauling hay, driving the tractor, and picking peaches and apples. The farm is where she learned what hard work brings in life, and where she developed her love for being outside.

Margo is a football official, a big fan of musicals, frequent traveler, embroidery nerd, wine snob, and lover of all things pink. She was named *Margo Janelle* after her dearest grandmothers, Margaret and Janice. She loves spending time with her family and traveling with her best friend, her husband. Margo happily lives in Saint Louis, Missouri where you can find her on a hike with her husband and two standard poodles in the spring, or wearing stripes on the football field in the fall.

Connect with Margo:

https://linktr.ee/margo.martinez

www.ingramcontent.com/pod-product-compliance
Lightning Source LLC
Chambersburg PA
CBHW041034120726

48005CB00005B/804